CULTURE OF EMPIRE

American Writers, Mexico, and

Mexican Immigrants, 1880–1930

CULTURE

OF

EMPIRE

Gilbert G. González

University of Texas Press, Austin

Requests for permission to reproduce material from this work should be sent to Permissions, University of Texas Press, P.O. Box 7819, Austin, TX 78713-7819.

∞ The paper used in this book meets the minimum requirements of ANSI/NISO z39.48-1992 (R1997) (Permanence of Paper).

Library of Congress Cataloging-in-Publication Data
Gonzalez, Gilbert G., 1941–
   Culture of empire : American writers, Mexico, and Mexican immigrants, 1880–1930 / Gilbert G. Gonzalez. — 1st ed.
      p.   cm.
Includes bibliographical references and index.
   ISBN 0-292-70186-1 (hardcover : alk. paper) — ISBN 0-292-70207-8 (pbk. : alk. paper)
   1. United States—Relations—Mexico—Historiography.   2. Mexico—Relations—United States—Historiography.   3. Mexico—Historiography.   4. Imperialism in literature.   5. United States—Foreign economic relations—Mexico.   6. Mexico—Foreign economic relations—United States.   7. Mexican Americans—Social conditions.   8. Mexican Americans—Education.   9. Mexicans—Migrations.   10. Immigrants—United States—Social conditions.   I. Title.
   E183.8.M6   G57   2004
   303.48′273072′09034—dc21

                                                          2003012088

CONTENTS

Photographs follow page 102.

ACKNOWLEDGMENTS

No book is purely the work of an individual, and this book is no different. I owe a sizable debt to friends, colleagues, and family, as well as a greater debt to others for their assistance than is usually the case. Colleagues have been instrumental in my theoretical and professional development. My friend and fellow faculty member at the University of California, Irvine, for the past three decades, Raúl Fernández, helped in no small measure with his open office door, which always allowed me to enter to ask for his take on a particular issue or topic. His suggestions for further reading and insights relating to my study were critical and afforded me a broader understanding of the subject matter. I gleaned numerous ideas from our discussions over the course of researching and writing, and these have enriched the text. University of California Professor Emeritus Robert V. Hine cordially agreed to take time from his own busy schedule to read several of the chapters. His evaluation and suggestions for improvement were, as always, offered in a spirit of camaraderie. I am grateful to his upbeat assessment, which stirred me to pursue my objective with greater resolve. Professor Nancy Page Fernández, California Polytechnic University, Pomona, recommended that I consult a number of sources that were of major significance in the revising phase of the manuscript, and her contribution is much appreciated.

My family also contributed to the making of this study. My wife, Frances, a pharmacologist as well as a history buff with an interest in writing, read several drafts of the introduction and the first three chapters. Frances always responded positively to invitations to read another chapter, and never failed to accommodate my hurried queries regarding her take on the reading at hand. Her assessments of drafts in various states of completion were always a motivating force to keep me on the task at hand.

Even though she was finishing the final editing of her MFA film, my daughter Xochitl kindly took the time to read the entire manuscript. Her comments, queries, and notations were gladly received and were incorporated into the final draft sent to the University of Texas Press.

Although there are no citations in the text to any of the contributors mentioned above, that does not diminish the significant improvement of the book provided by their friendship and unselfish collaboration.

I also want to thank Professor Sonny San Juan, University of Connecticut, Professor Richard Gibson, San Diego State University, Professor José Alamillo, of Washington State University, and Professor Chon Noriega, UCLA, for their support and interest in the topic. In addition, this work would never have been completed without the financial assistance of the University of California SCR 43 funds for research into California's Latino community, administered via the UC Irvine Chicano Latino Studies Program. I also wish to thank my colleagues in the UC Irvine Focused Research Program in Labor Studies for their continued collegial support, as well as the financial assistance offered through the program to complete research for the book. The UC Irvine Committee on Research also provided funding that afforded completion of an important research phase. Finally, I wish to thank Jesús Vega, Barbara Abell, Edna Mejía, Enrique Buelna, and Gillian Kumm of the UCI School of Social Sciences for their assistance. Over the several years that it took me to complete this study, I depended on them for various kinds of help, and I benefited in many ways from their unstinting support.

During the copyediting phase a very dear friend of mine, Robert M. Holstein Jr., suddenly passed away. Bob and I met in kindergarten, and over the years we remained friends and found that we shared much in common. He always supported my work and took the time to read my writing and offer his impressions. I asked Bob to read a chapter of this book while it was in draft form, and he suggested a reading, which proved very useful to my argument. Bob is not here to discuss my work with me, but his uncommon friendship is very much a part of this book.

Finally, I wish to express my appreciation to all the personnel at the University of Texas Press. The outside reviewers provided expert commentary that benefited the work in many ways. Theresa May, Editor-in-Chief at the University of Texas Press, was a pleasure to work with. She and her colleagues made the difficult passage from manuscript to book not only manageable but ultimately very satisfying.

CULTURE OF EMPIRE

INTRODUCTION

This book began several decades ago, when as a graduate student I set out to write a dissertation explaining the Chicano educational experience in Los Angeles during the 1920s. The object was to explain the roots of the unequal outcomes differentiating Chicano from Anglo American students in public schools and the origins of the Chicano protest movement that accused the educational system of deliberate discrimination. That dissertation later became the foundation for a book on Chicano education during the era of de jure segregation.[1] Again, the purpose was to review the origins of the Chicano educational experience and the causes of the discriminatory policies and unequal outcomes that formed the bookends of that experience. Both studies approached the topic by emphasizing the role that domestic capital interests played in shaping public school policies, particularly the use of racially inspired policies, and the predictable outcomes.

The prior studies are mentioned here because this book will resume the study of Chicano educational history but will follow a different approach. In my previous works the analyses remained within a national perspective, focusing on the schooling process as a strictly national question of policies that were explained as outcomes of domestic policy discourses shaped by the emerging corporate capitalist order. This study will expand that viewpoint to include a transnational perspective, but not a cultural transnational perspective, which has attracted attention in some circles. Here, the emphasis is on the American economic empire and its historical domination over the nation of Mexico. This is not to say that national policy discourses on such matters as racialized segregation, IQ testing, tracking, and vocational education should be tossed aside. However, that explanatory approach lacked a transnational component and consequently failed to fully explain the critical issues under review.

The present study adds the U.S. economic empire—the foremost element in the formation of public policy in general, and educational policy in particular, toward the Mexican immigrant community in the 1900–1930 period. The reader will notice that only one chapter (and the final chapter at that) is devoted to a discussion of the public education affecting the Mexican immigrant community. However, the necessity to foreground the U.S. economic empire and its offspring, the culture of empire, as well as its general impact on the emerging minority community, was unavoidable. Uncovering the significance of empire required an exploration into the cultural production by American writers of various stripes whose perspectives on Mexico and Mexican culture were critical to shaping U.S. domestic policy toward Mexican immigrants. This narrative explores, among other things, the rise of a culture of empire and the manner in which it constructed representations of Mexico and Mexicans.[2] The account then examines the ways that this maturing culture of empire impacted on the Mexican migrant community and the continuity of those imperial images as they followed migrants as they crossed the northern border.

The focus is on writers who fall outside the definition of novelist and emphasizes expository writing (novelists did not take up writing on Mexico till the 1920s, long after Mexico submitted to U.S. economic domination). I also chose to emphasize the voices of these writers and allow the story to flow as much as possible in a direct line from them, as if I held a tape recorder as they spoke. Of course, I glean their key ideas, assemble and analyze them, then place them into an interpretative framework. Simultaneously, in order to focus on the ideas of the architects of the culture of empire, I have tended to restrict relevant contemporary analyses supportive of my analysis to footnotes. While this study focuses on the 1880 to 1930 period, it is a limitation taken for the sake of establishing an initial and, hopefully, provocative discussion on the American economic empire and its offspring, the culture of empire, and about the impact of the culture of empire on U.S. domestic policy and social relations.

In the same manner that my dissertation and book were limited to a national focus, most students of the Chicano experience (and of the national experience as well) tend to keep their analyses within the boundaries of the United States. Once such authors have dealt with Mexican immigrants traveling north and settling into barrios and other enclaves, they virtually ignore U.S. economic domination over Mexico. The tendency to focus from the Mexican border north while ignoring the overwhelming presence of the United States in Mexico's economy and society severely limits the ability of research to explain the Chicano experience (and now the Latino experience) in all of its aspects.

Mention should also be made of the emphasis on culture that pervades the literature in Chicano and other minority studies. Virtually all discourses on minority histories fix upon race, that is, white racism, identity, and agency, an overriding emphasis that has stripped away any opportunity or sustained interest in an effective transnational methodology. The emphasis on culture partners with an overwhelming tendency, particularly among those writing the histories of Chicanos and other Latinos, to retain the analysis within a national framework. This work veers radically away from that exclusive emphasis on race, identity (whiteness, for example), agency, and other cultural themes to examine how the American economic empire has shaped social relations among peoples living within the United States. On the other hand, those discussions concerning American authors, primarily novelists writing on themes derived from experiences in Mexico, ignore, for the most part, any connections between the literature under analysis and the imperial nature of U.S.-Mexican relations.[3] These works generally examine and discuss literary issues—the themes, styles, and forms that novelists and other popular writers employed. International politics and economics are scarcely mentioned.

THE UNITED STATES EMPIRE

Although race and identity attract much attention, empire does not unless one is speaking of past colonial experiences. There has been among contemporary academics a decided reluctance to refer to the United States as an empire in the classical sense, despite its behavior over the past century, which has been cut from a classic imperial cloth. This reluctance has predominated even among social critics. In sidestepping U.S. imperialism and focusing on European colonialism, critical studies, as Amy Kaplan has so eloquently pointed out, too often unwittingly follow the "American Exceptionalism" trend in U.S. historiography.[4] Only a few are heard to refer to the United States as an empire, and, surprisingly, voices from the far right have taken up the banner celebrating the American empire.[5] William Rusher, editor of the *National Review* and Max Boot, opinion editor at the *Wall Street Journal*, have recently written of the good causes that the American empire can embark upon around the world. Boot, for example, writing in the conservative *Weekly Standard* (edited by Bill Kristol, former aide to vice presidential candidate Dan Quayle), makes the case for "U.S. imperialism—a liberal and humanitarian imperialism, to be sure, but imperialism all the same."[6] Rusher, on the other hand, compares the United States to the Roman and British Empires and proposes that the United States has inherited an imperial imperative that

it cannot relinquish.[7] Although both men make no excuses for their imperialist proposals, we should recognize that there is more than a grain of
truth in their testimonies. Their messages would never have appeared
were it not for a groundswell of opinions supportive of the United States
as the "new world empire."[8] While Rusher, Boot, and their ilk consider
empire an opportunity for spreading democracy, the opposite will be and
has been the consequence. All empires by their very definition are anti-
democratic; the domination of one nation by another is inherently opposed to equality among nations, a fundamental principle of democracy.

Unfortunately, the term "empire" seems not to have caught on in the
American historical or sociological imagination. When the expression
"empire" is used, it seems that it is quite appropriate for describing the
British colonial system of the nineteenth and twentieth centuries or for
condemning the Soviet bloc, the "evil empire" of the late twentieth century. It was safe for the British to proudly proclaim that the sun never set
on the British Empire, but Americans have been loath to use any such
metaphor to describe U.S. transnational relations with its Latin American
neighbors. Thus, the most powerful of all empires in the history of na-
tion-states, the United States, goes about its imperial business practically
undisturbed (and unrecognized) by historians and other academics, some
of whom might, in other contexts, condemn empires on moral grounds.

Americans generally prefer to identify the United States as a nation
that relates with all other nations on the basis of equality and respect for
sovereignty. Certainly, the mass media make no mention of an American
imperial vision or agenda, and political leadership flinches at the word.
More often, euphemisms for empire—"world power," "superpower,"
"global power"—are preferred to describe the actions taken by the
United States abroad. One former Reagan administration adviser referred
to the United States as the "greatest power the world has ever known,"
but the term "empire" runs against the grain of American nationalism, or
so it would seem.[9] The convention of explaining empire on the basis of
direct territorial control effectively relieves the United States of harbor-
ing imperial ambitions. Empire in the tradition of the Roman Empire or
the British Empire, which is the active seeking of territorial domination
and control over another nation, has been systematically privileged as the
defining element for all empires. Consequently, in the popular and official
viewpoints, since the United States has no apparent colonial possessions,
the United States is therefore not an empire. Puerto Rico escapes the des-
ignation "colony," which it rightly deserves, via another euphemism:
"commonwealth." And like the case of Puerto Rico, there are persuasive

arguments for considering Oceania and Hawaii as colonial possessions.[10] Despite examples of an active imperial agenda, popular belief that the United States is an imperialist power is absent and runs counter to the national political ethos in place for most of the twentieth century.

However, as this study hopes to demonstrate, U.S. foreign policy planners of the late nineteenth century seldom established territorial control as the key to empire building. In fact, in the discourse on empire taken by the world powers of that time, imperialism was never a neatly defined activity. Empire was conceived of as having many possible forms, including coaling stations, protectorates, outright territorial control, and economic domination (while nominally preserving the dominated nation's sovereignty). It will be shown that an overriding objective of U.S. foreign policy with regard to Mexico and Latin America was the establishment of economic control to satisfy the very same ambitions that the British entertained in the search for and acquisition of their colonial possessions.

The absence of empire as a prime focus of analysis in U.S. historiography evolves from the very nature of the American empire itself, which runs counter to the popular definition of all empires.[11] More often than not, empires are identified as territorial acquisition by force of a once independent nation or territory by another nation, that is, the outright colonization of one society or nation by a foreign people. In this sense, the United States has met this definition by having taken the Philippines, Hawaii, Puerto Rico, and setting a protectorate over Cuba, among other examples of imperial power wielding. Even within this narrower definition, then, the forcible separation of Panama from Colombia and building of the Panama Canal were certainly acts of territorial theft by international highwaymen. There are numerous other examples: the landing of Marines around the Caribbean at various times throughout the twentieth century comes to mind.[12] Although these are salient examples of classic imperial domination, in the main the essence of the American empire is not territorial control but wresting of economic control from another country and dominating that nation economically. Contemporary observers of the imperial territorial expansionism undertaken by the United States at the end of the nineteenth century rarely misunderstood that policy of expansionism. In the excitement of acquiring Cuba, Puerto Rico, and the Philippines, the prolific author and avowed apologist for imperialism Trumbull White wrote these candid lines:

For good or ill, the United States has entered upon a colonial policy, a policy of expansion, a policy which forces us into a position of world power, deep in the complications of international politics. . . . It is now too late to turn back. Once having reached this position, it is unnecessary to argue the importance of obtaining all the adequate knowledge available on the great questions involved. American citizens, with the welfare of the country at heart, are endeavoring to familiarize themselves with the conditions of these new dominions and in the countries adjacent to them. Without experience or precedents of our own colonial policy, we are forced into the position of creating one.[13]

White urged the elaboration of informed policies adequate for the effective governance of the recently acquired colonies. However, voices like those of White met opposition from a variety of quarters. Defenders of U.S. expansion into the Caribbean and Pacific were challenged by a minority of objectors led by such personages as John Dewey, vice-president of the Anti-Imperialist League from 1910 to 1920. Even though large-scale U.S. capital had previously captured Mexico's railroad and mining industry and was on the cusp of dominating its oil production, effectively transforming Mexico into an economic outpost of American capital interests, that form of expansionism met little, if any, opposition. Territorial expansion into the Caribbean and Pacific, on the other hand, caused a vigorous opposition movement on grounds not necessarily anti-imperialist, from a variety of quarters. However, for the most part the "peaceful conquest" of Mexico went unnoticed by those who would take up the flag of the anti-imperialist movement. Americans tended to make the connection between colonialism or imperialism and territorial conquest, but largely ignored economic domination, which amounted to imperialism by other means.[14]

While White and Dewey responded in their own way to the violent expansion into the Caribbean and the Pacific, a parallel albeit nonviolent policy had matured in relation to Mexico. It is in regard to this policy that the anti-imperialists, adhering to the territorial definition of empire, lost touch with events. This study will argue that in the post–Civil War period, the United States launched a concerted effort to economically dominate Mexico and subordinate that nation to the corporate interests that were then taking ascendance in economic and political affairs in the United States. By the late nineteenth century, Mexico had fallen to the economic domination of large-scale investors such as J. P. Morgan, Daniel Guggenheim, and Jay Gould, and to corporations like Phelps Dodge, American Smelting and Refining, Doheny Oil, Atchison Topeka and Santa Fe, and Union Pacific.[15] One should not assume that this domination happened by force, as in the case of the Spanish-American War; in fact, U.S. investors launched a determined drive to capture Mexico economically—termed "peaceful conquest" by the architects of that expansionism—soon after the Civil War and realized that objective by the turn of the century.

As the twentieth century approached, United States capital steered the Mexican economy and came to dominate its most important sectors. Meanwhile, the U.S. State Department placed the peaceful conquest of Mexico's economy at the center of the nation's foreign policy objectives and pursued it with single-minded dedication. For sure, not all Americans failed to define with exactness the ongoing imperial expansion. John Kenneth Turner called attention to the political consequences of the economic domination then overwhelming Mexico through his daring critique of, as Turner called it, the "partnership of Díaz and American capital." The critic noted the imperial outcomes propelled by the transnational enterprise, contending that it "wrecked Mexico as a national entity," which simultaneously bestowed on the U.S. government a "deciding voice in Mexican affairs."[16] Turner certainly understood, as did few of his contemporaries, the imperialist dimension of U.S. relations with Mexico.

U.S. corporate interests achieved their ambitious agenda with the cooperation of Mexico's elite landowner class led by Porfirio Díaz. Mexico adjusted its internal economic policies to the U.S. demand for an open door to foreign capital and virtually unlimited investment. Indeed, Díaz presaged the "globalization" schemes of the late twentieth century sponsored under the mantra of neoliberalism. Economic domination manifested in a billion dollars of U.S. capital, initially took the form of railroad construction; railroads then led to the domination of Mexico's mining and later Mexico's oil industry.[17] Mining and oil production summoned more than superprofits, as valuable natural resources were extracted using cheap native labor and transported to the United States for further processing in industrial production.

THE CULTURE OF EMPIRE

U.S. domination of key sectors of the Mexican economy set the stage for the creation of a culture of empire by American writers, who descended upon Mexico with the completion of U.S.-constructed and -owned railroads from the U.S. border into Mexico's center. As Mexico opened her doors to U.S.-inspired modernization, a cohort of writers that included professional travelers, Protestant missionaries, academics, journalists, business people, diplomats, engineers, tourists, and others descended on Mexico in increasingly large numbers. These in turn began to publish accounts of their travels or, in the case of businessmen, of their operations. A large body of literature appeared soon after 1880 and constituted a new genre in American writing. Numerous articles appeared in professional and popular journals such as *Collier's*, *Atlantic Monthly*, *Survey*, *The Independent*, and *National Geographic*. Indeed, the American public was treated to a virtual explosion of books and articles on Mexico, a sizable body of literature that was largely responsible for establishing a widespread view of Mexico, its culture, flora and fauna, and investment potential. Of importance for this study is the significance this literature had in explaining Mexico and Mexicans to the American audience and in legitimizing the economic domination then in process.

Mexico's economic subordination to the United States fostered the construction of colonial strategies expressed through popular writings. The imperialist Trumbull White, for example, prescribed the development of a knowledge base for effectively governing the "new possessions." In the case of Mexico, this is precisely what this body of literature did, by suggesting methods for securing economic expansion into the southern nation. Those narratives eventually provided the foundation for public policy directed at the emerging ethnic minority, the Mexican immigrant community that formed as a consequence of U.S. economic expansionism into Mexico.

The numerous authors' narratives read as if they came off an industrial production line, molded by a seemingly mystical template that guided them and controlled their pens. Their works often moved beyond words and included photographs illustrating Mexico's geography, archeology, villages, churches, holiday celebrations, women, children, work, and marketplaces. The manner in which Mexico, its culture, and its peoples were described to readers is most relevant to the question of empire. The economy generally attracted particular interest, and within the economy the importance of foreign capital, particularly American capital, to the inevitable process of modernization. Words and photographs combined to create images and draw conclusions—at best superficial and for the most part demeaning—of Mexico that the American audience would easily grasp. The works described Mexico in ways that paralleled the writing by the British of their colonial subjects.[18] Mexicans of the poor classes, the vast majority of Mexico's population, were described as a rather uncivilized species—dirty, unkempt, immoral, diseased, lazy, unambitious—and compared at length to Orientals (then the identifier for all colonial subjects) and despised for being peons. Wealthy elites of Mexico were treated with kid gloves, although more often than not in rather unflattering terms; nonetheless, the peons and not the wealthy were treated with overwhelming disdain.

Not surprisingly, it was the poor, the derided *peones*, who became the workforce for the myriad of industrial activities initiated and administered by American capital. Approximately 200,000 Mexicans worked for the mines, railroads, and petroleum sites. Most of them were recruited and transported from the central regions of Mexico to the main operations along the northern border states. The social consequence of the investment of foreign capital was the removal of hundreds of thousands of Mexican peasants from their communal villages, their ancestral lands; they migrated to towns and urban centers, from which they were recruited and transported to various industrial operations. From these internal migrations generated by the actions of U.S. capital, the flow moved into the United States, where Mexican settlements appeared in large numbers in the first decade of the century.[19] New sets of social relations marked by the segregation of nationalities were instantly injected into Mexico, with Americans on one side and Mexicans on the other. In the nearly three hundred mining camps in Mexico run by Americans, social segregation separating Mexicans from their American overseers became the norm, and in this setting a set of images and representations by American writers began to form.[20]

It was this emerging social order that Americans witnessed and experienced as they ventured into Mexico—some to live for an extended period, others for a brief visit, time enough to write a book or article. Some writers, as the reader will see, treated the settlements where Americans administered their enterprises as a facsimile of the social relations between British overseers and their colonial subjects. Some American writers even suggested the need for a Rudyard Kipling to capture the exact sense of the relations that they observed. In many respects, as the evidence demonstrates, these social relations would be repeated across the border as Mexican immigrant settlements spread across the Southwest. Thus, the social relations that greeted Mexicans across the border replicated in many ways the social relations constructed over several decades via the peaceful conquest of the Mexican economy.

Under the imperial watch, Mexico came to be titled the Land of Mañana, and Mexicans were described as inferior beings in comparison to Americans. Mexico was defined as a huge social problem, and the term "Mexican Problem" entered into literary discourse. The sum total of the cultural and character "defects" that distinguished Mexicans from the Anglo-Saxon or American norm defined the core of the problem. The solution to the problem, according to nearly every writer, could never be accomplished by Mexicans alone; only foreign guardianship could achieve the elimination of the Mexican Problem. And this meant the Americanization of Mexico, the panacea for Mexico's cultural and biological maladies. However, when writers used the term "Americanization," they invariably meant the expansion and deepening of the U.S. economic domination then in place. For these writers, the control of Mexico's railroad, mining, and oil industries represented the principal component of an effective and long-term Americanization to bring Mexico out of its cultural backwardness. Mexico, it was said, could never save itself without outside intervention, but not just any intervention. American writers and policy makers in Washington invariably upheld a predominant American right to intervene to ensure the realization of American objectives. A culture of imperialism, one that sanctioned the expansionary policies that Trumbull White found not only acceptable but also necessary, coursed through the literature.

This brings up the matter of what this all has to do with the educational experience of Mexican immigrants in the first third of the twentieth century. Briefly, the emerging genre of studies of Mexico appearing in book, journal, and article form shaped a representation of Mexicans that captured the American imagination. Derogatory images of Mexico and Mexicans took on a life of their own and became conventional wisdom regarding qualities characteristic of the average Mexican. This body of literature did not merely sit in libraries and collect dust. On the contrary, these visions by wanna-be specialists on everything to do with Mexico became an important source of information for those searching for clues as to the kind of public policy required for America's newest immigrant peoples. The entry of these studies appeared most visibly and significantly at the highest level of education, the university. The several American writers examined in this study who relied on this literature to define the Mexican immigrant were academics, but what is more important is that the literature surfaced prominently in the social sciences and subsequently the sociological analyses of Mexican immigrants. From there, the wide-ranging publications on Mexico entered into the public policy-making arena via university training of future school administrators, who relied on the information contained in the works to shape policy proposals. Dozens of graduate students who would later become teachers, principals, and school superintendents authored many of these academic explorations.

Just as American authors who wrote on Mexico discussed the Mexican Problem at length, so American officials at the federal, state, and local levels charged with formulating and implementing educational policy for the Mexican immigrant community incorporated that same conception without question. Interestingly, public policy makers relied extensively on the works of American writers and considered them specialists and reliable authorities. However, most of the writers were no more than one-time visitors and amateurs who jotted down their impressions in a notebook and, upon returning, turned the notes into a book. To be sure, some were not overnight specialists, especially the Protestant missionaries who hoped not only to convert Mexicans to Protestantism but Americanize Mexico as well. Common to all these writers was the near total pessimism concerning Mexican culture. This pessimism traveled into the United States and entered into the public policy arena, where it played a major role in shaping the educational program applied to the Mexican community.

The reader will notice that the point of departure for this study is the late nineteenth century, and that the narrative has very little to do with the Mexican-American War and annexation. Most historical accounts of the Chicano minority contend that the community originated with the Mexican-American War and the territorial conquest of 1848. Some argue that the annexation of one-half of Mexico's territory institutionalized a set of racial practices, which established a type of social relations that endured to the late twentieth century. These accounts also place racism at the center of the discussion. However, the present study differs in substantial respects from studies that focus on the annexation of the Southwest as the chief explanatory tool for interpreting Chicano history. In this study, the U.S. economic empire and the culture inspired by that empire are centered, and, it will be argued, this imperial expression explains the formation of public policy—in particular of educational policies and practices—applied to the ethnic Mexican community.

Surely there are some readers who will contend that the representations of Mexicans referred to above were voiced in the pre- and post-1848 periods. Mexicans, it will be said, were described in many of the same terms before the bevy of writers analyzed here took up their pens, and the critic might add that perhaps these writers merely continued a tradition, rather than establishing a new one. I grant that there may be some superficial continuity; however, the voices that were raised immediately following the 1848 conflict fell silent shortly thereafter. In his classic study of writing on Mexico and the Hispanic Southwest, Cecil Robinson noted a significant decline in American interest regarding the Southwest and its

Mexican population. The Civil War, Reconstruction, and the industrial-ization of the nation took precedence; a renaissance of writing on the Southwest surfaced but took on a romantic and nostalgic hue, like Helen Hunt Jackson's novel *Ramona*. The old images of the Spanish Mexican population fell out of circulation toward the latter nineteenth century; meanwhile, images of Mexico began to assume center stage in the national consciousness.[21]

Moreover, the objective of the contentious voices appalled at the Span-ish Mexican population of the postconquest Southwest was not empire. The sole objective of U.S. foreign policy and of the American settler cap-italists who traveled west after 1848 was the integration of the Southwest into the institutional framework of the United States. The war was one step in the construction of the American nation, and the Spanish Mexican population was perceived as an obstacle to that construction. This meant the removal of the original Mexican settlers from their land grants, the destruction of the old Spanish landowning system and the creation upon its ashes of a new society governed by capitalist principles.

On the other hand, the sole objective of foreign policy planners and writers who welcomed and sought empire in the late nineteenth century was not annexation; in fact, they stridently opposed annexation in favor of economic conquest. The logic that they expressed was not that of perma-nent settlers with a determination to expand the national economic and political boundaries. In contrast to the post-1848 period, during which the rancho or hacienda was viewed as an anachronism, in the peaceful conquest American capital was content to coexist with the hacienda sys-tem and even join politically with the landed elite who gleaned their wealth from that medieval institution. Consequently, the hacienda econ-omy was not touched by the imperial incursions; instead, it remained even stronger than before the arrival of U.S.-financed modernization. Imperial capital generated a retrogressive influence on the Mexican nation, pro-moting the retention of feudal forms while engendering modernization without national economic development.

Imperial capital sought to turn the nation of Mexico into an economic colony of the United States; the economic development of Mexico was not an objective unless it served U.S. capital interests. Writers who wit-nessed and embraced the process constructed a language that harmonized with that policy. The publications by these writers had little to do with the post-1848 Southwest and everything to do with the economic conquest of Mexico in the post-1880 period. The language of empire rose as if a single voice and by the turn of the century had captured the imagination of the northern nation. Finally, as one reads the public policy discourses, the works on Mexico written in the post-1880 period are of far greater importance than the information regarding Mexican residents remaining in the Southwest soon after 1848. The images of Mexico written in the post-1880 period, not the images of the old Mexican Southwest, took precedence in the public policy discussions between 1900 and 1930.

The key objective of this study is to illuminate one example of U.S. empire-making—the economic conquest of Mexico and the consequent migration of Mexicans to, and reception in, the United States—and to bring that example into the discourse on United States history and, in particular, into Chicano and Latino historiography. In addition, I hope to demonstrate that the U.S. empire has been central to the history of the ethnic Mexican community and that this study can be useful for those studying other immigrants, such as Central Americans, who are increasingly being forced into migratory paths within their respective nations and, as last resort, to the United States. This study will examine how the imperial, rather than merely transnational cultural, relationship that the United States developed with Mexico affected public policy, in particular educational policy affecting the Mexican immigrant community in the 1900–1930 period. The purpose here is to place the imperial domination exercised by U.S. capital over Mexico at the center of the discussion of Chicano history and of its social relations with the larger society. This study also seeks to challenge that long-standing misconception of the role of the United States on the world scene as a democratic influence by introducing the U.S. empire, a contradiction to the principle of democracy, into the discourse.

A case can be and has been made for demonstrating the continuity of the U.S. empire and of its domination over Mexico into the twenty-first century.[22] And just as in the first three decades of the past century, empire continues to impact the continually forming and re-forming ethnic Mexican community. However, this study will not engage in that larger project; instead, I hope to provide an invitation to further research into the interconnections between the U.S. empire and the formation and experience of the ethnic Mexican community. One might say that in twentieth-century U.S. history, empire not only matters, it stands at the center of that history.

1. THE ECONOMIC CONQUEST AND ITS SOCIAL RELATIONS

Mexico and the United States complement each other—the one furnishing tropical products of every variety, and the other standing in obvious need of a wider market for her farming implements, mining machinery, wagons, clocks and watches, and the thousand and one articles of invention that fill the American mills and warehouses. Something of what India is to England, Mexico could be and ought to be to the United States.

Solomon Bulkley Griffin, *Mexico of Today* (1886)

INTRODUCTION

American writers intent on informing readers of the newly opened-up nation to the south entered into a historic process of U.S.-Mexican relations. American capital entered Mexico at a dizzying pace in the last decades of the nineteenth century, a process that not only significantly altered Mexico's internal economy and social structure but also its relations with the then emerging world power to the north. While the interest of the authors lay in writing about the people and culture of Mexico, in doing so they could not avoid discussing the process of modernization inspired by U.S. capital, a development that had its parallel in European colonial expansionism.

While Europe's colonization projects swept through Asia, India, and Africa, the United States embarked on the American version of the Western colonial theme. The United States engaged in a calculated policy designed to construct a series of economic satellites subjected to an overriding economic influence tantamount to colonization. That policy deliberately avoided territorial annexation in favor of an economic domination that served the emerging corporate interests then in the process of assuming a commanding presence in the economic, social, and cultural spheres of the United States. Mexico provided the first encounter in an ultimately

successful endeavor to subject Latin America, considered the most critical geopolitical region affecting U.S. interests, to the economic supremacy
of the northern power.

While European imperialists added kingdoms, tribes, and clans of
Africa, Asia, and India to its dominion, the United States cast about for the
means to shape its own extraterritorial control. Mexico, the nation eventually to be touted as "Our Next-Door Neighbor," became the first experiment in U.S. imperial power. Long considered to contain vast stores
of natural treasures, gold, silver, and various metals vital to the industri-
alization processes, Mexico assumed an important place in the expansionary plans of the leading industrial powers of the world. None other than
the notorious imperialist Cecil Rhodes underscored the importance of
Mexico as the world's "treasure house." "I am not blind," he wrote,

> to the opinion as expressed by scientists and experts that Mexico will
> one day furnish the gold, silver and copper of the world; that from her
> hidden vaults, her subterranean treasure houses, will come the gold, sil-
> ver, copper and precious stones that will build the empires of to-
> morrow and make future cities of this world veritable New Jerusalems.[1]

Fortunately for the United States, no other power could compete with the
advantage that geographic propinquity gave it. European powers struggled
among themselves over regions that were accessible, geopolitically important, and economically beneficial. On the other hand, the United
States entered into Mexico nearly unchallenged and fulfilled Rhodes' pre-
diction that Mexico's resources would build the "empires of to-morrow."

THE THEORY OF ECONOMIC CONQUEST

Initial deliberations of U.S. expansion into Latin America appear within
a context of a growing domestic capital surplus and an active European
imperialism. The first stirrings of a national expansionism into Latin
America appeared in 1869, when a lively debate erupted between advo-
cates for the complete annexation of Mexico and a high-profile opposition
that advised an economic conquest of Mexico. A flurry of articles and
opinions in metropolitan newspapers, confident from the recent Northern victory, called for moving southward and to "take all of Mexico." As
soon as the annexationist drive surfaced, an opposition arose. William
Rosecrans, then minister to Mexico, assumed a central role in the contentious debate and strongly opposed annexation. In so doing, he laid out

what would eventually be the design of U.S. foreign policy toward all of Latin America.

An investor in railroads and a proponent of extending U.S. railroads into and throughout Mexico, Rosecrans contended that annexing Mexico would bring on more problems than benefits. He advised pursuing an economic conquest while leaving Mexico's sovereignty intact. "Pushing American enterprise up to, and within Mexico wherever it can profitably go," he exclaimed, "will give us advantages which force and money alone would hardly procure. It would give us a peaceful conquest of the country." [2] That claim was not lost on a generation of investors that took Rosecrans' dictum to heart. Edward Lee Plumb, for example, a representative for the International and Great Northern Railroad and onetime U.S. chargé d'affaires in Mexico City, wrote, "If we have their [Mexico's] trade and development we need not hasten the greater event [annexation]." None other than former president Ulysses S. Grant, along with his coinvestors in Mexico's railroads, shared the imperial economic vision that Rosecrans and Plumb championed. [3]

Apparently, some Americans remained open to either annexation or peaceful conquest (or possibly both). Rosecrans' contemporary F. E. Prendergast, for example, explicitly expressed an imperial policy when, in an 1881 article on Mexico's railroads appearing in *Harper's New Monthly*, he advised, "It is doubtful if any equal area on the face of the globe possesses larger deposits of the precious metals. . . . Now it is evident that any rapid progress in Mexico must come through colonization by some higher and more progressive race, or by the introduction of capital in large amounts to develop her natural resources by the aid of native races, who are generally peaceable and industrious." The United States chose the second option, much to Rosecrans' satisfaction. [4]

Although the practice of peaceful conquest had long been realized, the debate persisted into the second decade of the twentieth century. Fifty years after Rosecrans challenged the annexationists, Professor Chester Lloyd Jones was constrained to argue against annexation, which a sector of American investors was then proposing to protect investments threatened in the aftermath of the 1910 Mexican Revolution. Jones, a political scientist at the University of Wisconsin and onetime commercial attaché in the U.S. embassies in Paris, Madrid, and Havana, responded much like Rosecrans had done earlier. "The economic advantages that would result from annexation," he argued, "as contrasted to that which may follow independence and friendship is doubtful. Mexican trade, both import and export, is already almost inevitably American and investments will be increasingly so. . . . A friendly, strong, and independent Mexico will bring greater economic advantages than annexation."[5] The annexationist drumbeat continued, causing a renewed response. Five years after Jones' plea, the former head of President Woodrow Wilson's infamous Committee on Public Information, George Creel, also rallied in opposition to annexation. Creel claimed that annexation "would mean the attempted Americanization of fifteen million utterly alien races," warning that a racial problem would be unleashed upon the United States. He then added a significant clause intended to render the annexationist cause an anachronism: the "fortunes of the two countries are linked indissolubly." The peaceful conquest not only assumed a new definition, it made annexation a moot point. Economic conquest stood firmly implanted within U.S. foreign policy.[6]

Creel's contemporary, George B. Winton, professor of Latin American Studies at Vanderbilt University, used very similar phrasing: "The forcible annexation of all of Mexico would have brought the United States a throng of perplexities far greater than any that an independent Mexico can possibly produce."[7] One last example of a writer who opposed annexation in favor of economic conquest should finish demonstrating the point. J. Park Alexander, of Toledo, Ohio, wrote in the *Akron Daily Beacon*, "Let no patriotic American ever think of Mexican conquest. With Yankee energy and push in control and in cultivating the soil I have no doubt better results could be attained."[8]

Frederick Simpich, former U.S. consul at Nogales, Mexico, used different terminology to state what appeared to him to be the obvious. Simpich proudly noted the U.S. economic dominance in the Mexican nation. "It is our market now," he exclaimed, "linked with us by rail and sail and we must keep it."[9] Mexico, in the words of the former consul, is an entity defined as "our market," as if a form of property belonging to the United States. Note that both Creel and Simpich independently applied a deterministic appraisal to U.S.-Mexican relations. In the first the linkages are "indissoluble"; in the second, the linkages are "ours." And this is precisely how Consul-General Barlow described U.S.-Mexican economic relations in an official report titled *United States Enterprises in Mexico*, issued in 1902: "The commercial bond between the sister Republics is one that hardly can be broken, and is constantly growing in strength."[10]

Despite Wallace Thompson's shrill, opinionated works on Mexico, colored by unbridled racism, he can be credited with expressing the general thinking on the economic relations binding the United States and Mexico. Mexico not only carried a duty to itself, but it had a duty to the world— meaning the United States—as well. In *Trading with Mexico*, a work focused entirely on the U.S.-Mexican tie, Thompson (from whom we shall hear more later) applied a corollary to the peaceful conquest doctrine.

> Her resources, her gold and silver and oil, her henequen and rubber and coffee and lumber, her great labor supplies that wait so surely upon education and uplift, are forces which the white world cannot ignore. . . . Mexico cannot live in isolation, for her lands lie in the very heart of the world and her raw materials are sorely needed on all the seven seas.[11]

SURPLUS CAPITAL AND THE PEACEFUL CONQUEST

Economic conquest coupled with a nominal sovereignty, that is, governance of the country in the hands of collaborating elites, in the opinion of American economist James Arthur Conant, exemplified an imperial policy in the U.S. "sphere of influence." Conant, however, explained the root of expansionism to be the very success of industrial capitalism itself in causing rising levels of surplus capital without a domestic outlet—or, as he put it, "the great mass of capital seeking employment, and unable to find it at home." Writing in the last decade of the nineteenth century, Conant reflected on the source of the rising economic expansionism (which Rosecrans prescribed), a policy that Conant equated with European colonization, which he deemed as one possible remedy to overproduction of capital at home:

> The United States to-day seem about to enter upon a path marked out for them as children of the Anglo-Saxon race, not yet traveled because there has been so much to do at home. . . .
> The great civilized peoples have to-day at their command the means of developing the decadent nations of the world. These means, in their material aspects, consist of the great excess of saved capital which is the result of machine production. . . . how great this excess is at the present time, how profoundly it is disturbing economic conditions in the older countries, and how necessary to the salvation of these countries is an outlet for their surplus savings.

And later Conant drew an explicit parallel between European colonialism and the imperative facing the United States to resolve the problem of surplus capital:

> The energy with which the settled countries of Europe are seeking these opportunities for the investment of their capital has only recently begun to attract the attention of the American people. We have been

absorbed for many years in the development of our industries at home, and have only recently begun to feel the effects of diminished discount and interest rates and the pressure of surplus capital upon the means of its absorption.[12]

Conant clarified the meaning of empire as well, contending that empire can take various forms, including protectorates, coaling stations, military outposts, outright territorial control, and economic domination. Which course of action was eventually selected was not important, for what was important, according to Conant, was whether the domestic problem of overproduction and the consequent risk of permanent economic stagnation could be resolved. Whichever choice leaders decided upon, either territorial annexation or economic conquest, was relevant only to the extent that it met the problem of surplus at home. Each policy path was an equally valid means to secure the economic balance within the "home country." Deciding which route to take ultimately depended on the force of circumstances. There was no single path to accomplish the imperial mission. Whether by outright colonization or peaceful conquest, economic control remained the key to Conant's economic theory. For example, Conant argued that "the European nations were reaching out their commerce and political power in order to secure new outlets for their overproduction of finished goods and for their great accumulations of capital. . . . It was an economic necessity which precipitated the British occupation of Egypt; and it was the pressure of surplus capital which led to the opening up of the "Dark Continent."[13] Note that Conant chose to define imperial expansion as one driven by "economic necessity," rather than by a policy freely chosen by corporate executives and their partners in foreign policy offices. Imperialism, then, is not one of many possible policies; it is the only policy available to capitalist nations once they have reached a particular level of economic development.

Conant insisted that imperial expansion rewarded more than the stockholders and investors and that the working class also stood to gain. American labor allegedly held a profound stake in the success of economic expansion, not as laborers in economies abroad, but at home where the working class reaped the benefits of capital export and the consequent increased profits and thus higher wages. More than the fabled American Dream for workers was promised; for the owners of capital, class harmony evolved from a contented laboring force. Some labor leaders accepted the design for class collaboration, and these became known in corporate circles as the good labor leaders. One famous figure in U.S. labor history, Samuel Gompers, head of the American Federation of Labor from 1886 till his death in 1924, staunchly defended economic expansion as outlined by Conant. With the assistance of Robert Haberman, an informant for the FBI working with Mexican labor leaders, Gompers allied the AFL with U.S. policy toward Latin America and funneled AFL resources to Mexican labor leaders favorable to U.S. foreign policy toward Mexico. AFL organizers helped launch the first Mexican labor central in 1918, the Confederación Regional Obrera Mexicana, a government-controlled labor federation (with the American Haberman on its central committee) strongly allied with the AFL. The alliance lasted into the 1930s. The Mexican labor federation served to control labor and keep it on a course that harmonized with the peaceful conquest.[14]

Mexico's Elites and the Peaceful Conquest

Cooperation between U.S. proponents of the "pacific conquest" and Mexico's elite landowning classes was also fundamental to the realization of the transnational project's principal objectives. Under the administration of Porfirio Díaz, Matías Romero served as secretary of the Mexican legation, chargé in Washington for twenty-six years, including a continuous stint from 1882 to 1898. During those years, the United States expanded into Mexico on an unprecedented scale, and Romero can be credited with having assisted in that record increase. His activities in the United States as a representative of the Díaz administration exemplify the Mexican elites' boosterism of foreign capital, particularly U.S. capital. That cooperation made a nominal Mexican sovereignty not only defensible but also a critical element that provided cover for the economic conquest then in process. Perhaps the speech delivered by Romero at a New York City Democratic Club banquet in 1891 says it all:

> The capital, energy, and sagacity of the business men of this country will find a very large and profitable virgin field in Mexican enterprises.
>   . . . .
> When the settlement of the last territory of the United States shall make it difficult to find a new field for profitable enterprise, and before long it will be as difficult to find it here as it is now in Europe, the capital which this country is now so rapidly accumulating, and its enterprising activity, will have to look for new ventures. It will be an act of foresight to enter at once into the large and rich field offered by

Mexico, at the very doors of the United States. I sincerely hope that you will avail yourselves of this bountiful opportunity.[15]

Note that in revisiting Frederick Jackson Turner's famous Frontier Thesis, Romero also traversed the same explanatory path taken by Conant—and Rhodes, Prendergast, and Thompson—for justifying economic expansion abroad by the industrialized nations. The New York Democratic Club speech was followed by enthusiastic applause, as were the many speeches delivered by Romero that reiterated the same theme: that Mexico welcomed, more that it required, U.S. capital. American investors were more than happy to respond to Romero's invitation.

American Political Elites and Economic Expansion

Conant was undoubtedly familiar with the command of Mexico's railroads, oil, and mineral deposits by U.S. interests. These incursions fit the paradigm that the European industrial powers were busily incorporating, if not implementing, into their foreign policies. The United States, not wishing to be left behind the colonizing pack, acted to implement a foreign policy that satisfied the counsels of Conant, Rosecrans, and Jones.

Simultaneous with Conant's theoretical writing, for example, former secretaries of state Elihu Root (who served under Presidents McKinley and Roosevelt) and Charles Evans Hughes (under Presidents Harding and Coolidge) administered the policy of economic conquest. Root's views on Latin America were particularly significant, in that Root held the Latin American countries in contempt and harbored a missionary vision of U.S.-Latin American relations.[16] Root clearly understood the importance that surplus capital held in U.S. foreign policy formulation and focused on that surplus in his review of U.S.-Latin American policy. "Since the first election of President McKinley," he wrote,

> The people of the United States have for the first time accumulated a surplus of capital beyond the requirements of internal development. That surplus is increasing with extraordinary rapidity. . . . Our surplus energy is beginning to look beyond our own borders, throughout the world, to find profitable use of our surplus capital.[17]

Root's colleague Charles Evans Hughes added a corollary from the perspective of a policy manager working to protect the holder and investor of surplus capital. "The policy of the Government of the United States with relation to foreign investments should be well understood," he warned.

"There is the policy of the open door. We seek equality of opportunity for our nationals. . . . Given the open door, all who wish to are entitled to walk in. We resist policies of discrimination against American capital."[18]

Elihu Root, in his comments before the Mexican Academy of Legislation and Jurisprudence in 1907, summarized the "economic interdependence" then in process, stating, "We have turned our backs upon the old days of armed invasion . . . and are constantly engaged in the peaceable invasion."[19] Middle America came to the same conclusion. In the same year that Root addressed the Mexican Academy, author Nevin O. Winter, of Toledo, Ohio, described U.S. capital in Mexico as "another foreign invasion but with a pacific mission."[20] Chester Lloyd Jones would later coin the term "economic interdependence" (a term that became popular in the late twentieth century in reference to U.S.-Mexican relations) to describe the policy of capital export, that is, the peaceful conquest. Mexican elites, junior partners in the economic conquest, joined with Jones. The Mexican consul general in New York City, Juan N. Navarro, preferred "most intimate intercourse" for describing the economic relation.[21] The name changes notwithstanding, the policy and practice of "interdependence" (or "indissoluble" linkages or "intimate intercourse") remained consonant with Conant's guidelines.[22]

Joining the chorus, President Woodrow Wilson explicitly connected the introduction of capital around the globe with political power. "We have got to finance the world in some important degree," he told a conference of business people, "and those who finance the world must understand it and rule it with their spirits and their minds."[23] The transnational economic theory highlighting the necessity of the export of surplus capital for the survival of the economic order and its corollary, the peaceful conquest of undeveloped areas of the world, had by the end of the nineteenth century become a firmly entrenched axiom in U.S. foreign policy. The United States clearly understood the relation that Wilson drew between the export of capital and the political power that it embodied, and sought not only to maintain that power but to deepen and expand it as well, via military power if necessary.

To summarize, U.S. foreign policy toward Latin America, particularly that policy applied to Mexico, was largely a question rationalized upon (1) a constantly expanding surplus capital that threatened to bring down interest rates and plunge the nation into economic stagnation, and (2) the solution to the surplus, the Open Door policy (sometimes described as Dollar Diplomacy) and its corollary, the economic conquest of Latin America. Here I add two other requirements for the solution: the availability of cheap natural resources required for domestic industrial production and access to cheap labor to extract those natural resources. Together, these critical factors explain the late-nineteenth-century expansionism, titled the peaceful conquest by Rosecrans and his generation, into the undeveloped areas of the world overtaken by the United States and Europe.

THE PEACEFUL CONQUEST AND ITS SOCIAL RELATIONS

F. E. Powell, writing in 1920, noted that "the early eighties were years of optimism, and American capital flowed in increasing currents into Mexican railroads. The source of these funds was generally the larger financial interests, however; for it does not appear that securities were generally taken by small investors."[24] By 1910 no less than $500 million in American capital was invested in Mexico's railroads and another $500 million was sunk in mining, oil, and agriculture; all were key sectors of the Mexican economy. That half-billion invested in railroads formed 80 percent of the total capital invested in Mexico's railroads. Consequently, as one commentator noted in 1924, "practically all the capital invested in industrial enterprises in Mexico is foreign, while all the labor employed in these enterprises is Mexican."[25]

At least 300,000 people migrated from the central plateau to mining camps like Cananea, Batopilas, Santa Eulalia, and Nacozari; to the railway worker settlements that peppered the main rail lines between the border and Mexico City; and to the oil camps from Tampico to the Veracruz coast. These internal labor migrations northward, the social consequence of foreign capital, appeared first in the late 1890s and soon became a main current of Mexican population shifts that continued throughout the twentieth century. Ultimately, these demographic alterations foreshadowed the construction of the ethnic Mexican community in the United States (discussed in Chapter 4).[26]

Another related demographic shift occurring simultaneously brought into Mexico a steady movement of American citizens, not for purposes of immigrating permanently, but to administer the various enterprises established by American capital. By 1910 approximately 40,000 Americans lived across Mexico, the majority in Mexico City, with many living in the mining, oil, and rail sites established in the previous thirty years of an open door to capital.[27] The social relations rooted in the peaceful conquest appeared in bold relief throughout Mexico. The Penoles mine, a typical mine operated by American concerns, offered a generalized example of the new division of labor and the new social relations. One engineer commented,

> At present the mine is producing 500 tons of ore per day . . . and approximately 1200 men [are] underground. At the mine all the employees except superintendent, assistant master mechanic, electrician, head diamond setter, master mechanic . . . head pumpmen, head carpenter, foremen and cashier are Mexicans.[28]

The new relations of production were widespread. From his office in Mexico City, consulting engineer J. B. Empson commented that in some circumstances a "mine superintendent in Mexico has very often to rely on his own resources, especially in small mines where he may be the only white person employed."[29] Emil Blichfeldt observed an identical mining scene, which prompted him to write, "No white man above or below ground does manual work."[30] Mexican cheap labor on one side and American supervisors, administrators, and technicians, some with their families, on the other together produced critical commodities for export to the United States.[31] The pillars of commodity production in Mexico and its class relations assumed an imperial transnational character not unlike the social features of Europe's colonial conquests of the same time period.

Railroads: Modernizing Transportation

American expansionism first surfaced in a concerted fashion in the late 1870s. After amiable negotiations between railroad promoters and the Mexican elite, led by Porfirio Díaz, contractual agreements for construction of the Mexican railroad system were routinely signed. Contractual arrangements included generous concessions and a total of $32 million in subsidies. Enticing concessions led to "an astonishing rate" of U.S. capital moving into Mexico. By 1880 the process of rail development was in full swing, and by 1884 the first major railroad line extended from Mexico City to the U.S. border. Except for 400 miles, the entire railroad system of Mexico, comprising 15,000 miles, was eventually constructed by American capital. The lines connected Mexico City, the heart of Mexico, with major American lines like Union Pacific, Southern Pacific, and the Atchison, Topeka and Santa Fe. Indeed, the system builders ignored connecting Mexico internally, planning instead for a system of importing and exporting commodities between Mexico and the United States. Put another way, Mexico's railway system, for all practical purposes, formed an extension of the U.S. system. A foreign affairs expert went so far as to contend that the railroads of Mexico comprised "a part of the great railway building movement which between 1870 and 1890 threw a net-work of railways over . . . the United States and reached across to the distant Pacific."[32] The consequences wrought by railroads differed in Mexico from those which affected the United States. John W. Foster, former secretary of state and onetime minister to Mexico, writing for the *New York Tribune* unequivocally assessed that dissimilarity: "Mexico is now bound to the United States by the iron ties of four railroads."[33] No one ever mentioned or hinted that the railroads bound the United States to Mexico, but then again such a contention would have been patently false.

Among the investors were famed personages from the Robber Baron era like Jay Gould, J. P. Morgan, Russell Sage, U. S. Grant, E. H. Harriman, and C. P. Huntington.[34] Observers noted the critical role that large financial interests played in developing Mexico's rail system. In effect, U.S. railroad corporations and their stockholders funded, designed, built, and managed the railroad system using U.S. technology, generous Mexican government subsidies, and, most important, massive employment of cheap Mexican labor recruited from Mexico's central regions. Annually from 30,000 to 40,000 laborers worked in the various construction and maintenance sites, forming railroad boxcar camps up and down the lines, all under the supervision of American personnel.

The late nineteenth century introduced new and radical social relations into Mexico: the Mexican industrial working class began to take root.[35] However, these were not social relations originating from the operation of Mexican capital. On the contrary, U.S. economic expansionism spurred the enactment of Mexican legislation to "de-peasant" the land near planned and constructed railroads. These legislative decrees uprooted peasants from village lands on a massive scale, which resulted in their migration to cities and forming the surplus labor that railroad builders recruited, employed, and, when necessary, housed in company towns.[36] In addition, railroads ruined the mule packers' transport system, which could not compete with the cheaper and more efficient trains and was forced into the surplus labor supply.

Railroad construction and maintenance required thousands of unskilled laborers and experienced mechanics to build and repair the 15,000 miles of lines that extended the length of Mexico. In addition, spurs running from the main trunks connected remote mining and oil sites with transport facilities to and from the United States. Within this historical context, a permanent migration of workers established a new demographic pattern in Mexico. Railroad camps assumed a permanent place in the configuration of labor settlements spurred by foreign capital. Along railroad tracks and at construction sites, an entire train of boxcars often served as housing and, wrote the Englishwoman Mrs. Alec Tweedie, was "moved about as the necessity arose. . . . The workmen literally live on the spot. . . . The engineers have a series of tents . . . these can be moved as required." Workers also lived in settled communities which Tweedie described as "small wooden houses, forming a miniature village" and, at other locales, tent camps located about every 20 miles along the route. These "strange little settlements," as she called them, seemed as remote as the vast desert, canyons, and mountains that nestled around them.[37] One engineer encountered an unimaginable scene, a rather concentrated construction project in Sonora, which he described as a huge anthill consisting of a laboring army of 14,000 workers. Upon completing their shifts, workers lived in tents and on boarding trains. Across the desert, "a fascinating sight" intrigued the traveler. Here was a company store, which sold supplies at double their common selling price. Our engineer also pointed out that the general features of all American-sponsored railroad enterprises in Mexico appeared in these mobile villages. As he put it, "Two civilizations—the American and the old conservative Spanish— have adapted themselves."[38]

Again, novel social relations surfaced in the numerous railroad camps. American personnel administered a labor force consisting of displaced Mexican peasants. In the maintenance crews, the same relations obtained, and even the crews on the railcars seemed to be Americans. Train engineers, conductors, porters, and technicians were recruited from the United States and usually spoke only English. The racial component of American class relations obtained as well; porters and cooks were generally American blacks, although occasionally a Chinese servant was hired. The unskilled crews, particularly the construction and maintenance men (the American companies would have us believe that all Mexicans were unskilled), came from the growing surplus Mexican population. Thus the social fabric of Mexican society underwent a significant alteration with the peaceful conquest. An entire social and economic system was exported and grafted onto the Mexican nation.

Oil Exploration, Drilling, and Shipment

Oil and industry were inseparable. In the search for critical raw materials, oil paralleled copper, iron, and silver. Consequently, the market demand for oil would inevitably motivate exploration and production of this valuable industrial constituent. Foreign interests pioneered oil development with results that equaled those obtained in mining and railroads.[39] After success in the California oil fields, oil millionaire Edward L. Doheny, granted title by Mexico to lands measuring over 400,000 acres, developed the Mexican Petroleum Company, and in competition with such companies as Standard Oil and the Texas Company dominated the field. Clarence W. Barron, managing editor of the *Wall Street Journal*, celebrated the development of Mexico's oil by calling attention to the Americans who "cleared the jungle . . . built blacksmith shops, warehouses, water lines, and hospitals. They bored for oil . . . and brought forth the biggest oil gusher in the world. Pipe lines and railways preceded and followed the gushers."[40] In their critique of U.S. economic domination around the globe, Scott Nearing and Joseph Freeman noted, "The oil fields of Mexico were one of the richest economic prizes in the world."[41]

The oil industry, commented Wallace Thompson in 1920, "is overwhelmingly a foreign enterprise," with U.S. and to a lesser extent British oil companies competing for the coveted ingredient to industrial production.[42] Thompson added, with palpable pleasure, that "the story of the Tampico oil fields has been the story of the Americans. . . . No Mexican name and no Mexican interest are connected with the vast development which has come." Explorations, drilling, and shipping involved geologists, engineers, technicians, skilled oil workers, and investors who ultimately contributed to making Mexico the oil source for the railroads, as well as for the mining operations, including smelters and refineries and the electrical plants established by the mining companies. But more important, exports to the United States were considerable; in 1917, for example, no less than 14 million barrels were shipped to the United States and 4 million were sold to Union Oil Company for marketing in South America.[43] Oil investments totaled $125 million in 1915, and by the late 1920s the United States had eclipsed British concerns and sat safely in the driver's seat, controlling 95 percent of Mexico's petroleum production.

Soon after the turn of the century, at the center of oil production near and around Tampico on the Gulf of Mexico, a newly constructed port lined with "wharves, warehouses and hundreds of tanks of oil . . . ships, tankers and cargo boats" radically transformed the former fishing village.[44] And in the surrounding region along the coast, the tropical forest and vegetation gave way to clearings for oil drillings, pipelines and storage tanks, and administration offices; and nearby, makeshift camps and company towns housed thousands of Mexican laborers and their families.

In-migration of peasants recruited to work as cheap labor by contractors from the highlands, together with foreign skilled workers and managers, increased Tampico's population from 25,000 in 1905 to 75,000 ten years later, and by 1921 Tampico counted 150,000 inhabitants.[45] Company managers recruited workers through an *enganche* (recruitment) system of labor contractors, who plied their trade as far to the nation's center as Guanajuato with promises of free transport, bonuses, and good wages. At El Ebano oil fields, some 7,000 workers established their living quarters, while at Pánuco the onetime "little town" counted 10,000 living within its limits. Similar increases were recorded in the Tuxpan oil fields down the coast from Tampico and in northern Veracruz. Under the stimulus of the hunt for oil, the population of the state of Veracruz increased from 854,000 in 1895 to 1,133,000 fifteen years later.[46] A proletariat with a multitude of tasks associated with oil production took form along the Gulf. Together with the railroad and mining labor forces, oil workers exemplified the emerging social relations of the foreign-dominated modernization sweeping Mexico.

Edward D. Doheny, the American who opened up the oil fields around Tampico, frankly described the social relations as a "caste system" that sharply distinguished American personnel from the Mexican laborers.[47] Most workers established makeshift dwellings of sticks and bamboo, with earthen floors roofed with thatched palm leaves creating clusters of huts amid mango and banana groves and along lagoons. Beyond the thatched-roof houses ("replaced so easily when they wear out"), the company rented homes to the Mexican workers, two-room wooden "cottages" with a bedroom and kitchen but without cooking or laundry facilities. Apparently, women were expected to create their own cooking facilities and wash in the nearby oil-tinged river.[48] In the "metropolis of camps," workers who had migrated from peasant villages reestablished a community, with churches, street vendors, a marketplace and plaza, and other elements of Mexican village culture. Not far from their burgeoning settlements, former subsistence peasants worked for wages in all of the unskilled categories, carrying out the heavy lifting, digging, maintenance, and transporting. However, the social relations of the oil economy extended beyond the workers and their novel living conditions.

Along with the advent of peasants, American personnel arrived but assumed a place in the oil economy's social structure far removed from the "common quarters" of the men they were to manage. These separate residential patterns, including "a rigid grouping of the various classes of employees," fashioned what became known as the "Mexican village" and the

"American colony." According to Doheny, American mechanics (who stood below the administrative and managerial personnel) were housed in three-room houses with shared bathing and laundry facilities. For single men "occupying the higher and official positions the company provided a clubhouse which is the most complete structure of its kind in the Republic." Here the men enjoyed "reading rooms, billiard tables, tennis courts and complete bathing facilities." The clubhouse also served as a general gathering place for the American residents, where parties, celebrations, and receptions might be held.[49]

Doheny proudly described the company policy regarding its employees, particularly its housing for married personnel. "The houses for the American employees of the company," he told an interviewer, "consist of five room cottages, well kept, well cared for and presenting very attractive appearance." Together with the clubhouse, bookstore, and hospital, the needs of the American colony were well satisfied. For security, entry to the Pánuco quarters was restricted to residents and servants, the latter often Chinese brought to the camps. For the women living in the company-supplied quarters, life held a daily routine of unremitting leisure, often to excess. One visitor to Pánuco remarked that

> unless a woman throws off the spell and finds duties for herself, there is absolutely nothing for her to do in Pánuco. Chinamen cook the meals. Chinese boys come early to sweep the bungalow and bring drinking water. They call for the laundry and return it. They take care of the dooryards. The men of the household are far off in the fields from five o'clock in the morning until past six at night, when they return weary. . . . The women meanwhile, read until all novels and magazines seem alike. . . . They sleep and nap and sleep again.[50]

While life was "easy," the "slow tempo" led to boredom, depression, and longing to be "back home." One wife of an oil man was heard to remark, "I think if I don't get to the States before the rainy season starts, I'll go crazy."[51] However, the vast distance in experiences between the men and women of the laborers' camps and those of the American quarters stood out sharply.

More than the distinctions in residential areas and standards of living quarters differentiated the laboring population from the Americans. The centralization of power, inherent in all capitalistic enterprises, undergirded the colonial atmosphere. Americans managed, administered, and dominated the policies governing the workplace—and this usually meant control of the political balance of power—ensuring the ability of the company to enforce any and all policy decisions it chose. In search of a compliant workforce, administrators practiced welfare capitalism, which was displayed in Christmas parties and company barbecues served up by the American supervisory staff, common fare at the oil camps.[52] Ceremonial trappings concealed more important dealings with local political bosses. To ensure that its power remained unscathed, companies paid local *jefes políticos* for their services in controlling the labor force and quelling any potential for worker rebellion. Like their counterparts in the mining and railroad zones, officials of the oil companies joined with local, regional, state, and of course national bosses to politically dominate the population.

Like the legendary Ugly American, the Americans in Tampico lorded it over the Mexican population to the celebratory adulation of the imperial-minded Wallace Thompson. Of the economic conquest and of his compatriots he wrote:

> To-day there are 8,000 Americans and . . . the swaggering, free-money, noisy, busy atmosphere of the frontier, of oil fields, of the white man on his bully-ragging, destructive, inconsequential "education" of the dark brother round the world permeates the place. . . . Tampico is a monument to the genius and faith of the Americans who made it great.[53]

Mining and Smelting Company Towns

Railroads did more than connect the southern and central regions of Mexico with the United States; they also led to a massive investment in mining, particularly in Mexico's northern states. Shortly, railroads served as the pathway for accessing and exploiting Mexico's vast storehouse of mineral and metal resources and led some to title the rails "mineral railroads."[54] In 1908 no less than 48 percent of rail-borne cargo on the Mexican Central was "due directly or indirectly to the mining industry."[55] By opening up the mining industry, thousands of prospectors, American and Mexican, working to find a claim or perhaps rework an old abandoned mine, were soon put out of circulation. The new era of mining no longer allowed space for small individual operations or the preindustrial Mexican methods of mining. Mining in Mexico was transformed into a modern, industrialized operation similar in structure to that of the major industrial complexes in the United States. Not surprisingly, mining became the province of the wealthy investor—American investor, that is.

Within two decades of the completion of the first rail line, the mining industry, founded largely upon $300 million in American capital, reached

maturity. American investments overwhelmed the $15 million that origi-
nated from Mexican investors, junior partners in the modernization of
Mexico's archaic and often abandoned mining works. Mexico's main contribution consisted of nature's raw materials and cheap labor, the latter
numbering some 130,000 workers laboring for the various mining and
smelting operations across Mexico. Perhaps the most valuable commodity exploited by U.S. mining companies was the abundant cheap labor developed in large numbers through the operation of the railroads.

James W. Malcolmson, an experienced engineer in Mexican mines,
noted that in 1902, the heyday of mining, "a ton of ore can be mined in
Mexico to-day for 40 percent of what it could cost if the same ore were in
the United States."[56] Another wrote in 1905, "The cheapness of labor and
the absence of labor troubles have caused an enormous inflow of American capital, awakening the idle and slumbering regions of Sonora."[57] Of
course, what he meant by the "absence of labor troubles" was the milita-
rized social order provided by the iron-fisted rule of Porfirio Díaz. One
geologist with the U.S. Geological Survey wryly commented that in the
development of the mining industry, Mexico played an "extraordinarily
small part . . . except to furnish the resources and the labor and see the
profits go abroad."[58] Natural resources, cheap and politically controlled
labor, and an elite willing to bend to the "economic conquest" designed
by U.S. investors—all the essentials of an imperial relationship—endured throughout the century.

By 1900 engineers employed by the U.S. Geological Survey, advanc-
ing the interests of mining companies, had mapped out Mexico's geology,
noting the terrain and potential exploitation sites. Nothing was left to
chance.[59] Nearly 300 mining concessions managed by U.S.-based concerns sprouted overnight, causing a radical modernization and expansion
of the mining industry. By the early twentieth century, at least 160 U.S.-
based operations dotted four of Mexico's desert-like northern states, Chihuahua, Sonora, Sinaloa, and Durango. The words of engineer Malcolmson, written in 1903, confirm the dominant presence of foreign capital:

> The immense amount of American and foreign capital now coming
> into the Republic shows very clearly the confidence of the world in the
> future stability of political conditions in the country.
>
> It would appear to me safe to say that there are more prosperous
> mining camps in Mexico than any equal area of the world.[60]

Observations like Malcomson's appeared with regularity, particularly
with the use of the charged term "invasion," which invoked a militaristic

image of the entrance of American capital into Mexico. Walter D. Beverly, for example, pointed out that by the time he first visited Mexico in 1892 "the American invasion was well underway."[61] Another recalled that in the Santa Eulalia district, the period after 1883 "embraces the years of the American invasion."[62]

Mining operations often employed technology dependent on electricity. The absence of power sources led companies to develop power plants that did more than supply energy to mines; they also supplied energy to urban centers for private and public use, including urban transport.[63] Mining and its inseparable twin operation, smelting and refining, generated the founding of smelters, large and small, throughout the mining districts. However, Guggenheim's American Smelting and Refining Company, known in Mexico as ASARCO, controlled one-half of all smelting operations, a virtual monopoly.

Taken together, mining and smelting operations required a large-scale reorganization of Mexico's demography, settlement patterns, and labor relations. Internal migrations and the resulting surplus labor fostered by railroad construction were tapped by mining companies, creating a radical shift in the population from the central regions to the once sparsely populated northern tier of states. Companies actively recruited workers via agencies contracted to deliver men to the mines, causing "a constant movement of labor northward." One mining company alone imported 8,000 workers to the northern mines.[64] At the Corralitos and Minas de San Pedro mining district in Chihuahua, the population swelled to over 5,000 when an active "family importation" program delivered "carloads of miners and their families" from the state of Zacatecas.

Here in the company-built town, "long rows of two room houses" were assigned to those workers willing to assume a permanent place in the labor chain.[65] If recruiting agents failed to bring in the required number of workers, other methods might be employed. A western Chihuahua mine superintendent, for example, asked the local curate for assistance, who consented and provided a "miracle, a Virgin, for instance" who appeared and performed miracles. The mine owners found that with the religious flimflam "it was easy to secure all the required labor."[66] It appears that the use of religion to keep labor was not uncommon; one engineer advised that it should be a general policy to provide "the camp with a church or arranging for periodical visits of the curate. And if something is contributed occasionally to the *padre*, it will found to be a good investment, for his good will in keeping the men at work is a valuable investment."[67] The Compañía de Penoles used perks like free housing, baths, theater, school, hospital, drinking water, and loans to attract workers. However, most mining operations were reluctant to go beyond housing and a few diversions like company picnics and Fourth of July contests and relied upon the recruiter and labor contractor to bring labor to the mine.[68] New forms of social relations inevitably greeted Mexican labor as they entered into U.S.-owned operations. At the fabulously successful American mine at Penguico in Guanajuato, for example, a former American employee remarked, "No Mexican was permitted to eat with the Americans, not even the 'rough necks.'" He went on to state that at Penguico, "We addressed them [Mexicans] as inferiors."[69]

The impact of American capital and personnel was nowhere greater than in the mining and smelting industries. Across the northern tier of states, new mining operations recycled older claims and led to a radical alteration in demographic, social, and work patterns. A look at Chihuahua and Sonora tells the story, not only of a new era in Mexican mining and of economic relations with the United States, but of class relations as well. Cananea remains the best-known example of American mining in Mexico and rightfully deserves its recognition. On land that was once nothing more than scrub desert, Cananea turned into a small industrial metropolis of 25,000. Here, it was observed, stood "one of the most modern, orderly and best equipped American mining camps."[70] Some 5,000 workers lived in the housing built by Greene Consolidated Mining Company, while the American personnel lived in separate quarters. Americans in authority (and generally all Americans enjoyed some authority and privileges not held by Mexican workers) tended to be young, which one author likened to "the English officials in India." The parallel was more than merely one of age; the colonial analogy was summoned for other comparisons in many a writer's commentary on Mexico.[71] Rather than revisiting Cananea, the lesser-known but equally important mining sites of Batopilas and Monte del Cobre will be treated here to distill the radical transformations that foreign capital effected upon Mexican society.

Batopilas

Batopilas provides an especially interesting case of peaceful conquest whose history as a mining site precedes the arrival of Alexander Robey Shepherd, the onetime architect for Washington, D.C. After having been accused of corruption while managing the redesigning of the capital, and armed with the capital of a thousand investors, Shepherd turned an old and inefficient Spanish-era complex of mines into one of the richest silver producers in the world. Located in a remote, nearly inaccessible mountainous district of Chihuahua, the five mines at Batopilas exemplified the geographic distribution of the American mining establishment. At its height, Batopilas extracted anywhere from $50,000 to $100,000 in silver bullion per month; mule trains transported the heavy load over mountains, canyons, and desert to rail lines for shipment to the border. One visitor marveled that the mines of Batopilas "yielded many bonanzas and have produced some of the largest and most beautiful masses of native silver that have been exhibited in the world."[72] Batopilas made Shepherd "a millionaire several times over," which was not an uncommon feature of the new forms of wealth surfacing in the mining districts.[73]

As mining matured in Chihuahua, bullion worth several million dollars reached the state capital for transport to the United States. The success of American-dominated mining in Chihuahua led to the formation of the exclusive Chihuahua Club, which limited membership to 200 of the American colony's elite and was said to maintain a "large number on the waiting list."[74] By the mid-1880s the growing American colony in Chihuahua was large enough to support two newspapers, the *Chihuahua Mail* and the *Enterprise*. The *Mail* printed half of its columns in Spanish and was not shy of criticizing the local and state governments over matters of interest to American investors, and like the *Enterprise* its principle objective was the expansion of U.S. capital invested in northern Mexico. Based on the rapid influx of American capital invested in Chihuahua in the 1890s, the editors of the *Mail* and *Enterprise* must have beamed proudly at that outcome.[75] Marie Robinson Wright visited Mexico in 1910 on a book-writing tour (like many Americans before and after her) and was most impressed, not only by the financial Americanization of Chihuahua, but also by the cultural Americanization as well. She noted that "English is as much spoken as Spanish, and many American enterprises and manufactories give an air of progress."[76] She, of course, was not alone. James Wilson, a San Francisco newspaper editor, was pleased to find Chihuahua "largely Americanized."[77]

American investing had only just begun to enter Mexico when Alexander Shepherd concluded plans for his grand investment strategy. Upon receiving a handsome concession covering 61 square miles of territory (which, like all concessions, could be held and sold for a profit to another interest), Shepherd journeyed from Washington, D.C., with his entire family to Batopilas in 1880. Shepherd had already purchased an old hacienda located not far from the old mine plus two ranches comprising 1,600 acres. The sprawling colonial hacienda became the family residence, visitor center, and business headquarters. Here a retinue of *mozos*, or servants, not unlike those who worked for American families (and single men) throughout Mexico, cleaned, laundered, cooked, and looked after the children if needed. After modern equipment had been imported duty-free from the United States and installed for operation in the mine (and eventually technology for an electric plant), the problem of securing sufficient labor to successfully carry out the operation emerged. That problem evaporated rather quickly by hiring from the nearby settlements with a variety of carrots and some sticks.

Workers were summoned from distant towns and villages to engage in the numerous tasks associated with mining with the lure of good wages by the standards of Mexico, plus housing and credit at company stores. At Batopilas, 1,500 Mexican workers were regularly employed for manual work secured and organized through labor contractors; in addition, an assemblage of supervisors—chemists, a medical doctor, a schoolteacher, and several engineers, all Americans, some with families—rounded out the new enterprise. A new pattern of social relations sprouted overnight, with Mexicans numbering approximately 5,000, while about 50 Americans, the American colony, resided apart from the Mexican majority. For over twenty years, Shepherd and his staff not only administered the profitable mining operation but ran the town and the surrounding area as well. Upon his death in 1902, the company continued the same policies under the management of Shepherd's son.

As its general manager and major shareholder, the elder Shepherd occupied the center of the whole operation, not only in relation to the mining itself, but also related to the political establishment in the town and in the surrounding region. Indeed, Shepherd was more than merely an investor in mines and the head of a large mining operation; the company owned two large ranches and an electric generating plant. It was said at the time that the mine was "the sole support of the town and neighborhood." This put the manager "in the position of a sort of father to all."[78] Shepherd's paternalism created to some degree a measure of respect for the power wielded by the management hierarchy; some thought that it also resurrected the practices of the Middle Ages. One visitor depicted "life at Batopilas as a perfect type of the old feudal days." Isaac Marcosson praised Shepherd for "having created a whole empire," and noted that when the entrepreneur died "he was master of a domain of over 30 square miles."[79] Grant Shepherd, the elder Shepherd's son, described social order within the microempire as "a perfect discipline founded upon respect and affection for those in command." The younger Shepherd claimed that the respect was generated by a "personal interest taken by *El Patron Grande* [the Big Boss] and the *Patroncitos* [the Small Bosses] in the lives and welfare of all the employees."[80] Assertions by mine owners that they took care of their labor force did not extend to their trusting the workers. One observer noted that in a Mexican mine "the chief problem . . . thus far has been the dishonesty of the employees in the face of the extremely high-grade ore."[81] At the end of each shift, all mine workers except the American foremen and supervisors were stripped and searched on the lingering suspicion that Mexicans were by nature thieves and therefore, if given the opportunity, they would hide valuable ores in their clothes and even stash them in their tattered leather sandals.

For several generations, American personnel worked, vacationed (hiking trips were a favorite pastime), hunted and fished, enjoyed Sunday picnics in the countryside, and celebrated in the local and surrounding area. The region was a hunter's paradise, filled with deer, boar, peccary, and ducks, as well as ponds for those who preferred to fish. A visiting metallurgist recollected that the "American colony in Batopilas is a delightfully hospitable and happy lot."[82] Their easy access to servants of various kinds may have accounted for this hospitality. *Mozos,* the name given to all those who served as mule packers and guides as well as to household help, were indispensable, particularly on weekend hunting trips and when traveling. When journeying to and from distant points that were without rail connections, transportation consisted of mule rides over rough trails that traversed ravines and canyons and often required several days (from Batopilas to Chihuahua City took a week). In these instances, *mozos* were more than indispensable guides; in addition to cooking and general assisting, they guarded against highwaymen.

During the early years of mining development, geologists and engineers, accompanied by a guide, probed the regions for potential signs of high-grade ores. Mining engineer Mark R. Lamb traveled throughout western Chihuahua on a mine inspection tour, and of his experiences he remarked, "I have finally decided that the only danger in thus traveling without a *mozo* lies in the possibility of meeting with some accident with no help near." And later, "Over little used trails . . . it was easy to persuade me to take a *mozo.*[83] A foreign traveler in the company of a *mozo* became a distinguishing feature of the new Mexican social landscape. The presence of a *mozo* extended into the mines as well, where they worked as assistants to various American personnel, carrying equipment and materials associated with mining. One engineer warmly referred to his assistant as "my man Friday at my heels as usual."[84]

Within Batopilas, a *mozo* might hold a lantern on a late evening return from a party or dance, or act as a messenger sent with a note down the road or to a distant town. A specialty among casual Mexican laborers was that of the *cargador*, or load carrier, who hauled heavy loads often over fairly long distances, a feat that never failed to astound the Americans. The American colony quickly adjusted to a lifestyle in which mule packers, house servants, and *cargadores* serviced their basic and recreational needs. No task was beyond a *mozo* or *cargador*, so that when the need arose both were within earshot. In opposition to the philosophy of self-reliance, Americans seemed to integrate the tradition of having manual labor performed by others into their daily lives without much hesitation.

Known by the townspeople as El Patrón Grande, a term connoting power, Shepherd enjoyed friendly relations with the local *jefes políticos* to such an extent that he often collaborated in an official capacity in tracking down criminals or in putting down political insurrections.[85] Shepherd hobnobbed with state governors and enjoyed the confidence of Enrique Creel, the Mexican ambassador to the United States. Shepherd had enough clout to invite the state governor for an official dinner at his hacienda, an occasion described by Shepherd's son as "quite an affair. . . . The party congregated at the steps where the mounts were assembled, held by *mozos* arrayed in their resplendent best."[86] After dinner the two men were said to have "engaged in close and confidential conversation."

Beyond his ties with Mexico's *políticos*, Shepherd worked closely with the local U.S. consular and embassy officials. Consuls were generally selected from the regional American colony (whose members traditionally recommended them for the office) and usually had practical ties with American investors, if they were not investors themselves. In general, U.S. officials, from the embassy to the local consulate level, were eager to protect American interests, and consequently managers of American firms and consuls interacted on a consistent basis. These broader networks, together with ties to local and national politically powerful personages, secured for Shepherd the image of a political boss. Thus his unofficial title, El Patrón Grande, became the common term used by the laboring force and townspeople. Not surprisingly, Shepherd proudly defended the policies of the Díaz administration and showed his support symbolically by the name of a major mine excavation: the Porfirio Díaz Tunnel. Beyond symbolism, he actively collaborated with the government and had a special interest in protecting the Díaz administration from political opponents and their propensity to instigate *pronunciamientos*, or insurrections. Every now and then an aspiring *jefe* would proclaim a political uprising, which would cause Shepherd and the local *jefe político* to make plans for "repulsing any attack that might be made."[87] Plans included equipping the American and Mexican employees with weapons and ammunition. After the overthrow of Díaz in 1910, Shepherd, like many of his contemporaries, feared a rollback of Díaz era policies, although guarantees issued by the succeeding governments protected American investments and the right to continue the Open Door policy. Nonetheless, Shepherd's contemporaries fondly reminisced on the unimpeded flood of U.S. capital that entered Mexico during the Díaz years.

Monte del Cobre

Life at Monte del Cobre, also located in Chihuahua, exhibited many of the geologic and social conditions found in Batopilas. Daily life in the camp was centered around the mine headquarters, which, in a classic industrial scene, was next to an immense mill that reverberated with the clapping of steel machinery topped by a belching smokestack. Nearby were a blacksmith shop, idle equipment, railcars for hauling ores, hoists and, of course, the deep, cavernous, and always dangerous mine. One writer's comment on an ASARCO plant applied to Monte. "It is," he wrote, "a cross-section of Pittsburgh transplanted to the Coahuila plain."[88] These industrial outcroppings formed a self-contained system of production that appeared strangely out of place on the otherwise precapitalist agrarian landscape. Here labor contractors vied for the privilege of bringing a crew of men, at a certain rate of pay and for a set number of days or weeks to work. It was one thing for the hiring office to hire a crew, another to hold the men for several years or even for a season. Companies settled on towns built and operated by the company, which seemed to solve the problem of securing sufficient numbers of men for set periods of time.

At Monte the 60 or so Americans resided in what was commonly known as the American colony, situated high on a hill and segregated from the Mexican section below, known as the Mexican town, which was comprised of wooden company housing and a separate section of houses that some of the workers built of adobe and cast-off materials.[89] An engineer described the distinctive character of each sector from an American viewpoint: "The peaceful quiet of the [American] colony gave way to the swarming life of the Mexican town."[90] The Americans enjoyed what were described as "attractive little houses," each with its "irrigated garden" lining Pershing Drive, as the main walkway in the colony came to be known during the Mexican Revolution. Each company house enjoyed the convenience of electricity and generally employed a young Mexican woman to cook and keep house. The variance in habits and customs between the Mexican help and their employers caused no little friction. Ralph Ingersoll, a veteran mining engineer in Cobre, found that wives of American personnel seldom learned to speak Spanish, preferring instead that the Mexican maids learn English. Moreover, he asserted, Americans "were convinced of the inferiority of Mexicans" and generally complained that "the natives . . . were clumsy in waiting on table and did not know how to make beds." As in other colonial settings, boredom continually affected the residents, particularly the wives of the men managing the operations. One miner looked back and recalled, "They all wanted more than anything else to be back in that rarefied air that they had left."[91] Regardless of the American wives' psychological depressions, across the array of social relations that brought Mexicans and Americans into contact, the Americans in Batopilas and those of Monte del Cobre enforced a set of common norms that Mexicans were obligated to observe.[92]

In Monte del Cobre's Mexican section, mine workers living on a dollar and half per day were assigned a hillside row of "one room shacks" measuring not more than fifteen square feet. The shanties were rented at premium prices, and it was not unusual for workers to double up and share their quarters with another family. While the company houses for the Americans exhibited "geometrical lines" the worker-built houses were constructed without a plan, houses here and there, wherever space was available. At one mine in the district, the "homes of the mine workmen were spread all over the landscape, and for the most part were mere jacales, hovels, and huts."[93] Here, Mexican families lived in what was described as a display of "sordid poverty" on a street "no more than a washed out gulley." Americans never found much to appreciate in the Mexican section, whether company-built housing or worker-built. Of the latter, engineer Ralph A. Ingersoll wrote in his memoir that

> every balcony had its own tangled garden in rusty tin cans, its assortment of half-washed clothes drying in the sun, and a disorder and color that defied the geometrical lines of the company-built houses. I could not see the interiors, but there was a constant traffic, going in and coming out, of toddling babies and odd-colored pigs.[94]

For the "benefit" of the Mexican quarter, the company operated its own store for Mexican trade that, like the general run of company stores, gouged the worker as a way of securing labor by having them pay off their debt. Of this one writer offered:

It is custom throughout the district for every company to operate a store and expect the employees to deal there exclusively; in the towns this is sometimes a hardship as there are plenty of store-keepers willing to sell at prices lower than the company stores. But in the less settled parts the company store is a boon, in that it brings a greater amount of variety of goods into the district than any individual could do. The men are expected to take out their pay in orders on the company's store, and with a storekeeper who knows how to handle the men, but a small amount of actual cash will be needed at the end of the month.[95]

One veteran of mining in Sinaloa, Mexico, confirmed, "Perhaps the greatest injustice worked on the laborers . . . was the system of company stores. Especially this was true of the mining companies."[96] Not only did the company store extend credit to workers and take the repayment out of their weekly pay, but local businesses found it hard to compete. In addition, company stores as a rule made a profit of as much as 30 to 40 percent "on the actual cost of goods."[97]

The people of the Mexican town never abandoned their cultural practices in their new surroundings and maintained their traditional plaza, church, small shops, cantina, and numerous religious celebrations. In the mining districts, if the Mexican section was fortunate enough to have its own school, only Mexican children attended it. In Monte, up on the hill, the dozen or so American children attended a one-room school reserved exclusively for American employees. One long-time resident described the women brought in to run the school as "two young American schoolteachers with bobbed hair and sport shirts."[98] Their appearance symbolized the deep divisions between the American colony high on the hill and the Mexican town below. As one miner put it, "Two races were represented here, each worshipping its own idols, in temples facing each other across the street."[99] Two social worlds existed side by side without much interchange except for interactions as employers and employees. Perhaps one should temper this somewhat. Certainly, Americans came to enjoy the Mexican landscape, cuisine, and folk art among other things; and Mexicans adapted a substantial number of English words to Spanish, like *traque*, *poste*, and *quequi* for railroad track, post, and cake, respectively. However, the social and political distinction was only underscored by such exchanges.[100]

Americans were extremely conscious of class and inequality dividing the Mexican from the American, and of a valuation that came with that distinction. Most Americans came from Main Street towns and had a desire to move up the social scale, possibly to escape their mediocre and humdrum past. Americans emphasized cultural differences and ignored the subtle ways in which differing cultures can have similar customs. Americans defined the culture of Mexico within the context of the invasion of capital, leading inevitably to situating all things Mexican within the standards of the United States. Consequently, the cultural response on the part of Americans not only justified the dominant presence of American capital but urged an expansion and the deepening of that presence as well.

Thus social life in the "American colony on the hill" remained self-contained and insulated, its inhabitants preferring to gather at semiformal Saturday evening dinners (by invitation only). Engineer Ingersoll recalled that the colony's dinners were always served by "a shy, dark skinned girl in misfitting calico." Diversions included bridge and mah jong parties, birthdays, and dances at the club. The company-built residences for the American personnel included a dormitory for single men and for the women hired to teach the colony's children. The dormitory included a recreation center where dances, birthday and Fourth of July celebrations, Christmas gatherings, and company parties pulled the entire colony together. At the dormitory, a lounge equipped with a phonograph player and sufficient recordings provided space for dances, which were held every other Saturday and were described as a "great civilizing agent . . . and Cobre takes it very seriously." [101] Behind the dormitory stood the tennis court (an "excellent tennis court"), the scene of frequent serious competitions. In the valley below the town reposed the six-hole golf course, where every round stirred an "intensity of enthusiasm . . . in comparison with which the spirit of St. Andrews was that of a disinterested spectator."

Extracurricular activities beyond the community's borders always beckoned to the males. Single men sometimes ventured into the Mexican section for a nightcap but more often to satisfy a "desire for adventure," as one mine engineer put it. A Saturday night to Sunday morning of dancing and other pleasurable stress releases (prostitution was available and appears to have been used by some of the men) was never a far ride away. To the uninitiated, the cantina was not easily found, located among "long adobe buildings without windows; little gleams of light coming from the cracks around the single door of each, and the sound of music and merrymaking within." [102] However, more often than not, satisfying the spirit of adventure meant a visit to the nearby and more generally acceptable saloon, appropriately named the American Club, which met their daily drinking and testosterone-laced conversation requirements at the end of the day's shift. There the men lounged with their feet propped up over a

balcony railing, with beer in hand to exchange gossip and view the sun retire behind the distant peaks.[103]

Despite the potential for reckless and dangerous extracurricular behavior, a firm discipline permeated the town, the operation of the mine,
and its ancillary industries. As at Batopilas, the company's attitude toward
the Mexicans was, in the words of a long-time mining engineer, "necessarily paternal. . . . the people dealt with are children and must be looked
after and guarded, to insure any production whatever." Americans willingly assumed the role of social and racial superiors and benefactors while
reaping the rewards of the peaceful conquest.

Other mining centers in the region replicated the Batopilas and Monte
del Cobre experiences, particularly the San Pedro mining center in
Sonora. At San Pedro, American mine personnel enjoyed the pleasures of
a tennis court and the "hunting of deer, duck, quail, and dove." Sundays
were spent at picnics at choice spots in the mountains several miles from the
mine. There the mine manager, Britton Davis, and the state governor were
"a congenial pair" who shared traditions of "good society, good wine, and
how to entertain," according to an old-time mining engineer who worked
the mine. For security, Rurales, the Mexican federal security police, regularly visited the mine to inquire which, if any, Mexican miners exhibited re-
bellious tendencies. According to Morris B. Parker, an engineer at the
mine, handing over alleged culprits "was our main outlet for suspected or
known trouble makers." Parker also told of the time that he was offered an
official authorization from a local chief of police to "shoot to kill" bandits
and of a nearby American merchant, mine owner, and large rancher who
acted like a "medieval baron."[104] Certainly, American interests enjoyed the
security offered by state-sponsored social and political control.

The Mexico City American Colony

The 40,000 Americans living in Mexico soon after the turn of the century
comprised the largest foreign element in Mexico and were particularly
visible in Mexico City, where they numbered somewhere around 15,000.
Considered the largest foreign element there, Americans quickly became
"well established" and resided near Churubusco, a section of Mexico City
that came to be known as the American colony.[105] American-style residences along streets modeled on upper-class areas of U.S. cities impressed
visitors. Here the heads of the mining, railroad, oil, and agricultural corporations congregated among their class and, more often, their national
brethren. The English language newspaper, the *Mexican Herald*, brought

them the kinds of information that they required for their businesses and lifestyles through the daily column "Society," devoted exclusively to the colony.[106] The *Herald* offered more than society chatter, particularly during the tumultuous civil war period when the popular newspaper acted as a voice for U.S. investors. Former U.S. ambassador to Mexico Henry Lane Wilson (who assisted in the overthrow of President Madero in 1912) characterized the *Herald*'s actions as a "courageous . . . stand of staunchly defending in every instance Americans and American interests."[107]

More than upscale residences comforted the residents; the colony boasted of its own country club, placed "at the midst of large grounds and on the borders of a lake, clear as crystal, fed by an artesian well."[108] The well-appointed club included the obligatory golf course ("the chief attraction") and tennis courts, and furnished a "place for dances, theatricals and concerts and a residential club in one."[109] Businesspeople networked and exchanged information at the American business club. No American ever needed to visit a Mexican hospital, since the colony enjoyed its own. A baseball diamond and a football field for the men provided weekend diversions, and the women's club offered "afternoon teas [and] literary circles." Former secretary of state John W. Foster praised the colony in a special for the *National Geographic*, contending that it had "all the paraphernalia of a well ordered society intent on getting the most out of life."[110] The sheer numbers of Americans were making a significant cultural impact, reflected in the predominant use of English on "the principal business streets and in business hours."[111] As occurred in Chihuahua, a cultural Americanization was making inroads into the once insular nation. And yet, Americans seemed never to become Mexicanized, which led one author to write:

> Foreigners have rarely become Mexican citizens. If they made money they took it elsewhere to spend it. If they lost money they went home disillusioned, but "home" was always elsewhere—never Mexico.[112]

CONCLUSION

In a span of a quarter of a century, the American financial and social presence appeared to many to have overwhelmed or at least transformed Mexico. American capital may have captured the Mexican oil, mining, and transportation sectors, but it did so without propelling any meaningful development in Mexican industry or manufacturing and tended to preserve the feudal landowning system. The latter economic formation was ignored by American modernization, hidden by an overriding interest in the Americanization of Mexico. However, new social relations introduced into Mexico by foreign capital bore a striking resemblance to the colonial pattern whereby foreigners design, administer, and enrich themselves from the country's important economic undertakings with the assistance of local elites. Meanwhile, Mexicans performed the physical labor while Americans supervised the enterprises.

Economic conquest, the peaceful conquest elaborated by Rosecrans in 1869 and fulfilled by 1900, constructed the economic relations between the United States and Mexico that endured throughout the twentieth century. In the late nineteenth and early twentieth centuries, these relations in turn shaped the thinking of a legion of American writers who descended upon Mexico on a scale never seen before with expectations of a conquest of their own. In the practice of their craft, writers of various professional stripes launched a celebration and a defense of the American empire.

2. AMERICAN WRITERS INVADE MEXICO

Mexico is a marvelous conglomerate of the ancient and the modern—the pathetic and the ludicrous. To gaze upon a country and mingle with a people of whom he had read much in various books had long been a cherished desire of his heart. And to be able to gratify that desire constituted an epoch in his life.

Reverend J. Hendrickson McCarty, D.D., *Two Thousand Miles through the Heart of Mexico* (1886)

INTRODUCTION

Railroads and writing about Mexico developed in tandem. As one writer mentioned, "Until the railroads of the last few years opened up the country, Mexico's isolation was complete."[1] Around the mid-1880s, with the travel opportunities to Mexico vastly increased, legions of Americans trekked to Mexico for a wide variety of objectives and purposes. One could travel from Washington, D.C., to Mexico City practically nonstop via railroads. What was once a fairly arduous and time-consuming trip had become a "comparatively easy matter," noted one. And another mentioned that by the late nineteenth century, an "annual invasion" of "personally conducted tourists" swarmed into the capital on a regular basis.

A market for books on Mexico sprouted, presenting titles like *Two Thousand Miles through the Heart of Mexico* (1886), *A White Umbrella in Mexico* (1895), *Mexico of the Twentieth Century* (1907), *In Indian Mexico* (1908), *Mexico Today: Social, Religious, and Political Conditions* (1913), and *The Mexican Problem* (1917). Meanwhile, countless articles in professional and popular journals and magazines complemented the books. Here we are concerned with all those who wrote about Mexico, whether they traveled as tourists, interested investors, or simply authors on the lookout for interesting (and commercially viable) subjects.[2] These accounts published in book and article form served as reference points for readers regarding

Mexico; and just as important, they provide the reader of the twenty-first century a window to the culture of a gradually evolving imperial society.

Not only did this literature attract a widespread readership, but more important, it affirmed and popularized U.S. foreign policy, from which investor interests in Mexico clearly benefited. Indeed, this literature became a key channel for information regarding Mexico in general and, in particular, the varied U.S.-based industrial and business processes initiated under the aegis of peaceful conquest.

Authors focused great attention on the supposed benefits that U.S. capital and American know-how brought to Mexico and were not shy in explaining in substantial detail why Mexico needed the United States' guidance and its expertise in order to modernize. Not a few authors appeared to pitch their works as a case for completing the "peaceful invasion" and reconstructing Mexico using the United States as the paradigm. In these instances, the euphemism for "peaceful conquest" became simply "Americanization." In tandem with Americanization, heroic representations of Porfirio Díaz for having welcomed U.S. capital appeared throughout the literature.

WRITING FRATERNITY

Except for a few extraordinary cases, nearly all authors examined in this study were enthralled by the peaceful conquest and devoted extensive space, attention, and nationalistic rhetoric in support of it. Writers traveled with a variety of motives. A few wrote of their experiences as mining engineers, others accounted for Protestant missionary works in search of converts, professional travelers sought novelty, some wrote articles for a local newspaper and later published them in book form. In one instance, a newspaper editor's letters to his family evolved into a privately published book on travel in Mexico. Artists searched for inspiration, geologists hoped to master Mexico's natural terrain, anthropologists envisioned a map of Mexico's ethnography, and the wife of a businessman exercised a repressed literary bent.

One author wrote that the only reason he visited Mexico was for the "purpose of mastering the language"; however, he could not keep from turning his visit into a book.[3] The curator of the Chicago Academy of Sciences, Frank Collins Baker, toured the Yucatán and southern Mexico "to collect data and specimens illustrating the fauna, flora, and geology."[4] Another wrote to satisfy a romantic penchant; his was, as he said, "simply a case of going to a land remote far beyond its distance in miles; shrouded in an atmosphere of mystery and danger."[5] Marie Robinson Wright made no excuses for her work; she unabashedly intended to celebrate the centennial of Mexico's independence and the dictatorial reign of Porfirio Díaz.[6] Several authors published accounts of excursions by professional groups. Articles in the *Engineering and Mining Journal* gave extensive coverage to the 1901 annual meeting of the American Institute of Mining Engineers in Mexico City and the 200 engineers in attendance who toured widely in Mexico. George G. Street recorded an 1883 journey of railroad managers and agents plus newspaper reporters on a sojourn to the city of Chihuahua. The latter trip brought 64 men to the northern mining and commercial center where, it was said, "every object of interest was visited."[7]

The literature seemed to revolve around common themes to such an extent that its writers appeared to have been influenced by a generalized model. And indeed, this was due in part to the cross-fertilization that was so apparent among many of the books. Above all, writers bought into the idea of economic conquest and worked within the context of U.S. economic expansionism and, except for one or two, never critiqued U.S. economic policy toward Mexico. Authors often quoted from each other or made reference to each other's works, and photographs were repeated in various texts. Clearly, they were aware of an emerging genre of works dedicated to Mexico (later to be known in academia as Latin American studies), and they partook in the process of its development. Charles Beebe noted in 1905 that studies of the people, culture, and markets of Mexico "may be found in half a hundred volumes."[8] He did not exaggerate. That he knew the contents of a considerable body of literature on Mexico signals that at the very least he had read that literature. Beebe was not alone. In preparation for his 1908 tour of Mexico, author William E. Carson "carefully consulted the best works on Mexico, statistical, historical and descriptive."[9]

The level of interactions reflected in substantial cross-referencing among the various players also indicates that they consulted each other's work, which may account for the overall topical coherence and repetition of themes. A brief (and partial) listing of the pervasive exchange among authors demonstrates a lively fraternizing. A few examples taken from the literature exhibit a wide-ranging informal coordination: the Reverend Francis Borton borrowed material from the anthropologist Frederick Starr and the eminent sociologist Edward A. Ross, and also dedicated his book to Starr; Francis Hopkinson Smith quoted David A. Wells; Nevin O. Winter quoted Francis Hopkinson Smith and Fanny Chambers Gooch;

E. D. Trowbridge and Emil Blichfeldt quoted extensively from Charles Flandrau; Chester Lloyd Jones praised Wallace Thompson; H. A. C. Jenison cited Robert Glass Cleland; and Ellsworth Huntington, Earnest Gruening, and Edward A. Ross quoted passages from Thompson, while Thompson noted debts to Huntington and the Doheny Research Foundation's unpublished investigation "Mexico: An Impartial Survey" (the latter prepared under auspices of University of California researchers).[10]

Networking occurred in informal and formal settings. Conferences on Mexico brought many writers into face-to-face discussions, particularly after 1920. Pomona College, located near Los Angeles, hosted annual Friends of Mexico conferences convened by the historian James Batten; Clark University convened a conference on Mexico and the Caribbean in 1920 attended by authors Frederick Starr, James Carson, E. D. Trowbridge, Samuel Guy Inman, and Ellsworth Huntington. Each presented a paper on topics relating to their varied expertise on Mexico, and the papers were later turned into a book edited by George H. Blakeslee.[11] Contemporaneously, Earnest Gruening, Frederick Starr, Frank Tannenbaum, and Stuart Chase, among others, were pioneering the field of Latin American studies. Clearly, Mexico assumed an important place not only in the academic world but in the world of popular and investor literature as well.

RIDING THE RAILS AND OTHER MEANS OF TRAVEL

Methods of travel from the United States to Mexico and within Mexico varied from the early years of the 1880s to the 1900s. Early travelers, that is, those embarking before the advent of railroads, usually crossed the U.S.-Mexican border in carriages, but as railroads opened up the first-class coach took precedence. Before railroads, a few took steamships from New York, New Orleans, or Houston and landed at Veracruz. As transportation facilities improved, the great majority took first-class Pullman cars originating at Chicago, New York, or Saint Louis, crossing at El Paso and on to points south.

Travel within Mexico often required abandoning the beaten path and stepping beyond the reach of railroads, which meant riding in carriages, called *diligencias;* many rode mules or went on horseback, while a few, mainly women, were conveyed in sedan chairs. Mrs. Shepherd, wife of Alexander Shepherd, mine superintendent at Batopilas, regularly traveled in the environs of Batopilas borne "by eight good men."[12] From such vantage points and experiences, writers jotted their first observations of the nation that had assumed a central position on the U.S. foreign policy agenda. Starting at the border and continuing throughout their travels in Mexico, their notes recorded that which most impressed, intrigued, distressed, or interested them. Seldom were they without an opinion on practically all things Mexican, from the scenery to weather, geology, history, racial origins, moral character, meteorology, architecture, dress, phenotypes, diet, culture, and religion.

Achieving a Foot in the Door

Most authors traveled with purpose and itinerary in mind, while only one or two just seemed to take one day at a time as they meandered across Mexico. However, letters of introduction and advice from insider acquaintances—either high-ranking Mexican officials or through contacts with U.S. investors—were often secured. These documents and recommendations allowed them access to influential Americans and Mexican officials at key points on the trip. A few with good contacts reached the presidential chambers of Mexico. Nearly all had a meeting or two with Mexican or American officials, from American consuls to Mexican governors and senators. Charles William Beebe and his assistant (Mrs. Beebe) obtained letters of introduction from Secretary of State John Hay and the virulent racial doctrinaire Madison Grant, an advantage that Beebe declared "proved invaluable" and allowed him "innumerable courtesies extended to us."[13]

A lucky few received the royal treatment, as did Marie Robinson Wright. On her first trip in 1897, she acknowledged a debt to Major Robert G. Gorsuch, a key investor in Mexico's railroads and official representative for Collis P. Huntington's Mexican interests. She cited Gorsuch for having "been my faithful advisor and kind friend in all matters of importance in connection with this great undertaking," as she put it. Doors were opened wherever she traveled and she eventually met with Díaz, who opened more doors. Consequently, in her book she acknowledged the "generous assistance and kind courtesy of President Díaz, who furnished letters to the governors of all the states through which we passed."[14] Howard Conkling's travels in 1883, noted in his book *Mexico and the Mexicans*, were undoubtedly colored by the assistance offered by the Mexican minister in Washington, Matías Romero. Conkling made sure to note the favor in his preface. "I gladly avail myself of this opportunity," he wrote, "to record my grateful sense of obligation to Señor Don Matías Romero, the Mexican minister at Washington, for the valuable aid, and in the prosecution of my plans, which he has so kindly favored me." Through such favors Conkling met with President Manuel González and "various other gentlemen of official and social distinction."[15]

University of Chicago anthropologist Frederick Starr's ethnographic study owed a great debt to the Mexican minister of development under Díaz, Manuel Fernández Leal. Minister Leal provided Starr with "every aid and assistance in his power," reaching down to state governors who in turn granted a letters of introduction to local *jefes políticos.* These letters allowed entry to the remotest villages, but more important they imparted an element of official authority, which Starr used freely to leverage indigenous peoples to permit body measurements and to make plaster of paris body casts, thereby realizing his research goals.[16] Starr completed his trip with a personal meeting with Porfirio Díaz, at which the social scientist and specialist on Mexico's indigenous peoples presented Díaz with a copy of his book *Indians of Southern Mexico.*

One final example is that of T. A. Rickard, author of *Journeys of Observation* (1907), a description of Guanajuato's historic mining industries. His inside track originated from a stint as editor of the *Engineering and Mining Journal,* which not only devoted substantial space to U.S. mining operations in Mexico but also served as a voice of mining interests in Mexico. Rickard needed no more than his personal credentials, which provided him an open path to the mining districts and the regional political clout that they wielded.[17]

Scrutinizing Mexico

As Americans crossed the border and set foot on Mexican soil, their initial impressions seemed to set the tone for the entire trip. Most were overwhelmed by what they observed, particularly if on their first trip to Mexico. Even letters of introduction and the like, which opened official doors, failed to suppress the shock and queasy wonder that they experienced at first sight of Mexico and Mexicans. A number of examples convey the quality, uniformity, and depth of those impressions that readers encountered as they turned the first pages of the their books and articles:

> As I gazed upon them it almost seemed that I had been transported into a new world. If one should go up in a balloon, and drift away into space . . . he would not find himself surrounded by more unaccustomed scenery or more strangely appearing people than he will meet in crossing the Rio Grande into Mexico.[18]

The entire change of customs and of language has a temporarily depressing effect on the traveller, though the train hands are Americans. The new order is rudely emphasized.[19]

As we land upon the south bank, it does seem as though we had really alighted upon a new world. The people look, appear, and talk so strangely. The land and buildings are unlike anything which we have in the states.[20]

It is strange that so small a stream as the Rio Grande should separate two races, two civilizations, two cycles. From the Anglo-Saxon civilization of to-day we pass, upon crossing the river, to the Spanish-American civilization of one hundred and fifty years ago. As we file out of the train to the custom house we see only dark faces, and sombrero-hatted serape-draped figures, and, most foreign of all, we are treated by custom house officials with a gentle courtesy alien to our experiences.[21]

As we drew up to the railroad station, a lazy, listless, bareheaded, dark-skinned crowd of men, women, and children welcomed us with staring eyes to Mexican soil.[22]

The journey was made without event. Our stops were short, the country uninviting, and the natives more so.[23]

First impressions cried out unequivocally that nothing seemed more utterly distinct in every way from the United States than the nation bordering it to the south. One traveler, overwhelmed by the contrast, wrote in his notebook, "I did not think it possible that anywhere could be such absolute strangeness in everything as here. One might have been in the remotest part of the East."[24] Mexico represented more than a unique society; it was incomprehensible and puzzling, and whatever descriptions came to mind only begged explanation. Americans were more than pleased to bear a self-imposed responsibility for explicating Mexico, not just to the American public, but also to the world at large. And as they elucidated Mexico to a more or less uninformed public, the images that they created were soon turned into conventional wisdom and their expressions entered the common, everyday lexicon. Writers assumed themselves a class of specialists in their field.

First impressions notwithstanding, every writer had something good to say about Mexico's natural environment, scenery, and colors, which drew the acclaim of all. Accordingly, Marie Robinson Wright titled her book *Picturesque Mexico*. Some went as far as Nevin O. Winter, who exclaimed in a romantic transport, "Mexico possesses the strongest possible attractions for the tourist. Its scenic wonders are unsurpassed in any other part of the globe in natural picturesqueness."[25] While observing a town below the towering volcanic peak Orizaba, Albert Zabriskie Gray found that "it was everywhere like a garden of beauty and fertility, with the quaint old city nestled most picturesquely and invitingly in the midst."[26] The contrasts (and contradictions) between the picturesque charm and the poverty of the people of Mexico, which jolted them, were retold endlessly. Winter noted that "dirt is everywhere and poverty abounds," but that "even these are removed from the commonplace by the brilliant color on every hand." And to emphasize this point, Winter quoted from Francis Hopkinson Smith's *A White Umbrella in Mexico* (an equally romantic composition):

> A land of white sunshine, redolent with flowers; a land of gay costumes, crumbling churches, and old convents. . . . It was more than enough to revel in an Italian sun, lighting up the semi-tropical land; to look up to white-capped peaks, towering into blue; to look down upon windswept plains, encircled by ragged chains of mountains. . . . Mexico is the most marvelously picturesque county under the sun. . . . A semi-barbarous Spain.[27]

George B. Winton seemed to think the same thoughts as Winter and Smith. In his training textbook for Protestant missionaries studying under the auspices of the Missionary Education Movement, Winton opened the introductory chapter with a lengthy discourse on the land. "Mexico is a picture book for the study of geography," wrote Winton. "Nowhere can mountain and plain, valley and foothill, river, lake, forest and field be seen in sharper outline or examined on a more beautiful map of gray and green and gold."[28] Few writers disagreed with Winter, Winton, Gray, Wright, and Smith. Apart from abundant natural resources, the only real beauty of Mexico resided in its "picturesque charm." But if asked whether it was the picturesque charm or the eminently exploitable natural resources and cheap labor that made Mexico truly attractive, our authors would have chosen natural resources and cheap labor.

TRAVELING INTO MEXICO

From Chihuahua to Yucatán, from Mexico City to the smallest village, Americans harbored at haciendas, village *posadas* (inns), open-air campgrounds, and the one or two adequate and occasionally upscale hotels in many of the larger cities of Mexico. However, wherever Americans traveled an American presence surrounded them. American ships and American railroads brought them to Mexico. American railroads then took them across the country. When in Mexico City, electricity from El Oro Mining Company supplied energy to run the streetcars built in the United States. American industrial enterprises and their spin-offs—all built with U.S.-made machinery—were visible at many points and became subjects for writers, particularly the mining towns, oil camps, and the American colonies in numerous cities and towns.

Americans may have traveled to a foreign country, but they seemed never to leave their native land—at least they never adopted or admired a Mexican view of things unless it came from a member of Mexico's elite. In addition to the social, industrial, and financial Americanization appearing throughout Mexico, the political climate seemed to converge at one central point as well. This was particularly true when surveying opinions about the peaceful conquest and Mexico's culture. Cultural differences were highlighted, and writers seemed transfixed by Mexico's cultural collage, sifting through it for possible clues to Mexico's state of affairs. While carrying out their investigations, Americans never left the politico-cultural atmosphere of the United States, and this was true even for those who were aware that Americans in Mexico stuck out wherever they went, even though they wished to blend in.

A few traveled purely as tourists, as did James A. Wilson, who wrote an account of four Americans visiting major archaeological sites from Mexico City to Yucatán. Most, however, had a more complex plan in mind. Authors found the mining and oil companies and railroads not only a safe haven but also a wonderful subject upon which to practice their craft. Frederick Ober may have been one of the first Americans to visit Batopilas and its equally productive neighbor, Santa Eulalia; his experience became the stuff of a chapter titled "Chihuahua, the Great Frontier State." James H. Wilkins journeyed to another mining enterprise, the California Mining Company in the state of Durango. Here Wilkins struck up a friendship with the owner, Colonel C. D. Burns, who, like Wilkins, was originally from San Francisco and, Wilkins reported, "overlooks and directs an immense industry."[29] Not surprisingly, Wilkins spoke most approvingly of Burns, a man he described as "full of enterprise" and as the cause of the district's mining revival (at least in Wilkin's mind).

William Henry Bishop's *Old Mexico and Her Lost Provinces* featured two chapters on railroads and another on mining. Naturally, he partook of each personally, exclaiming that railroads "have made the modern world elsewhere . . . and why should they fail of the usual effect here?"[30] Alfred Oscar Coffin spent considerable time in Mexico City's American colony, which led him to observe that the "business portion looks like an American city." Frank Collins Baker, curator at the Chicago Academy of Sciences, enjoyed the extended hospitality of railroad builder Colonel Glenn and his wife while on a research trip through northern Yucatán. (The title "colonel" seems to have been taken up by few entrepreneurs.) Despite Baker's stated intention of studying the zoology of the area, his study *A Naturalist in Mexico* had the same general course of nearly every other book on Mexico, regardless of title.[31]

Marian Storm's "Wells at the World's End," written for *Atlantic Monthly*, offered a most engaging view of the oil camps around Tampico. Her lengthy and detailed report on the oil camps, on the social life led by the Americans, and on the larger social relations is revealing and informative. Like her compatriots, she praised the American invasion for having provided improved living conditions for the Mexican workers (while companies reaped profits in the process). Among her intentions, she aimed to dispel notions that Mexican laborers were treated badly; on the contrary, she wrote, "The oil field peon lives in a Paradise."[32]

Americans were acutely aware of the role that their compatriots played in Mexico's economy and society in general. A trip on the first-class Pullman was enough to make them aware of the important place occupied by Americans, given that generally only foreigners and Mexico's elites traveled first-class. For Nevin O. Winter, boarding the train offered a satisfying patriotic experience. "It was a real pleasure," he explained, "to step into a fine American coach drawn by an American engine and run by an American crew bound for the chief town of the Isthmus and the one that gave it its name."[33] In a review of thirty years of experience as a Protestant missionary, Alden Buell Case fondly remembered the security offered in the railroads' Americanized environment. "So long as one is on an American-conducted train," he recalled, "with a few American travelers, what matters if he does not *sabe* [know] a dozen Spanish words?"[34]

When Mexican peasants (who comprised the great majority of the population) rode the train, they congregated in third class, a place that Americans studiously avoided. And in the dining car Americans, together with other "foreigners and the best-class of Mexicans," congregated in the same area of the coach.[35] Wallace Gillpatrick found this social segregation to be instructional. While on the northern route of the Mexican Central, he noticed that all of the Americans were "returning to the mines." Gillpatrick related that they exchanged "fabulous tales of wealth and adventure that were quite past belief." Gillpatrick must have come across a pilgrimage making its way through the mining regions—the sort of tour that one consul reported upon to the American Embassy. The consul wrote, "Almost daily there arrive in Durango new investors to look over the field, bringing with them American capital to be put into some one or other of the paying industries the country affords—generally mining. This, of course, means an increase in American interests, [and] a greater number of American residents."[36] Our author's doubts were dispelled upon visiting the very successful La Candelaria mine in Durango— owned by an American whom everyone called "colonel"—and having an extended and apparently enjoyable stay in the area.[37]

THE OMNIPRESENT AND INDISPENSABLE *MOZO*

Fortunately, reported one author, "the entire area of Mexico is open to exploration," a condition which led Americans to investigate the far corners and remote crevices of Mexico. Since few knew the details of their travels before arriving and, consequently, what they were getting themselves into, they readily came to depend on the services of *mozos*—that is, servants—and in so doing closely resembled the British colonials in their dependence on servants.[38] Of all the cultural practices that Americans felt an affinity with, the Mexican custom among the wealthier classes of utilizing a *mozo* for a wide variety of everyday needs ranked well up there. Guides and mule packers assisted with trips into the interior, including archaeological sites and tropical forests, in climbing the snowbound Mount Popocatépetl, and in maneuvering among the archaeological and historical attractions in and around cities. Moreover, a guide often served as cook, mule packer, interpreter, and general handyman. Guides were particularly important to the explorations and research trips taken by anthropologists and naturalists.

On their research excursion to Mexico, William Beebe and his wife depended on their *mozos* for a variety of functions. With the assistance of the several *mozos* which they employed, or rather bartered for at various times, mules were packed, tents pitched, meals cooked, and canyons, rivers, and gorges crossed. On their initial foray into uncharted territory, they reported, their *mozo* loaded "our tents, cots, provisions, and other baggage, and we prepared to start out at daybreak for the wildest *barranca* on the edge of the tableland." There, as at the various campsites that they set up, they viewed birds and "wild Mexican life under many conditions and at varying altitudes." At one site, the Beebes employed the service of a *mozo* named Ricardo, described as their "clever little Mexican cook and general aide-de-camp, [who] had the supper prepared before the short twilight fell." In the case of the Beebe expedition, when a *mozo* remained for an extended period of time, he inevitably came to be known as "our Mexican" and on occasion, "our Mexican boy." For certain, the Beebes were grateful for the easy acquisition of a *mozo*, particularly their service, described in detail by Mrs. Beebe in the final pages of their book. "I hope every party may be as fortunate in its cook as we were in ours," she advised. "He was cook, dish-washer, guide, and when occasion demanded more fluent Spanish than was at our command, he was interpreter."[39]

Traveling into the hinterlands required at the very least a good guide. James Wilson's journey to the California Mining Company took him over trails that could only be traversed by mules. "You are absolutely dependent on the mule for motive power and the mule is dependent on the muleteer," he counseled.[40] T. A. Rickard's visit to Guanajuato impressed him as well with the value of the *mozos*, in particular those who specialized in transporting cargo on their backs. "Like the Turk," wrote an astonished Rickard, "the native Mexican is a great porter."[41] Travelers were not of one mind that a *mozo* was a godsend, but most seemed to find them a great boon. Such was the opinion of Percy F. Martin, who commented that "the mozo remains the same faithful, trustworthy and careful servant . . . as loyal and as dependable as one could meet anywhere in the wide world."[42]

Every now and then a note of displeasure broke the near unanimity of admiration for *mozos*. During his lengthy investigation of indigenous body forms, anthropologist Frederick Starr was greatly distressed at the conduct one *mozo* that he employed. Yet, he found that another filled the bill. His words fairly well indicated his views of the importance of *mozos* for research and pleasure in Mexico. Note his use of animalistic characteristics in describing his *mozo*. We shall see that such descriptions were not uncommon:

> The cargador . . . was a comfort, after the wretched sluggards whom we had lately. With our instruments upon his shoulders, he trotted, like a faithful dog, directly at out side, from start to finish, never showing the least weariness or sense of burden.[43]

While visiting the lakes around Mexico City and caught in a rainstorm, William Henry Bishop sought lodging and secured help to lead the way. Of his good fortune on that stormy night, Bishop wrote, "A mozo preceded us, like a great fire-bug, sheltering a burning candle under a straw mat as best he could, to aid us in keeping out of the deeper puddles."[44]

A *mozo* served all sorts of traveler's needs, whether in the country or city, and writers were quick to point this out. Solomon B. Griffin, author of *Mexico of Today*, advised his readers, "These fellows can be hired in the city for $3 a week to give you undivided service, and they are a feature of Mexican life that fits like a glove to the necessities of a lazy man's vacation."[45] For certain, Wallace Gillpatrick's travels greatly benefited from his *mozo*. As he commented:

> In the mountains, the heat is seldom oppressive save at midday. Then your mozo finds a cool spot, near a stream if possible, for our luncheon or siesta. Your mozo is nearly always a cheerful, obliging individual, of sanguine temperament, trained to servitude and hardship, expecting little, yet accepting without effusiveness the little luxuries you may care to bestow. After a long day's ride, he unsaddles the animals, has a fire blazing in a jiffy, and cooks your supper; while you lie on the ground and stretch your tired legs, inhaling the grateful fumes of meat on the coals.[46]

As soon as they alighted at a train station, travelers were surrounded by *cargadores* willing to carry baggage to their hotel for a pittance. At their hotel, *mozos* were continually at their service. One author wrote of hotel servants as creating a kind of heaven by being at the ready for every beck and call. "The servants are models of their kind," recounted Alfred E. Coffin. "With their sandaled feet they glide about without noise and do their work without murmur. . . . the serving class is more servile than can be found anywhere." And later, Coffin commented, "Mexican servants are the best in the world."[47] Americans easily accustomed themselves to the privileges long enjoyed by the hacendados of Mexico.

CELEBRATING PORFIRIO DÍAZ

Americans expressed universal acclaim for Mexico's political order, above all for the administration's adjustment to the exigencies of peaceful conquest. Not surprisingly, Porfirio Díaz emerged as the one universally acclaimed hero in the literature, a figure even bigger than in life. Or so it seemed to James Wilkins, who described Díaz as an "enlightened statesman," and to Harriott Wight Sherrat, who went a bit further, proclaiming that "President Porfirio Díaz is as intelligent and as progressive as the best American."[48] Several books, including Reau Campbell's popular *Complete Guide and Descriptive Book—Mexico* (1899) and Sullivan Holman McCollester's *Mexico: Old and New, A Wonderland*, featured a photograph of Díaz opposite the title page.[49] Most were content to genuflect before him with lofty phrases in captions under photographs of a proudly uniformed and richly decorated Díaz accompanied by his wife in formal dress. (Harriott Wight Sherrat featured a photograph of Mrs. Díaz opposite the title page.)

Marie Robinson Wright even dedicated her book to Díaz, employing hyperbole that probably swayed most readers. "To Señor General Don Porfirio Díaz," she began, "The Illustrious President of Mexico, Whose Intrepid Moral Character, Distinguished Statesmanship, and Devoted Patriotism Make Him the Pride and Glory of His Country." When it came to Díaz, such language probably seemed appropriate for the times (1910), although the length to which Wright decorated Díaz went beyond what most authors recorded. Nevertheless, Wright's praise encountered its match here and there. Wallace Gillpatrick's *The Man Who Likes Mexico* (1911), written while on assignment for the voice of the American colony in Mexico City, the *Mexican Herald*, serves as example. After having met Díaz at the presidential palace during the centennial celebration, Gillpatrick waxed ardent, stating that Díaz "has long elevated himself above any personal ambition or self interest. His identity is merged completely with national life. And in the future peace and prosperity of Mexico he will continue to find happiness."[50] On the title page Gillpatrick disingenuously described his book as "The Spirited Chronicle of Adventurous Wanderings in Mexican Highways and Byways."

Spirit notwithstanding, pro-Díaz sentiments (meaning boosterism for economic conquest) like those of Gillpatrick peppered the literature. On the other hand, investments rather than an adventuring spirit motivated Grant Shepherd, of Batopilas fame, who dedicated an entire chapter to extolling the alleged virtues of Díaz. Several decades after the 1910 revolution, Shepherd looked back on the Díaz era with nostalgia and noted that Díaz "was astute and strong; he knew men . . . [he was] a man of enormous courage."[51] We should expect such praise from someone whose family's investments were protected by the open door that Díaz ensured for U.S. investors.

The pervasive pro-Díaz sentiment expressed in elevated and more often stilted praise suggests an anticipation that Díaz, together with U.S. assistance, would remake Mexico into a comprehensible, even a democratic and modern nation. That prospect prompted Maturin Ballou to write of Díaz, "His principle purpose is plainly to modernize Mexico."[52] In a similar vein, Frederick Guernsey, editor of the *Mexican Herald* in Mexico City, confirmed Díaz as "the modernizer of his country" in the pages of the *Atlantic Monthly*.[53] San Francisco newspaper publisher James A. Wilson chimed in and glorified Díaz as "the greatest of Mexicans . . . the one man who has made Mexico what it is today."[54] Undoubtedly, the real virtue of Díaz rested in having "invited foreigners to come in and show his people how to keep house." Modernization by way of foreign capital, according to Edward M. Conley in the *Atlantic Monthly Review of Reviews,* provided unassailable evidence of "his farseeing statesmanship."[55]

Given the widespread adulation of Díaz, a book dedicated to the Mexican ruler appears, in retrospect, a bit unnecessary—yet that book did appear. James Creelman's *Díaz, Master of Mexico* in 1911 went to great lengths to assign to Díaz every available heroic attribute, from his physical features ("deep-set, dark, soul searching eyes") to his moral courage ("the grace and strength of an old warrior").[56] Creelman claimed to have strictly observed the rules of objective and unbiased reporting, yet he epitomized the genre in which, as he put it, "the thrilling story of Porfirio Díaz has been told many times."[57]

In work after work, Díaz shone brightly, even in the accounts by Protestant missionaries who, like foreign capitalists, were granted an open door to Mexico and who proselytized freely. It would not be far off the mark to interpret their efforts as an attempt to carry out a religious conquest of Mexico. Economic conquest and religious conversion were inseparable, as if two sides of the same coin. Reverend Francis S. Borton, of the Methodist Episcopal Church, praised the Díaz era in religious terms: "Mexico is beginning to stretch her hands toward God. We have a grand and God-directed Díaz at the helm of the nation, and he is our friend."[58] Conceivably, Borton and his associates understood modernization via foreign capital to be the work of God.

Not all authors employed religious metaphors, but nearly all paraded generous encomiums praising Díaz. As one author noted, "To the foreigner, the one bright spot in Mexican history is the reign of the Dictator, Porfirio Díaz."[59] In this context, the triumvirate of Díaz, the various mining, railroad, and oil enterprises operated by Americans, and the conversion of Mexico to Protestantism all worked toward the same objective (more on this in the following chapter). The many authors covered in this study, which include Protestant missionaries and U.S. investors, were of one mind with Díaz regarding the virtues of foreign capital for modernizing and democratizing Mexico and, in the bargain, redeeming Mexico's souls.

More than the Open Door policy provoked the lyrics sung to Díaz; many were enthralled by the strong-arm tactics used to quell rebellion, which, of course, served to maintain cheap labor on a short leash. What one author said of Díaz—"above all, he knows how to maintain the peace"—assured mine owners of a nonunionized, unorganized, and compliant labor supply.[60] Consequently, the Rurales, the rural federal police force formed under Díaz that was comprised largely of former criminals, were held in high esteem for allegedly having "pacified a disorderly society."[61] Guidebook author Reau Campbell put his readers' fears of travel to Mexico to rest, informing those planning a trip to Mexico that the Rurales were "fine specimens of humanity, stout and well built."[62] The kind of state-sponsored violence that would not have been tolerated in the United States—or at least would have been intolerable to the upper classes—seemed a perfectly satisfactory and appropriate method of administering justice in Mexico, but only to Mexicans. Conditions were such that only a strong ruler employing an iron hand could nurture the kind of progress that Americans had in mind.

Americans served as a sort of cheering section for the Díaz method of justice. On his travels through Mexico in 1884, Frederick Ober found the Rurales "a pleasure." He then acknowledged that "the present government has taken energetic measures looking toward a gradual reformation, if possible, of this worst portion of the criminal class, and the beneficial bullet has disposed of many of those who indulged in the pastime of highwayman."[63] Another wrote of Díaz and the Rurales, "The outlaws were given no rest or mercy. One by one, they were hunted down to their death. . . . Today I should consider Mexico one of the safest countries to travel through."[64] After having lived in Mexico for several years, Fanny Chambers Gooch reached the same conclusion and found the Rurales to be "the most competent preservers of public peace within her borders."[65]

Modernization and democracy, it seemed, required extreme versions of undemocratic and nonmodern methods of administering justice. As one author wrote, "There is no sickly sentimentality wasted upon law breakers."[66] Accordingly, the dictatorship was justified as a reasonable approach to democratizing, and therefore modernizing, the country. All the key elements were in order: the right man, Díaz; the right method, dictatorship (often qualified as "enlightened" and "benevolent"); and the right time. Despite fawning circumlocutions offered in defense of Díaz (who personified Mexico's reactionary landowning class), the dictator gladly received the many florid tributes bestowed on him by American writers.[67]

POPULAR BOOSTERS FOR THE ECONOMIC CONQUEST

Following the 1870s, a vocal chorus of writers publishing in popular and professional journals espoused the export of capital as a patriotic article of faith, and professed that Mexico could not develop—indeed, could not exist—without U.S. capital. Susan Hale's observation in 1888 that the

"Yankee pervades Mexico," appears to have been what Isaac F. Marcosson celebrated in the popular *Collier's Magazine* (1916). In his words, "The vision of Harriman, the masterful ambition of Huntington, the doggedness of Palmer, the tenacity of Guggenheim, the faith of "Boss" Shepherd, the constructive genius of half a dozen other noted empire builders all found expression in the making of Mexico."[68] Given the commentary of Americans visiting Mexico, one would have concluded, as did Emil Blichfeldt in a series for *Chautauqua Magazine*, that the Open Door policy was alive and well. After a journey of observation through Mexico, Blichfeldt returned to an old theme: "The pacific conquest is going on, though it does not look at all toward political union."[69]

Despite the flood of American capital, a few alleged that insufficient U.S. investments entered Mexico, a charge that persisted among many writers, particularly after the Mexican Revolution of 1910. More capital for the peaceful conquest now became a central theme. Frederick Simpich, for example, argued, "Mexico still needs more capital" and recommended Mexican legislation to open the door still wider to foreign capital.[70] Another of the dissatisfied, James Carson, national councillor at the American Chamber of Commerce of Mexico, the headquarters for U.S. businesses located in Mexico, advocated a greater presence of U.S. capital. In a 1920 university conference on Mexico, Carson urged, "What is wanted now is an invasion of capital"—as if such had not already taken place on a grand scale.[71] Railroad historian Fred Wilbur Powell bluntly summarized his perspective on U.S.-Mexican "economic interdependence." He claimed that "no intelligent or responsible Mexican can hope to see his country prosper without foreign capital."[72]

Like many before and after him, Arizona mining engineer Franklin Wheaton Smith noted, "Mexico is practically wholly dependent on foreign capital," and furthermore "is not yet strong enough to undertake unaided its own development."[73] Herbert Corey concurred with Smith in a 1922 issue of *The National Geographic*, in which he explained that Mexico "has been about as thoroughly developed as is possible without the aid of foreign capital."[74] For the dissatisfied, the final chapter of the peaceful conquest remained to be completed. However, most observers agreed that a continual flow of U.S. investment capital to Mexico was the best of all possible scenarios.

ADVISING AMERICAN INVESTORS

Most authors at least mentioned the investment potential that Mexico presented to foreigners, making it appear that the writers were well aware of and interested in the peaceful invasion then in progress. Several, however, made it a point to concentrate substantial attention on the investment opportunities that abounded in Mexico. And one or two seemed to have written their works solely for the benefit of those with surplus cash on their hands. Kamar Al-Shimas (pen name for Morton F. Brand) in *The Mexican Southland* (1922) informed the readers up front of his interest in economic opportunity, advising them that "certain of the chapters are written largely for those who are looking to Mexico as a field for investment."[75] The title of a work often told the story, as did Frederick Simpich's for a *National Geographic* article: "A Mexican Land of Canaan: Marvelous Riches of the Wonderful West Coast of Our Neighbor Republic." Focusing on the "vast level plantations of cane, corn, beans and tomatoes," all under U.S. management, he painted a romantic Mexico, "a land of wondrous lure, rich in romance and adventure."[76] Like Kamar Al-Shimas, Maturin Ballou devoted substantial space to the investment opportunities that Mexico offered with the advent of railroads. His optimistic advice, offered prior to the trade benefits acquired with the colonization of Cuba, must have impressed many a reader:

> The Monterey and Mexican Gulf Railway has lately opened access to most excellent lands, suitable for sugar plantations, equal to the best in Louisiana devoted to this purpose, and which can be brought for a mere song, as the saying goes. . . . In the opening of these tropical districts by the railroad . . . we have offered us the opportunity to secure all the products which we now get from Cuba.[77]

Percy F. Martin's 1906 review of American and British mining operations in Guanajuato borrowed the title, *Mexico's Treasure House*, from Cecil Rhodes' effusiveness (cited above) concerning Mexico's natural wealth. Martin contended that "it is fit and proper that a mining district possessed of such a remarkable record as that of Guanajuato, and providing, as I believe it will, so fine a field for future developments, should have a volume . . . devoted entirely to its consideration." Martin considered the production at Guanajuato to equal that of the Rand in the Transvaal of South Africa and warned investors not to tarry, for "the opportunities which exist today for participating in this attractive enterprise may soon fade away."[78]

Sometimes a book had multiple purposes, not all of which were readily apparent. For example, Reau Campbell's guidebooks were published in Chicago, but Campbell worked under the auspices of the Sonora News Agency, which served Mexico's English speakers, tourists, and American residents by providing English-language publications at stores, favorite tourist destination points, and railroad stations throughout Mexico. More important, the guidebooks have all the qualities of a handbook for investors intending to reside in Mexico, as well as being a guide for the occasional traveler.

Other obvious attempts to stir the American capitalist to invest in Mexico included U.S. Department of Labor publications, *Engineering and Mining Journal*, and the upscale and popular *National Geographic*. The Department of Labor's 1902 publication *Labor Conditions in Mexico* informed investors of the wages and characteristics of the typical Mexican laborer. Researcher Walter Weyl concluded that an optimal labor supply—meaning cheap and industrious labor—awaited the investor in Mexico.

The U.S. Government Printing Office published books and pamphlets illuminating the investment opportunities. One publication with the intriguing title *Mexico: Geographical Sketch, Natural Resources, Laws, Economic Conditions, Actual Development, Prospects of Future Growth* offered a primer for novice investors interested in data relative to making good investment choices. Government-sponsored publications differed little from the general run of American publications, and this one, as in the case of privately written books and articles, emphasized that "the commercial bond between the sister Republics is one that can hardly be broken, and is constantly growing in strength."[79] The bonds created by economic conquest were a theme picked up in other books and defined in numerous ways. Juan N. Navarro, Mexico's consul general in New York, described U.S.-Mexican relations as an "intimate intercourse," and George Creel observed over a decade later that the economic relations between the United States and Mexico were "indissoluble."[80]

The *Engineering and Mining Journal* regularly published articles and informational notes of interests to mining corporations and investors, while the *National Geographic* offered its readers numerous descriptive as well as informational reviews of Mexico's peoples, culture, and particularly its natural resources. A 1902 issue devoted entirely to Mexico included articles with titles like "The Luster of Mexico," and "The Treasure Chest of Mercurial Mexico."[81]

Marie Robinson Wright's *Picturesque Mexico* (1897) and her homage to Díaz, *Mexico: A History of Progress and Development in One Hundred Years* (1910) were frank endorsements for the continued flow of U.S. capital into Mexico. Both works were extraordinarily detailed and contained material that would have interested investors, including a healthy listing of the spectrum of crops, natural resources, available labor supplies, and cultural patterns in the various regions of Mexico. In addition, investors must have been taken in by the guarantees that Díaz promised to anyone with an investment scheme in Mexico, which Wright made sure to emphasize. Her advice here summarized must have teased a few with spare capital:

> A careful study of the business conditions and opportunities of Mexico develops two facts,—viz., that the resources of the country are almost illimitable and that the application of proper business methods will bring results that are most satisfactory. Mexico is, in short, the coming country.[82]

As mentioned earlier, Colonel Robert Gorsuch, who held an important stake in Mexico's railroads, greatly influenced her book.

The War of 1848 and the cession of the northern half of Mexico to the United States prompted James H. Wilkins to compare the possibilities offered by Mexico at the turn of the century to the transfer of Mexican ranchos to American capitalists in 1849. "I cannot imagine," he surmised,

> an investment more sure to yield a rich return in the future than the purchase of real property in Mexico, in those sections where it can be had pretty much at the buyer's figures. The conditions are very much the same as in California in 1849, when ranchos were transferred for a few hundred dollars that are worth millions today. And we have here what we did not have there—and abundance of effective labor to develop our opportunities.[83]

There is one important difference that Wilkins overlooked. Annexation destroyed the precapitalist Mexican economic core, the hacienda, in the United States; economic conquest, on the other hand, operated alongside and cooperatively with the hacienda system in Mexico. Thus economic conquest posed no challenges to the economic foundations of Mexico; it only asked for the privilege of investing and exploiting at will.

In the interests of those wanting to know more about the manual labor available for Americans in Mexico, authors explored examples of "typical" Mexican behavior patterns, foibles, values, and traditions. Ruminations about the "Mexican psyche" were expected to prepare the reader for engaging Mexico on its own terms or at least lead to an understanding of "the real Mexico." Authors touched on those elements of Mexican culture that seemed the opposite or at least removed from that which Americans practiced. Topics like the "typical" Mexican's courtesies and politeness, extended family, sense of time ("they're always late"), and what seemed to be irrational religious practices (the Basílica de La Virgin de Guadalupe often served as an example) were placed under a microscope and dissected repeatedly.

Among those searching for the cultural reality of Mexico (and claiming that they discovered Mexico's cultural heart), perhaps none other stands out like Wallace Thompson. Several of his works ostensibly focused on culture and psychology, but his underlying purpose was to rally the reader to the necessity for the continued invasion of American capital into Mexico, particularly after the momentary glitch brought on by the 1910 revolution. Written in response to that protracted civil war, Thompson intended *Trading with Mexico*, as he said, to confront "the Mexican trade problem as it is." Thompson bluntly embraced a "deep faith in the American businessman" and wished to ensure the continuation and extension of the American economic invasion. In so doing, he extolled the interests of "the American pioneer . . . in his new conquest of the New World" whose "weapons of conquest are dollars and brains and energy." [84]

For those expecting to participate in the economic invasion, the virtue of learning Spanish was highly recommended for effectively dealing with Mexican clients and government officials. Writing in the *Atlantic Monthly*, Charles Johnston suggested that American investors in Mexico learn from the British experience in India. There, he wrote, the

> traders of the East India Company began by studying the languages of India, purely for commercial ends. When destiny forced them into administrative relations with the peoples of India, they went deeper and set themselves really to master the Indian tongues.

Armed with the "sympathy, insight, [and] a truer understanding" that knowledge of the native language endowed them with, traders inevitably encountered improved (meaning more efficacious) social relations. In the bargain, "administrative relations" improved as well. [85] Without a doubt, Wallace Thompson would have supported Johnston's recommendation, in that language facility furthered the new conquest.

Americans were joined by Mexican elites writing in the very same journals; even the titles of their respective works were on occasion similar if not identical. Dr. Don Juan N. Navarro published "Mexico of Today" in *National Geographic* to convince readers that Mexico's "commercial attractions . . . make it one of the best places in which to invest capital." [86] A host of authors painted similar rosy investment scenarios. George B. Winston's *Mexico Today*, Solomon Bulkley Griffin's *Mexico of Today*, Nevin O. Winter's *Mexico and Her People of To-Day*, and E. D. Trowbridge's *Mexico Today and Tomorrow* contained many of the same optimistic assertions made by Navarro, a repetition hinted at by the similarity of titles.[87]

Overall, authors suggested to potential investors seeking a successful endeavor that they adjust to Mexico's cultural ethos and work with it, that is, take advantage of the opportunities thereof, without necessarily being absorbed or captured by them. Readers were counseled that one need not embrace Mexico in order to succeed, but that certain key methods were considered indispensable for achieving the inevitable success that awaited the informed and therefore expert businessperson. Former secretary of state John Foster strongly suggested the same in an address before the National Geographic Society. After pointing out that Americans led in the mining, railroad, and agricultural development of Mexico, he added that some adaptations were nevertheless necessary. "Our citizens who voluntarily go to Mexico," he wrote,

> should bear in mind that they are in a community of a different race, language, religion, customs, and system of judicial procedure from ours, and if they adapt themselves to these changes they are quite unlikely to encounter embarrassment or trouble.[88]

The former minister may have confused the subject and object; Mexico underwent the main adapting, as Americans went about the business of refashioning Mexico's economy and society.

CELEBRATING COLONIAL SOCIAL RELATIONS

While visiting Mexico in 1905, Charles Macomb Flandrau noticed a strong similarity between the foreigners in Mexico (particularly the English and Americans) and those in Rudyard Kipling's writings.[89] Unlike most writers, Flandrau was generally at odds with Americans, particularly tourists, and often critiqued their behavior, yet he was not alone in suggesting a Kipling analogy. Generally, writers were eager to extol the peaceful conquest and urge a greater American presence. They were also quick to evoke colonial analogies that defined the essence of this peaceful conquest, analogies that legitimized the economic domination. The example of Great Britain's colonial expansion seemed most appropriate to at least three writers besides Flandrau, who insisted that America's role in Mexico bore a Kiplingesque character.

Of the west coast of Mexico, Herbert Corey wrote, "One thinks of Kipling in the Fuerte River country. . . . the resemblances . . . are striking." And, he continued,

The Americans dress for dinner, and meet twice a week for dancing and bridge, now and then spending a weekend on a houseboat.

Add the swarming natives in their thin cotton, paddling about barefooted, and ox-carts, donkeys, fine horses . . . and alligators in the lagoon, bears in the mountain, and a bad cat the natives call a tiger. All the country needs is a Kipling.[90]

A decade later, on his 1931 visit to the same "lovely valley of the Rio Fuerte," Harry Carr recorded in greater detail the same impressionistic scene brimming with colonial images:

It is in the heart of the sugar-cane country. All the land, the sugar mills, the hotel, and most of the business firms are owned by Americans. The plantations are operated with modern American efficiency. The planters live a life that reminds one of Rudyard Kipling's stories of the life of the English in India. They have their tennis clubs, polo fields, golf links, dances, bridge parties.[91]

Like Herbert Corey, Marian Storm also regretted the absence of a Kipling, as her reaction to visiting the Tampico oil fields indicates. "There has been no Kipling," she lamented,

to celebrate the strange life of the great oil-fields south and west of Tampico. What themes have been missed! What sagas of sweat and courage, of fierce nights and stern days, of wild hopes drooped and faint hopes blossomed! What life would beat in the true song of the Pánuco![92]

Romanticizing the peaceful conquest often meant resorting to comparing U.S. economic policy toward Mexico with British imperialism. Clearly there were abundant similarities between the Mexican state of affairs in Mexico and European colonialism, and examples were trotted out when the occasion seemed appropriate. The British model seemed to serve as the perfect paradigm, the ideal description of the United States in Mexico. Like several of his cohorts mentioned above, former U.S. consul Frederick Simpich turned to Britain's colonial possessions as he reflected on the imperial social scene in the same region described by Corey and Carr. "Life among the American merchants and planters settled on this West Coast," he suggested, "is not unlike that of the colonials in India, China, or the Philippines. Servants are numerous and cheap. . . . Nervous breakdowns and "worry" headaches are unheard of."[93] In comparing the United States to the then reigning imperial power, writers implicitly justified the American economic empire as a rational and legitimate international undertaking. Indeed, they applied clearly identifiable imperial examples—India, China, Africa, and the Philippines—when analyzing and describing Mexico and its people for their readers.

Bear in mind that to the American writer Mexico existed *only* in relationship to the United States. Seldom, if ever, did writers conceive of a Mexico independent of the United States, whether culturally, economically, or politically. Even though most authors stopped short of explicit comparisons of the United States in Mexico to the British Empire, nonetheless, perspectives on economic expansionism involving Mexico unmistakably reflected the culture of an empire. Naturally, the economic and social relations between Mexico and the United States candidly illustrated through colonial representations opened a window of opportunity for recommending British methods of colonial governance. Accordingly, William Carson imagined for a moment what kind of government would best suit Mexico in the absence of Díaz; his conclusion indicated his intellectual debt to British imperialism:

> The truth is that what Mexico needs is a strong central government headed by a man such as Lord Kitchener, one of unblemished record, a soldier, statesman and administrator; and what Lord Kitchener accomplished in Egypt might, to a great extent, be brought about in Mexico. But as a Kitchener is not to be found in Mexico to-day, the place must needs be filled by a Mexican substitute—a man of strong character, who understands his countrymen, who has the confidence of the army and is able to restore order.[94]

Either a Mexican proxy governing in the place of a colonial administrator (one thinks of Díaz here) or a colonial administrator appointed by the United States may have been what Carson had in mind. For certain, he thought that to be consistent with the needs of Mexico and to protect American interests in the bargain, the methods employed by a British colonial administrator in Egypt was the most appropriate for governing Mexico.

CONCLUSION

The opportunities available for traveling to Mexico increased at a rate that reflected the progress of the peaceful conquest. The immediate reaction of authors upon entering Mexico for the first time was that the nation to the south was strange, unlike anything they had imagined, at odds with, if not opposite to, their cultural experiences. However, as they settled into a traveling routine, they interacted with certain elements of Mexican society that seemed compatible with their notions of good and bad. Servants as guides, cooks, mule packers, and backpackers became a mainstay of many tourists and writers. Americans often traveled with other Americans and entered into settings where American business and other activities were prominent, and thus were well aware of the overriding influence of American capital on the Mexican economy.

American travelers entered Mexico as that nation experienced modernization inspired, designed, and directed by foreigners. In unison, writers applauded that economic process and contextualized their accounts within what they termed the "American invasion." Indeed, they participated in that economic invasion by writing nationalistic apologias about the powerful American presence and provided information of interest to the potential investor. Not only did they write overt defenses of U.S. economic domination over Mexico, they also compared U.S.-Mexican relations to British colonialism in the process.

As writers surveyed the social landscape of Mexico, and as they thought of ways to realistically portray Mexico, the striking similarities between Mexico and British colonial possessions stirred their imagination. Some even thought that Mexico was to the United States as India was to Britain. The image of Mexico as an American colony assumed a life of its own in American literature and in the popular imagination. Evaluating everything Mexican, particularly the people and their culture, also figured into the literature. The substantial number of writers who found India under England an appropriate model for describing Mexico dominated by U.S. capital were not exaggerating or fantasizing. The social relations then in process of construction via foreign-inspired modernization, relations that included segregation, servitude, company towns, and unequal pay, not only reminded authors of India but also concretely represented social relations between a real colonizer and a real colony.

3. THE IMPERIAL BURDEN: THE MEXICAN PROBLEM AND AMERICANIZATION

The depth of Mexico's ignorance, in childhood and in adulthood, in life and in business, literally passes comprehension. The active, curious minds of the Indian youngsters grow quickly into sodden stupidity; the keen and vivid intelligences of the children of the middle and upper classes expend their growing forces in sensuality and plunge themselves and their country into debilitating excesses—because there is no training to give them a life above the animals.

Wallace Thompson, *Trading with Mexico* (1921)

INTRODUCTION

Wallace Thompson's *Trading with Mexico*, one of his three books on Mexico, contained a wide-ranging set of ideas that were not very original or novel. If anything, his uncompromising disgust (and despair) with just about all things related to the peoples and culture of Mexico summarized many an author's thinking. But what is much more important than the literature's lockstep critique of all things Mexican is the near universal acceptance of the colonizer's lexicon for explaining the domestic problems besetting Mexico, problems which, it was alleged, harmed the ability of the United States to continue business as usual in Mexico.

By now the reader has come across references to many authors' use of the language of empire and of sundry comparisons to European colonialism in India, China, Turkey, and Africa. These analogies and comparisons were not mistaken identities; on the contrary, authors borrowed freely from the only examples that they could realistically link with the American presence in Mexico. European colonialism and the American economic empire exhibited more than similarities: they were two forms of empire-building, and consequently the analogies accurately struck to the core of U.S.-Mexican relations.

Apart from comparisons, writers also exhibited and practiced a language of empire. Mexico was represented in a spectrum of colonial images, such as subservient mozos, in Kipling-like representations of social and economic relations between Americans and Mexicans, and of Mexican workers as lesser intelligent human forms. But, above all, Mexico existed primarily for the benefit of the United States and only secondarily for Mexicans. In order to make this distinction, writers sketched strong, if clumsy, racialized images of Mexico, of its culture and peoples, which not only justified the economic domination then in place, but simultaneously argued for an expansion of American capital and personnel in Mexico.

Of course, not all writers felt the need to portray Mexico in such a negative manner. In a critical vein, Frederick A. Ober pointed out that among his colleagues, "it is the custom to abuse the Mexicans, to affirm that no good thing can, ever did, or will come from their country." [1] Still his displeasure did not stop him from praising Porfirio Díaz for "pacifying" Mexico or from alleging that every beggar is a thief. And so, Ober, perhaps unconsciously carried out the pervasive tradition that he criticized.

Here we examine that literary portrait of Mexico painted in broad strokes by Americans for the exclusive viewing by the American public. The narratives generally included a historical sketch and then proceeded to construct an impressionistic definition of Mexico, one that distinguished it from the developed nations of the world. In the process, authors identified something called the Mexican Problem and recommended a long-term strong dose of Americanization as a solution.

HISTORY AND RACIAL BIOGRAPHY

Americans of the late nineteenth and early twentieth centuries were (and still are) extremely naïve not only about Latin America in general but about Mexico in particular. Knowing this gap from their own personal experience, writers focused on the historical background of the modern Mexican nation, a discussion that prepared the way for later themes critical to explaining contemporary Mexico to the American public. Generally, narratives began by examining the indigenous past, proceeding to the Spanish conquest and then the independence movement and national period. Each of these epochs, the narratives told, added an element crucial for explaining Mexico, above all, for defining its racial origins and the consequent cultural and behavioral patterns. Writers asked, as did Wallace Thompson, "What is a Mexican? What is his racial, his cultural background? Whence did he come? What did he bring with him beyond the glow of his recorded history?"[2] Authors answered uniformly.

Mexico's history begins with the indigenous peoples, Olmecs, Aztecs, Toltecs, Chichimecs, Huastecs, Mayas, and various other societies that inhabited what would later be Mexico, from the northern deserts to the southern peninsula. Their lifestyles, settlement patterns, religious practices, and war and governing systems were briefly, and in a popular vein, reviewed. One learned that Mexico City once was comprised of three city-states settled on lakes connected by causeways. *Chinampas*, or farming patches built on the lakes, provided the space for agricultural production. Particular interest was expressed in their astronomy, mathematics, and architectural construction, and that Aztecs were a brave warrior people. Writers marveled at the impressive pyramids, temples, hieroglyphics, gold and silver work, and what must have at one time been beautiful wall paintings but recoiled at the human sacrifices. Titles of books and articles express the abiding interest in the historical record; one reads of "The Luster of Ancient Mexico," (excerpts reprinted from William H. Prescott's *History of the Conquest of Mexico*), *Aztec Land*, and chapters titled "Traditions of the Toltecs," or "Mexico, Past and Present."[3] Solomon Griffin began the latter chapter with "Mexico has a magnificent background upon which her story should be painted." Guidebook author Reau Campbell devoted a section of his second chapter to extolling the "superior" virtues of the ancient Mexican peoples and tribes.

Unfortunately, whatever magnificence there was receded into a "magnificent background" with the passage of time. With the arrival of Hernando Cortez and his Spanish conquistadors in 1519, the once great social advancements of Middle America all came crashing down. Instead of further advances, the development experienced by the various peoples came to a halt and perhaps may have regressed. In the process, the indigenous peoples and Spanish soldiers eventually intermarried or cohabited, and the mestizo, a hybrid component of the Mexican population, was formed. Eventually the resulting populace of Mexico presented three main discrete populations: Spanish whites, mestizos (often labeled "halfbreeds"), and Indians. This questionable mixture gained Mexico its independence as a sovereign nation. Unfortunately, none of the alleged racial populations—Spaniards, Indians, and mestizos—had the resources to lead Mexico into modernity. Of the three, only the Spanish might have been able to do so, but even they were constrained by their circumstances.

Indians and mestizos, the vast majority of the Mexican population at the end of the nineteenth century, totaled 12 million out of the 15 million and hung around Mexico's neck like the proverbial albatross. Without exception, the racial breakdown held the attention of writers and seldom did they ignore the percentages of each. Readers were continually fed images of Mexico that emphasized the "blood lines." In his general treatment of Mexico, William Showalter, for example, offered this "typical" street scene: "Here you will see a Mexican half-breed, barefooted, wearing a dollar pair of trousers, a fifty-cent shirt, and a ten-dollar sombrero."[4] Few would have questioned Nevin O. Winter's generalization that "the vast majority of the inhabitants of Mexico are descendants of the Indian races," with less than 20 percent white.[5]

Wallace Thompson advised that the "racial intermingling" doomed Mexico. To explain Mexico, he relentlessly emphasized the genetically inherited characteristics of a "people inheriting the worst traits of both and burying the virtues of both deep beneath the skins darkening ever to the lower type, with minds which do not seek even the natural goods of the poorer of the two elements."[6] In his racist exhibitionism, Thompson was no exception. Others spoke from the same script. C. S. Babbitt's *A Remedy for the Decadence of the Latin Race* (dedicated to David Starr Jordan, a treatise that Starr would have appreciated) is based entirely on a theory of "mongrelization." Like Thompson, Babbitt deplored *mestizaje,* or the mixing of races, which in Mexico exemplified the "breeding of inferiors." "The Spaniards," declared Babbitt, "mixed to an extent with the Moors, and the resultant cross emigrated to Mexico and South America, and intermixed with the brown natives, Indians and negro slaves, exhibiting an example of breeding downward on a gigantic scale."[7]

Such talk was not the expression of extremists or eccentrics. Former U.S. diplomat Chester Lloyd Jones agreed with Babbitt's hypothesis. He offered, "It must be confessed that [mestizos] often exhibit the known tendency to follow the vices and weaknesses of both sides of their ancestry rather than the virtues."[8] In essence, Mexico was its own enemy.

On occasion some dissonance regarding the perils of Mexico's ancestry surfaced. Protestant missionary George B. Winton, guided by an optimistic missionary spirit, intended to correct what he thought to be a general misconception. "In the opinion of most observers," he suggested, "[the mestizo] is an improved stock as compared to the aborigines, quick to learn but inconstant in the applications of the lessons taught."[9] His qualified correction only added a slight twist to the general pessimism affecting American writers when it came to Mexico's racial stock. In the very same publication, Winton later gave a different reading to the matter of interbreeding: "It is unfortunately true, nevertheless, that the law that people of mixed blood tend to inherit the vices of both sides of their ancestry, rather than the virtues, has operated in Mexico."[10] University of Chicago anthropologist Frederick Starr, speaking at a university conference on Mexico, offered students and faculty this bit of conventional knowledge on the mestizo: "He is the common, every-day mixed-blood Mexican. Poor, miserable greaser—ignorant, superstitious, eminently pious; gay, thoughtless, improvident."[11] A field geologist with years of experience in the Tampico oil fields, Charles Hamilton, hastened to point out in his memoirs that the "lazy louts tourists sometime see along the streets and highways of Mexico are more often than not Mestizos."[12] On Jack London's visit to the same Tampico oil fields visited by Marian Storm and Hamilton, the celebrated man of letters repeated a well-known chant: "The mixed breed is unveracious, dishonest, and treacherous."[13]

The "mixed blood" discourse entered into the "peaceful conquest" policy as well, exemplified in the 1902 U.S. Department of Labor's publication *Labor Conditions in Mexico*. The study opens with the largest section of the study on population and its racial and cultural characteristics. The author, Walter Weyl, noted that the growing "mixed race" is "an important fact, and one which makes any study of labor as well as of political and economic conditions in Mexico of special interest to the sociologist."[14]

However, the unfortunate stock and ensuing regressive hybridization fell short of satisfactorily describing to the reader, much less explaining, all the circumstances that historically constructed Mexico. A more effective method would be to insert a real-life example and compare it with Mexico for similarities, parallels, and exact duplications, if any. The colonial system, a choice not chosen by a metaphorical impulse, held a greater explanatory power for delving into Mexico's present, and thus it entered into the conventional discourse on Mexico. Consequently, the option fell to exploring linkages with the Orient, particularly with "the Oriental" and all the racial and colonial implications that the term contained.

ORIENTALISM

How to inform the reader of the precise qualities that distinguished Mexicans from other peoples (Europeans) while simultaneously explaining Mexico by ascribing those qualities that mirrored peoples from other areas of the world challenged the writer. Among the many possible elements available to contemporary authors seeking to construct an identity for Mexicans, the term Oriental and all that it implied seemed a perfect fit.

Again, the colonial experience was appropriated wholesale and without interrogation. The nearest living relative to Mexico seemed unequivocally to be the Oriental peoples, a consistently impressionistic connection that carried more than superficial comparisons. American writers, travelers, diplomats, academics, and businesspersons deliberately employed the Oriental comparison. Seldom did an author ignore the Oriental analogy as if it were a fundamental element, much like the mixed-breed theme, of Mexico's history and culture that required a close examination. Mexico, it was said, was the Orient of the West, or as Sullivan McCollester noted, "There is far more of the Orient here than of the Occident." [15] Unsurprisingly, Reau Campbell dubbed his first guidebook, *Mexico: Tours through the Egypt of the New World*, [16] and Nevin Winter titled a chapter "A Glimpse of the Oriental in the Occident," while Winton unequivocally testified that Mexico "is the Old World in the New. It is the Egypt of the Occident." [17] Winter observed what he imagined could exist in no other part of the world than the East. "So this unique panorama continued all the afternoon," he exclaimed as he toured southern Mexico,

> I could not think of anything but Palestine, as I gazed at this unceasing procession of donkeys, Egyptian carts, women with their shawls folded and worn on their heads in Eastern fashion; and in the background the white walls, red tiled roofs and domes of the churches of Oaxaca. For a moment I wondered if I were not mistaken, and had suddenly strayed into some corner of the Orient, and found myself involuntarily looking for the mosque, and listening to the cry of the muezzin calling the faithful to prayer. [18]

Mexican wealthy elites echoed the foreign voices; the Mexican minister in Washington, Matías Romero, in comparing Mexico to Egypt, asserted that "there is no doubt that between the legends and romance with which the history of each of these countries abounds there is a striking resemblance." [19]

Writers followed with comparisons of Mexico's architecture, dress, scenery, religious traditions, sexual practices, cultural traditions, climate, and mental abilities to the Orient. "It is all Oriental," exclaimed Mary Elizabeth Blake in an article for the *Boston Globe*, "even to the dogs that howl through the streets." Margaret Sullivan, coauthor with Blake of their book *Mexico*, published in 1888, added:

> As the mystic symbols on the monuments of Egypt have only begun to yield their secrets to the archeologist, we need not despair of yet know-

ing something of antiquity of a country whose age is beyond present estimates, and whose earliest civilization, as indicated by her superstitions, architecture, costumes, and myths, was Oriental.[20]

Upon visiting Tehuantepec, in southern Mexico, Herbert Corey likened the city to Moroccan villages: "One walked against a backdrop of Moorish houses."[21] The traditions of agricultural cultivation, of embracing when greeting, and of funeral customs were firm evidences of an Arab distinction thought Marie Robinson Wright. She noted, "In the small villages and country sections where the millions of Indians dwell, Oriental scenes are plentiful . . . distinctively Oriental."[22] In emphasizing the prevalence of the Oriental theme and the thoroughness with which it defined Mexico, C. Reginald Enock noted, "It has been said that, from his headdress to his sandaled feet, the native Mexican is Hispano-Egyptian."[23]

Various points within the Orient seemed to fit the Mexican case so that the comparisons and parallels were drawn with Japan, India, Africa, Burma, Ceylon, or Egypt. One traveler wrote, "The Mexicans have been compared by experienced travelers to the early Egyptians, and many points of striking similarity undoubtedly exist between these two widely-separated people."[24] The arguments for the Mexico as Orient theme crept in from every direction. Blichfeldt asked, "Is it not an Oriental fact about them that they can be fed upon almost nothing, and are they not Oriental in the calm continuance of their own ways of dress and their own style of habitation?"[25] Ballou found parallels between the climate of Mexico and that of Egypt, with a "striking resemblance between them."[26] Ballou, like his contemporaries, contended that climate shaped cultural patterns: the hotter the climate, the more enervating the effect and the less energetic the people, with a resulting economic developmental pattern. Physically, Mexicans were said to markedly resemble peoples of the Orient. Williams Bishop described poor peasants as bearing "an analogy to the Chinese type."[27]

Often the pyramids were perceived as examples of a parallel with the East and were but one step removed from identifying the traditional indigenous religion of Mexico with the Orient. It fell to Charles Johnston to fashion the argument that more than similarity marked the connection between the Indian peoples of Mexico and the ancient religion of India. Although he agreed that there might not be an airtight case for an identity between the "aborigines of Mexico" and the "life of Prince Siddhartha," he nonetheless argued, "There is much that strongly suggests them." And later he dismissed any doubts and contended that "in the mountains of

Western Mexico, in the twentieth century, what is for all intents and purposes the Vedic religion, with its hymns and ceremonial, [is] still in active
operation. . . . hymns strongly resembling those that our Aryan kinsmen
chanted among the tributaries of the Upper Indus."[28]

Others found striking similarities in architecture and design, particularly houses, fountains, and the layout of villages, among others. In *Mexico:
Past and Present*, published in 1928, Winton observed a similar pattern.

> In their manner of life, both in city and country, the Mexicans have
> much in common with the peoples of western Asia and northern
> Africa. So manifest is the resemblance to the latter that, taken with cer-
> tain traits of the stone carving and architecture of the pre-European
> period, it has suggested to many a racial connection with Egypt.[29]

Another Protestant missionary who spent thirteen years in Mexico documented a similar conclusion in letter to his family. "Their [Mexicans']
habits and modes of thought," wrote Charles Drees, "seem very Oriental
and patriarchal, so that they move in masses."[30] Again I refer to Winton
and his effort to accurately report on the character of the Mexican people.
Opposite the first page of his *Mexico To-Day*, he presented a quotation
from William Wallace, probably a missionary colleague, which is indica-
tive of the depth of Orientalism among American writers and Protestant
missionaries. Wrote Wallace,

> Now with regard to the character of the people, they are as Oriental in
> type, in thought, and in habits as the Orientals themselves. It is true they
> have a veneer of European civilization; but underneath this veneer, on
> studying the people and becoming better acquainted with them, we
> find that they are genuine Asiatics. They have some of the fatalism, the
> same tendency for speculation on the impractical side of life and reli-
> gion, the same opposition to the building of industries, the same tradi-
> tionalism and respect for the usages of antiquity.[31]

Academics joined in the parade. Ernest Gruening, a distinguished inves-
tigator and expresser of Mexico's economic and political problems and
prospects, could not resist applying the Oriental analogy. He, like others,
linked the behavior patterns supposedly inherent in the Oriental psyche
with the representations of Orientalism he observed in Mexico. Mexicans
are "a race whose outlook is essentially Eastern," argued Gruening, applying the accepted dichotomy that divided the world into modern and
backward:

The Western outlook is active, aggressive, restless, ambitious, proselytizing in what it considers a good cause; the Eastern outlook is calm, gentle, courteous,—though in the case [of] the American Indian, prone to violence when roused—passive, reflective, artistic, self-sufficient. The former seeks outlet in the imposition of his will, be it on the forces of nature or on his fellow-men; the latter flowers in artistic creation and in the unfolding of mind and soul.[32]

Mexico's political history followed an Oriental design making democracy difficult if not impossible. James Creelman's defense for the Díaz dictatorship touched on the place of the Oriental in Mexico's history. In the manner of his contemporaries, Creelman maintained that

one finds enough to explain the Mexico of today in the practical certainty that the brown-skinned and yellow-skinned races, and their hybrids, which make up at least three quarters of the republic's population, descend from Oriental bloods, to which truly democratic political institutions are alien if not impossible.[33]

Despite the ritualistic assertions that Mexico and the Orient were, if not one and the same, related or at least compatible, authors staked out a new cultural turf for identifying and explaining Mexico. Yet, originality eluded them. The British colonial rulers, represented in the works of Rudyard Kipling, had previously applied the very same definitions to the meaning of Oriental that American writers ascribed to the Mexican. Kipling's distinction between the Orient and the West resonated in the literature on Mexico by Americans: "The outcomes of human genius which we have been taught are to be found for the seeking, are few and very far between. It is necessary first to peruse infinity of trivialities before we arrive at anything which may fairly be held to represent oriental *thought*. The rest is dream piled on dream and phantasm on phantasm— unprofitable, and to [the] Western mind, at least, foolish."[34]

Like his American counterparts' thinking on the Mexican subject, Kipling believed that the average adult Oriental's intellectual abilities reached at best the level of the Western child. Of one of Rudyard Kipling's passages on the native Indian, Thomas Pinney writes in his critique, "That is the paternalistic, official stereotype of the native fully developed: caste-ridden, venal, incompetent—a sort of larger child capable of falling into trouble if left to himself. . . . Kipling actually believed this."[35] And so did Americans, whether diplomats, Protestant missionaries, travelers, or businesspeople in Mexico.

Although Orientalism held the status of article of faith in the minds of most "Mexico hands," it became apparent that Mexico also exhibited particular social patterns that implied uniqueness. This did not mean that the Oriental theme was jettisoned, only that it was joined with a focus on the culture and behavior of the majority of the Mexican population, the *peones*, or the peasantry, bound and free, and all unskilled laborers. Writers Anglicized *peones*, pronouncing it "peons," and in the process created a term that accommodated the peaceful conquest in much the same way that Oriental satisfied British colonialism. Writers explained the social condition of Mexico and the importance of the U.S. economic presence in meeting Mexico's fundamental needs and removing obstacles in the path of modernity. It was not the geography, climate, or soil of Mexico that prevented modernization; on the contrary, the nation was endowed with great natural wealth. Rather, the majority of Mexico's population, Indians, mestizos, and peons, who like their Oriental cousins stood in the path of Western progress and needed the hand of their American superiors to lift them from the deep morass.

PEONISM

Just as in the case of the British and the Oriental colonized subject, the mass and poorest of the Mexican population were scrutinized, dissected, analyzed, and defined. First, authors generally declared the peon an obstacle to modernization. Second, authors sought to answer why—that is, what was it about the peon that made him or her a source of backwardness?—and questioned whether the peon displayed any redeeming qualities. The verdict on the peon, synonymous for Indian in the mind of authors, practically condemned him or her to a life of cheap labor.[36] So distinctive were their alleged characteristics that peons were essentially perceived as a racial category unto themselves.

Protestant missionary Alden Buell Case, for example, offered a very general definition of who comprised the peon population. They were, according to Case, "the numerous class of unskilled laborers." William Carson correctly asserted that Mexico, "could not do without him," and then added, "He not only cultivates the soil, works the mines, and does all the hard labor, but also acts as servant."[37] Beyond a simple identification of his role in the Mexican economy and society, from *peon* to *minero* and *mozo*, Americans defined the peon's main "instinctive" characteristics and then suggested methods of dealing with them so that peons might perform their role in the peaceful conquest satisfactorily. From heads of mining corporations to touring vacationer, peons were, for better or worse, considered the backbone of Mexico. Whether Americans liked them or not, the peons was here to stay, and Americans had to make the best of it.

The Peon as a Drag on Progress

Percy F. Martin believed he had identified the answer to the riddle-vexed American commentators on Mexico: "The great deterrence to the complete regeneration of Mexico has been the native peons."[38] After all was said and done, peons were said to waste "their time in lust, dancing, singing, drinking, playing cards, gambling, cock-fighting, riding, thieving, stabbing in quarrels and other indulgences of their passions." Few disagreed. Hubert Howe Bancroft had said as much twenty years before. As for the peon, he declared, the "least possible labor provides for these wants, and careless for the morrow, they squander the surplus on drinking. . . ."[39] By 1930 such thinking had become conventional wisdom.

Mining corporations, among others, were particularly interested in the peon's inner self. Wallace Gillpatrick suggested that peons were instinctive wanderers and, therefore unreliable. He advised that the

> peons, in fact all the people who work in mines, interest me. . . . A Mexican miner is indolent, and no power on earth can make him work very hard. He is by instinct a rover. He may be comfortably housed, with fair pay and credit at the company store; but when the fever to wander is on him . . .[40]

Using the American experience, several writers made note of the behavioral similarities between peons and American blacks. The writer of an article for *National Geographic* related, "The Mexican peon knows that he is born to serve, as did the southern darky, and caste and class distinction is emphasized on all occasions."[41] Mining engineer Allen H. Rogers defined the peon in ways that most Americans could readily understand. The peon, wrote Rogers, is

> of mild and humble nature, much like the plantation field hands before the war. . . . like the southern darkey, he lived in quarters at the home ranch or at outlying ranches under the supervision of a majordomo and from working constantly under the sun his skin, naturally dark, was blackened to the hue of the African.[42]

One need not say the same thing by reference to American blacks. One author found the peon exhibiting fatalistic traits, an "abject submission to a miserable state."[43]

In search of scenes for his canvas, artist Francis Hopkinson Smith sketched an image of peons in his book. Smith alleged that peons have no "idea of present economy or of providing for the future. . . . most of them seem to be occupied in obtaining food and amusement for the passing hour, without either hope or desire for a better future."[44] Mining engineer Evan Fraser-Campbell, motivated by similar impressions, devoted the first paragraph of his article on managing Mexican labor to a discussion of the peculiarities said to inhere in peons. He cautioned mine administrators to get beneath the surface of the peon's behavior in order to adjust him to the company's requirements.

> To manage Mexican labor successfully it is necessary at the outset to take into consideration the fact that the peon is of a race whose habits and characteristics are those of a simple-minded people, accustomed for generations to conditions not far removed from actual servitude and who have not yet learned to act on their own initiative. . . . The successful manager is the one who understands the limitations of the people and is willing to adapt his methods to their capabilities.[45]

Fraser-Campbell claimed that one mine supervisor who followed his instructions cut labor costs by 20 percent in three months. Armed with knowledge of the habits and the way of thinking of the peon, managing him became a simple *and* profitable matter.

Others were not so quick to find an easy solution. Carson, for example, concluded that the average peon was "mentally and physically lethargic [and] improvident . . . without ambition . . . untruthful." Mining engineer J. Nelson Nevius similarly reasoned, "The Mexican laboring classes have a highly developed lazy strain in their blood."[46] So did a journalist for the *Nation*, who concluded that the Mexican adheres "to a complete disregard for the basic need for work [and] regards it as an evil."[47] And to make matters worse, the Mexican was prone to gambling and drinking. Moreover, although laborious when working, the peon worked in an "old fashioned, slow way, and he will not work even in that way unless he is watched."[48] However, employers could not do without the peon.

Railroad administrators must have been equally interested in the efficient management of Mexican labor. One newspaper reporter found that experiences similar to those of the mine operators exasperated American rail bosses. "The good-natured peons," wrote Griffin, "who handle the freight that makes up the larger share of our load, work with a pleasant listlessness that would infuriate a New England railroad man." But, on the other hand, Griffin noted that the Mexican Central, "winding around the hills" through Zacatecas, "was built with earth carried on the backs of peons."[49] While their place in the new economy made them indispensable, the image portrayed of them did them no favors. They were described variously as dirty, lazy, indolent, unambitious, gamblers, sexually overindulgent, and to top it off, the peon "has little concern about yesterday, to-day, or to-morrow."[50]

THE BAD IS GOOD

A 1902 U.S. Department of Commerce and Labor *Bulletin*'s analysis of labor in Mexico emphasized that the generally attributed qualities were the sum of the peons' very being and that wages above the standard only increased "idleness."[51] Still, peons supplied labor, and regardless of the coarse images that made them distinct, peons as cheap laborers made it possible to extract great riches from Mexico. Part of their low cost, a supposed ability to survive on very little, motivated a substantial commentary. No use to supply the peons with modern plows, since they can only grasp "primeval simplicity," warned Carson. Since "his ideal of life is to be idle, . . . he only desires his little mud-brick hut, his piece of ground, his pig, his tortillas and his frijoles." No purpose would be served with higher wages either, as "his wants are easily supplied, there is really no incentive to be progressive."[52]

Writing in the *National Geographic*, Herbert Corey framed an image that suggested that the pitiful wages paid were reasonable, given the peon's nature. The "peon is impervious to discomfort," claimed Corey, "He rarely shivers. When he gets ready to go to bed, he selects the nearest wall and curls down upon the stones of the street."[53] Writers' wording and themes were so similar and sometimes bordering on the identical that it seemed they plagiarized from each other freely. In step with Corey, J. Park Alexander recalled that while cold weather "drives us indoors and compels us to cut wood, . . . a Mexican just curls up in the sun alongside his adobe hut and sleeps it out."[54] Each of the various tasks assumed by peons were addressed and allotted a particular ascriptive characteristic. Peons formed the mass of Mexican *cargadores*, which prompted Winter to mention that these mozos "come and go," and that each generation is like the last. They are happy in that they want but little and that little is easily supplied. They are contented because they live for to-day and worry not for the morrow. They are satisfied to go through life as the bearers of other people's burdens.[55]

Newspaper correspondent for the *Los Angeles Times* Charles Lummis offered a similar diagnosis, one that defended American capital from any criticism regarding treatment of Mexican labor. "It is fair to add," wrote Lummis, "that the current pity of the Mexican laborer is altogether wasted. He has a climate decent to be lived in—wherein it is estimated, twelve days' work in the year is enough to supply one peon with the necessities of life." Lummis then added, "If he gets higher pay he works fewer days. . . . the only object of work is to get enough to live on."[56]

Using a similar if not identical logic, David Wells quoted David Strother, the former U.S. consul general in southern Mexico, to back up his claim that peons were satisfied with little: "None of the working-classes of Mexico have any idea of present economy, or of providing for the future. The lives of most of them seem to be occupied in obtaining food and amusement for the passing hour."[57] Strother's contemporary, J. H. Bates arrived at the same conclusion, "This land is a loafers' paradise—little clothing, little food, and less shelter being needed."[58] Consequently, the consensus seemed to be that the treatment of Mexican laborers and the institutionalization of the "Mexican wage" prevalent in all the industries operated by Americans was by all measures justified.

That the peon allegedly exhibited but "little inventive but sufficient imitative talent" only added to their value as a labor force according to Bishop. Combined with their quality as cheap labor, previous training in small self-sufficient forms of production prepared excellent mill hands "for capital, to work up into manufactures the raw materials with which the country abound[s]."[59] Winter used a similar argument in this passage:

> The little brown man with back bent under a load has a countenance which is full of rest and patient philosophy as a modern financier's face is of care and wrinkles of anxiety. It is almost unfair to the simple-minded, patient and docile peon of Mexico to speak of him as an Indian for he is at once confused with the bloodthirsty redskin of the north. He is a peaceful, if improvident, character, and is child in nature. He represents cheap labour and is one of the great attractions that brings wealth to Mexico.[60]

THE PEON AS CHILD

Frequently, readers came across terms such as "horde," "a bunch," "swarming," or "rabble" for describing any grouping of Mexicans, which connoted a formless, anarchic collection of individuals without intelligent purpose. Peon easily segued into images of children, and in the scramble to define the Mexican, peon and childlike served well enough. The Mexican-as-child theme appears frequently in narratives, suggesting that from the perspective of the observer, Mexican customs and norms were inherently determined sets of actions and ideas that worked their way into the politics and economics of the country. Jack London, for example, described Mexican revolutionary forces in the Tampico region as "child-minded men, incapable of government, playing with the weapons of giants."[61]

The "child-like quality about the Mexicans," alluded to by Harry L. Foster in a 1924 work with the revealing title *A Gringo in Mañana-Land*, seemed to many writers the fundamental characteristic of Mexico's peons.[62] Consonant with books on Mexico, newspaper editorial cartoons commonly depicted Mexicans in particular and Latin Americans in general in childlike postures before an Uncle Sam intent on correcting incorrigible Latins.[63] Editorial caricatures followed the example provided by such chroniclers of Mexico as the "Father of American Sociology," Edward A. Ross. The famed sociologist traveled in Mexico in the early 1920s and recounted his visit in *The Social Revolution in Mexico*. Among topics covered in the work, the intellectual abilities of peons were prominent. He argued that not only was the general run of Mexicans endowed with levels of genetically determined intelligence less than that considered "normal," but that the "common folk" as well were said to "have less alertness, less mental 'edge' than the bucolic Chinese." In language familiar to Evan Fraser-Campbell, Ross later concluded that the peon "is as easily led as a child, and the master who understands him and means right generally has no difficulty in managing him."[64] Ross stated the common wisdom of the era of "peaceful conquest." Nearly forty years previous, a Protestant missionary declared that the peon's "wants are few, for they are children of nature, with whom a little goes a long way."[65]

Like many tourists and corporate personnel living in Mexico, retired mining engineer Ralph Ingersoll felt assured that the success of an enterprise in Mexico required an appreciation that "all Mexicans are children and have to be treated accordingly. The engineer has to be a sort of amateur god."[66] Ingersoll's contemporary, mining engineer C. S. Thomas, wrote from the same script. Even though the peon is childlike, stated Thomas, and "in spite of their provoking stupidity at times, they furnish a never failing source of amusement. They are faithful . . . if treated properly."[67] Peon labor may have been slow, reticent, and unskilled but their childlike qualities worked in favor of employers advised one mining engineer. "Peon temperament and economic conditions," wrote Franklin Smith, "make it improbable that powerful and coherent labor unions will ever be formed." However, if supervision is left in the hands of men "ignorant of the language . . . and customs of the country," disaster might very well ensue.[68]

Perhaps no other commentator stated the "peon as child" theme as clearly and vehemently as did Wallace Thompson in his *The Mexican Mind: A Study in National Psychology* (1922). After Thompson cited rampant promiscuity and compulsive sex drives as the Mexican norm, he dealt with the matter of maturity. "The Mexican," he confidently professed, "seems to have a child's or a savage's unwavering grasp of the details of desire and of the things he hopes for,—a heritage from the Indian which centuries of white rule and oceans of white blood have never eradicated."[69] He then extended the racially determined maturation thesis using the example of Mexican humor: "There is indeed true humor and a great deal of it in the Mexicans, although it is accented by but little levity, and is more often childlike and wantonly cruel."[70] Thompson was hardly original; four decades earlier Hubert Howe Bancroft asserted a similar line of thought:

> The Mexican—the mestizo now being dominant and representative—has remained in a state of adolescence, as indicated by his capricious, thoughtless, and even puerile traits. . . . he can be ferociously cruel; treachery and fidelity go hand in hand; his generosity degenerates into prodigality; lofty desires sink for want of patience and determination. . . . in short . . . he lacks reflecting prudence and sustained purpose.[71]

The peon and the Oriental stood on an equal plane; both were objects far removed from the Western ideal and both were candidates for a cultural cleansing.

Peons as Grotesque

Not infrequently, mean and vicious metaphors debased the subject peoples. Metaphors using animal and insect forms and behaviors were on occasion employed to describe peons, whether at work or residing in their villages, and only added more emphasis to an already depressing image of peons. Griffin explained that, as a people, peons "were happy as lizards, more content under a heat that would broil an American."[72] From the vantage point of a first-class coach, Bishop thought that peons appeared like a variety of insects. "Here and there a cluster of white tents is seen at a distance," observed our traveler, "and cotton-clad peons delving in gulch or on mountain-side are like some strange species of white insects."[73] Ballou applied the same metaphor to "the eddies of busy life" near Mexico City, where "the natives assume the size of huge insects crawling about in bright colors."[74] The focus sharpened to identify the insect. In laying the rail line in northern Mexico, an engineer portrayed the labor-intensive industry by reference to ants. "In less than a month the line was literally alive with these human ants," reported Cy Warman. "Red ants, fleece clad from the mountains, naked ants from the Terre Coliente [*sic*], and black ants from Sonora."[75] In an article for the *National Geographic*, Frederick Simpich employed the same metaphor and assured his readers that Mexicans were, as a people, "as aimless as the inhabitants of a disturbed ant hill."[76]

From within the processes of a mining, oil, or railroad camp, peons earned considerable recognition for at least being cheap and somewhat readily accessible. On the other hand, in their homes, villages, and cities, they became the focus of uneasy attention if not rebuke, and physical and social distances were maintained. When the occasion required the peons to gather up close, Americans generally found them reprehensible. The images of "swarms of street beggars and thieves" were more than J. Park Alexander could bear, and he complained in a series of articles appearing in the *Akron Beacon* that "a visit to Mexico intensifies one's love of home."[77] While touring on the first-class coach, Stanton Kirkham experienced a moment of tense discomfort when suddenly surrounded by peons. In the comfort of his first-class seating, the train overflowed with peons celebrating a saint's feast day. Kirkham described what was to him an uninviting but (fortunately for him) a short-lived scene: "The train filled up with peons, who eventually invaded the sanctity of the first-class coach, cluttering the aisles with bunches of bananas, baskets of zapotes and live chickens."[78]

In a similar experience to Kirkham's, Carson bemoaned having to share the dining coach with other than his first-class coach mates. Interlopers invaded his privileged compartment, described as a "motley company of unwashed natives whose manners constantly remind you that fingers were invented before forks." However, to avoid the unpleasant natives on that trip, Carson mentioned that he and the other "white passengers . . . usually gather at one table."[79] Travelers, particularly foreign travelers, commonly collected among themselves in restaurants, hotels, and on trains to form a kind of protective *cordon sanitaire* separating Mexicans from Americans. In Monterrey, for example, one writer found that Americans actively sought to implement the "color line" to divide Mexicans from Americans.[80] That color line existed throughout the various labor camps that sprouted as U.S. capital "invaded" Mexico. For sure, it was this widespread social distinction that prompted writers to suggest that only a Rudyard Kipling could effectively and realistically convey the images engendered by Americans in Mexico.

The Positive Attributes of Peons

Mexican images that clashed with modern U.S. culture occupied page after page of narratives, and yet authors, in the same breath, admitted that Mexican culture displayed many positive attributes. These features, which entertained and pleased Americans, failed, however, to modify damning critiques; nonetheless, readers were continually reminded that Mexicans had something of value to offer the world. Congratulations were extended for a number of supposed instinctive traits, including artistry and imitation, and in relation to Indians, a supposed "natural" form of society untrammeled by industrialism and its materialistic emphasis. Weyl described the artistic quality as "beyond all question," while imitation rendered them adept at learning new trades. Griffin, like many others, found that "the love of music and art is born in these Indians" (and at the same time noted that they were inveterate thieves).[81] A refined courteousness and a "kind-hearted" generosity taken to a fault were also listed among the qualities Americans found in abundance among Mexicans.[82] Sociologist Ross summarized the positive: "A racial gift of sensitivity to beauty . . . lovers or makers of good music . . . love of color . . . politeness at all levels."[83] The good juxtaposed with the bad did not always inspire. "If every thing one sees here," complained the Reverend J. Hendrickson McCarty, "were as good as the music, then Mexico would be a paradise indeed."[84] But, few things in Mexico reached the level of music, artistry, or courteousness.

Moreover, the positives—love of color and flowers, willingness to share, and politeness—and the negatives—apathy, indolence, and thievery—existed independently of each other. Each cluster originated from an innate psychological wellspring and was writ in stone, so to speak. On balance, the negative far outweighed the positive and set the stage for addressing the redemption to a people bound by an instinctive nature to a subordinate role on the world stage. Again, the threads binding the fortune (or misfortune) of the Oriental and the peon stood out in bold relief.

THE MEXICAN PROBLEM

In 1911 James Creelman published his famous paean to Porfirio Díaz, *Díaz, Master of Mexico*, with its penultimate chapter entitled "The Real Mexican Problem." In short, the Mexican Problem defined Mexico as a society not yet ready for democracy or for economic development styled along the lines of the United States. Creelman very briefly touched on his explanation for the Mexican Problem, saying, "The condition of things is largely due to the natural laziness and political indifference of the Indians and part Indians who constitute more than three quarters of the whole citizenship of the country." Although many understood Creelman's explanation for the state of Mexico's political and economic underdevelopment, the concept of a Mexican Problem would not occupy center stage till the 1910 Mexican Revolution.[85] However, Creelman's explanation stood the test of time.

After the blast of cannons and violent battles of the 1910 civil war had subsided, a war fought over causes not always clearly delineated nor with a defined ideological framework, Americans expressed deep concern not so much for Mexico and its people as for the future of the Open Door policy. Despite the invasion of American capital and the rich profits derived from those enterprises, Americans sounded shrill alarms, announcing that Mexico was no longer a sure bet to open its door widely to the foreign capital as it once had been under Porfirio Díaz. Something called the Mexican Problem entered into the language of both American diplomats and American writers concerned about the turn of political events in Mexico, an issue that brought forth a discourse on the nature and causes of the problem and how to best resolve it. After a considerable discussion over the future of Mexico at a 1920 conference held at Clark University, convener George H. Blakeslee concluded, "Mexico admittedly presents a genuine problem . . . one due primarily to the inherent weakness and political instability of the country. How may it develop into a law abiding, capable nation, with an effective, educated, reliable middle class."[86] Mexico was a problem for the United States to solve, but as Blakeslee mentioned, "No general agreement exists as to its proper solution." What is of great importance was the place assumed by the United States in defining the Mexican Problem and in securing its resolution.

Not unlike many of his contemporaries, and similar to Creelman a dozen years earlier, Wallace Thompson contextualized the Mexican Problem squarely within the matter of genes or as he said, "Every phase of Mexican history and every Mexican problem has its race correspondence."[87] Former diplomat, Chester Lloyd Jones agreed, suggesting that in order to know the Mexican Problem in all of its ramifications, one needs a grasp of "the racial endowment of the people."[88] However, no author better expressed the question than Clarence Barron, manager of the *Wall Street Journal*. First, the candid title for his book, *The Mexican Problem* published in 1917 brought the matter to the public's attention. Second, he succinctly addressed the nature of the problem and its solution. Barron's first concern was the preservation of Mexico within the U.S. economic orbit given that Mexico, as he said,

> has so much to give us; fruits of the tropics, mineral and oil, wealth of a continent compressed into an isthmus, capacity for the happy, healthful, helpful labor of, not fifteen million but fifty million people . . . Of natural wealth she has abundance. Of helping hands, kindly direction, and organization she has woeful need.[89]

Jones said the same in slightly different wording in his analysis of the Mexican Problem: "The great wealth of Mexico makes it a region in which the adjustment of its political and economic relations with the rest of the world is of great importance."[90]

Of course, Barron, much like Jones, proposed that the United States supply the "kindly direction" and lead Mexico out of its abyss. And what was the cause of the Mexican Problem, asked Barron. He answered: "At the present time the larger part of the good people of Mexico are children who want to be in debt and at the same time care-free." And later Barron followed up his clarification of the origins of the Mexican Problem, suggesting that "Mexico is not a difficult proposition once you understand the Mexican character. He is the same childlike, dependent, trusting fellow whether at work, play, or revolution. He is simply in need of a strong helping hand."[91]

Jones agreed without adding much variation to the discourse that occupied American writers for nearly half a century. From Jones' perspective, the Mexican Problem boiled down to a "varied population, native, mestizo, and white, without a cultural basis upon which to create a uniform civilization," who, as a society, were "non-industrial and, up to the present, as a rule non-industrous."[92] And even though mestizos were "an improved lot [over the Indians]," they were nonetheless "inconstant in the application of lessons taught." Jones repeated the conventional critiques of the Mexican character, a character which he claimed lacked the "wholesome unrest and dynamic element" found in colder countries, and summarized it in one brief statement: "Life is too easy."[93] From Creelman to Barron, Jones, and Thompson, the Mexican Problem rested on the same racial foundations. In good imperial fashion, they also designed a solution to the problem.

SOLVING THE MEXICAN PROBLEM: THE AMERICANIZATION OF MEXICO

Americans had long felt that redemption for Mexico, commonly defined as the Americanization of Mexico, was ultimately a process of removing or constraining those obstacles and characteristics that allegedly hung like an albatross around Mexico's neck. Americans assumed the mantle of civilizing agents. Ross expressed a variation on the theme, asserting, "As you go about you reflect what a paradise this Mexico might be if it possessed the moral character and the social institutions of the descendents of the Puritans. Nature has done her part. It is man that does not fill out the picture."[94]

In terms Kipling probably would have well understood, Harriott Wight Sherrat suggested that although Mexicans "often seem to us childish and puerile, we may, nevertheless . . . [lead] our neighbors up the steep grade of civilization."[95] For others, civilization, modernization, and Americanization all carried the same definition. As Edward Conley put it (in an article appropriately titled "The Americanization of Mexico") "Modernization and Americanization are almost synonymous terms." Conley celebrated the Americanization already in progress by the late nineteenth century, or as he put it, "We have by our example and our commercial products, taught the Mexican peon to wear shoes and a hat, and have increased his wages all over the republic." The author underscored other examples and predicted that "twenty years hence the Mexican family life will be on an American basis" and that "each year the American way of living is taking a deeper hold on the Mexican people."[96]

Nonetheless, many writers felt that whatever Americanization had taken place fell wide and short of the mark. Nevin Winter, for example, complained, "Things cannot be changed to Anglo-Saxon standards in a year, or two years, or even a generation. To Americanize Mexico will be a difficult if not impossible undertaking, and there are no signs of such a transition."[97] William Showalter reached the same frustrated conclusion.

He conceded, "It will be a long, long climb until its population, four-fifths Indians and half-breeds, will reach the point in their national destiny where they can possess a government like our own." Nonetheless, the task could not be ignored or avoided. "American intelligence and capital," he optimistically claimed, "have done much . . . and will do much more in the future." A mining engineer challenged his fellow Americans in Mexico to "make an American out of him or leave him to his happy indolence."[98] Winter warmly observed that "their neighbors to the north of the Rio Grande [are] ready to lend a helping hand."[99]

Such progress was notable by 1890, according to an upbeat Ballou, who pointed to a number of American practices that were in evidence, including the use of English, which signified that "matters of higher civilization were in progress."[100] The increasing use of English seemed to be a standard measure of civilization, or so thought Griffin, who noted, "Young Mexico is learning with pride to speak English as it takes up American ways and Northern ambitions."[101] More than English entered into the formula; a city thoroughfare, the use of a certain style of clothing, or a new dance craze could be evidence of Americanization, and each would be a sign of progress away from a once unfettered culture of peon mestizos and Indians. Simpich added that on the west coast of Mexico, where he imagined that Americans enjoyed the life similar to that of the British in India, Mexicans "achieve better results with the stimulus of foreign aid and example."[102]

Deep draughts of Americanization came with the railroads, or at least many writers urged readers to believe so. Howard Conkling's reference to the passive but important influence of railroads was echoed throughout the literature. In a chapter appropriately titled "The Railroads," Conkling wrote, "The railroad is at once the expression and instrument of modern civilization," and he added that when the rails were completed, a golden age would "dawn upon the country."[103] Not a few thought that more than railroads brought civilization in its wake. By the term "Americanizing," contended Ober, "I would imply that great civilizing force that is permeating the Southern republic, opening its mines, spanning its deserts with bands of steel and electric wires, thus materially aiding the central government."[104]

The task required a recognition that inadequate problem-solving methods were being applied by Mexicans. In such a search, Kirkham divided the Latin mind from the Anglo-Saxon's; whereas in the former "life is surrender," in the latter "it is assertion."[105] The Mexican mind formed the

Mexican Problem. "The problem," argued Wallace Thompson, "is essentially psychological and essentially one which, because of the failures and neglect of the mestizos and of the Indians, the white world must meet and solve."[106] In using the term "white world," Thompson meant Americans; however, he, like his British colonial counterparts, placed the resolution within the context of a civilizing mission taken by Americans to the less fortunate "brown brothers."

Whatever effort was to be undertaken, cautioned Thompson, it must operate within the framework of the Mexican's innately conditioned potential. Ultimately, for Thompson and his colleagues interested in civilizing Mexico, "foreign companies are the business world of Mexico," and therefore the "solution is in the hands of American business men."[107] The deeper message decreed that by themselves Mexicans cannot achieve modernization, and that the United States must actively take on the responsibility of tutoring Mexico to adulthood. Barron minced no words: "The redemption of Mexico must be from the invasion of business, forcing upon the natives—the good people of Mexico—technical training, higher wages, bank accounts, financial independence, and the rights of citizenship and accumulation."[108]

Americans were well aware of the condition of colonized nations subjected to European powers and of the difficulty in maintaining a measure of control over the colonies. Not surprisingly, Barron related that the Mexican Problem was "a problem belting the world," the same as that which affected China and Egypt (and implicitly Britain and other industrial powers). "The problem of Mexico," suggested Gruening, "is the dilemma of a so-called "backward" nation, which, while having a culture of its own, is backward in adopting the modern industrial civilization."[109] The widespread sentiment seemed to be that the northern power, the representation of the modern and, therefore, civilization must and will triumph over the Mexican Problem, the representation of a dysfunctional culture, sometimes referred to as a backward culture, in contact with a harmonious, progressive and dynamic culture. The consensus opinion declared that the backward must adjust, forcibly if need be, to the self-proclaimed superiority of the modern nation. Thomson spoke for a generation of "Mexico hands" claiming that "the white man is still the greatest of the world's teachers . . . and he will carry the mixed-blood and the Indian of Mexico forward surely—and indeed not slowly—to the formation of his new civilization."[110] Mexico, styled by Americans as their nation's burden, entered into a new stage in its national history.

Protestant Missionaries and Americanization

The U.S. peaceful conquest had numerous parallels with the British colonial experience, particularly in the case of efforts at religious conversion of the colonized subject. In the American case, Protestant missionaries accompanied the business entrepreneurs. They came not in a group fashion but as independent agents for an Americanization program that operated under the mantle of religious conversion. Protestants were quick to condemn the Catholic Church for a variety of overt and covert actions that allegedly left the people of Mexico lodged somewhere between a pagan and a Christian state. In seeking to convert Mexico, the Protestant missionaries believed that they were also eliminating an obstacle to modernization, the Catholic Church, which promoted blind faith, mass ignorance, despotism, idolatry, and greed. In other words, the foundation for the backwardness of Mexico rested to a significant extent on the dogma of the Catholic Church. Missionaries and many other writers frankly pointed to the "priest-ridden" Catholic Church for causing Mexico's political difficulties over the centuries.[111]

More than conversion to Protestantism resulted from the missions. Converting Mexico supposedly complemented and aided the peaceful invasion and was celebrated by many authors who also noted the importance of Protestant missions in extending an Americanizing influence over Mexico.[112] On the other hand, Protestant missionaries returned the compliment and believed that American capital undermined the backward cultural outlook allegedly fostered by the Catholic Church. Railroads and mining companies brought modern forms of thinking and behavior, or so thought George B. Winton in his work for the Missionary Education Movement. Winton assured his readers that the "entrance of foreign capital . . . and the immigration of many forceful and efficient foreigners have all wrought directly upon the mental habits of the Mexican people."[113] He energetically made the case for railroads as a "a huge entering wedge for modern ideas." Winton welcomed the influence and described the method of Americanization wrought by the mere presence of American companies. "If a tract of a jungle or a wild mountain gorge was considered impenetrable," he exclaimed,

> straightaway these *americanos* plowed through it a chasm for their steel rails and shrieking locomotives. It is not surprising, therefore, that ideas in the moral and intellectual realm that long had been accepted as settled began to lose their fixity and finality. The resourcefulness and independence of their new friends were for the Mexicans conta-

gious. That spirit of self-reliance, of determined self-assertion got abroad among them.[114]

Railroads and mining camps alone could not supply the needed energy to move Mexico into the twenty-first century, as Mrs. John Butler surmised in an article for the *Missionary Review of the World.* "These poor people need wise and loving help," she explained. "They need someone to take an interest in them . . . until there are better homes; until people learn the sacredness of family ties and have better ideas of morality, very little progress can be made." Mrs. Butler offered the example of Protestant schools for "sending young women . . . to great and glorious tasks" propelling social change.[115]

In the spirit of cooperation, the missionaries enjoyed the support of the American diplomatic service in Mexico, which took "very strong measures" to protect the Protestants. Missionary John Butler (husband of the Mrs. Butler cited above) made note of the help extended by the ambassador and various consular officials who "earned the gratitude of missionaries."[116] Support did not end there. According to a missionary with thirteen years of experience in Mexico, American investors were on friendly terms with Protestant missionaries and were known to extend such favors as reduced fares on trains.[117] The language of empire spoken by missionaries and investors mirrored common objectives, reflected in this passage quoted by Reverend McCarty: "Her destiny is ultimately to be associated, if not identified, with ours. She is a sister republic, feeble, burdened with heterogeneous and debased elements. . . . Her natural resources and enterprise are steadily inviting the investment of our capital and enterprise. Their importance is conceded, and sagacious statesmen cannot but recognize the claims to national sympathy which she presents."[118]

Protestant missions worked hand-in-hand with the overall objectives of U.S. foreign policy. Missionaries set up schools for instruction in the proper lifestyle appropriate to a modern society. Its educational projects, which sociologist E. A. Ross visited on his trip to Mexico, convinced him that "an American mission school" provided Mexicans with an "example of what a school should be." A pleased Thompson placed "American business men, American teachers and American missionaries," on an equal footing; together they constituted "the hope of the downtrodden majority."[119] The Boot Strap philosophy applied at the Hampton Institute exclusively for American blacks bore more than a similarity here. Thompson was not alone in envisioning the Hampton method as the model for raising the Mexican population to a higher cultural level.[120]

The connections with India borne by American Protestant ministers were practical reminders of the role of religion in the imperial mission. American missionaries returning from missions in India in 1869 launched a Women's Foreign Missionary Society in Boston with intentions of "up-lifting" the condition of women in India. Although the original discussions that led to its founding focused on women in India (where it was alleged that the Catholic Church not only failed to uproot "paganism" but accommodated it) as the guide for the society's work, no change in direction was required when it established its first Mexican mission in 1873.[121] In the thinking of missionaries, India and Mexico presented an identical set of problems: the temporizing of the Roman Catholic Church and the persistence of pagan customs, dress, and religious practices and the absence of capitalist forms of production.

The Methodist Church began its mission campaign in Mexico with the return of the Reverend William Butler from India. One Protestant chronicler noted, "With the memory of his work in India to strengthen his heart and faith he joyfully began the task of founding the Methodist Church in the land covered with the ruins of ancient Aztec idolatry."[122] The example of India's colonial experience presented a rich opportunity to compare it with the transnational relation binding the United States and Mexico. That opportunity, which we have seen, found a place in many writers' frame of reference. Emil Blichfeldt's declaration made in his 1912 study, *A Mexican Journey*, succinctly summarized the point: "Protestant missions are as legitimate and almost as sorely needed in Mexico as in India."[123]

ANTI-IMPERIAL IMPERIALISM: WINNING THE HEARTS AND MINDS

Americans were acutely aware of the nationalist response on the part of labor and the middle classes in Mexico to the domineering presence of Americans. Additionally, the First World War and the prospect of a possible German ally next door added to a sense of alarm. The possibility of an economic nationalism breaking the economic ties motivated Washington to respond with policies adjusted to the times, policies that ensured the maintenance of the status quo. Moreover, the Mexican Revolution added a great sense that all could be lost, a consequence that the United States sought to prevent and succeeded through President Woodrow Wilson's policy of quiet negotiation to protect the Open Door policy under threat of armed intervention and de facto recognition of the Venustiano Carranza regime. Nevertheless, renewed calls came for the annexation of Mexico and even the setting up of some sort of buffer state, a new twist on the theme of conquest. Territorial annexation was once again on the front pages.

On the other hand, many Americans, particularly intellectuals and expatriates who found in Mexico a kind of exotic and unsullied paradise, began to react negatively to the "Ugly American" syndrome that coursed through the literature. One critic noted the unfortunate returns from "uncouth tourists" and "loud voiced" and insensitive Americans who displayed behavior patterns disrespectful and insulting toward Mexico and Mexicans. Many worried that the United States was needlessly losing the "hearts and minds" of Mexico and in the process creating dangerous political discontent in addition to becoming overlords throughout the region. Voices like that of the anti-imperialist George Inman juxtaposed the stereotyped undiplomatic American with those "good" Americans:

> [Those who learn] the language of the people, come to appreciate their good points, make the most intimate friendships with Mexicans, and publicly declare they had rather live in Mexico than any other country in the world, have done more than it is possible to estimate to offset the bad impressions . . . Many American firms and individual business men have been real missionaries to the people, with their introduction of higher wages, improved machinery, welfare work, schools and better housing for their employees.[124]

Meanwhile, the term "invasion" formerly used to describe the flow of Americans and American capital into Mexico disappeared from the literature. Fears that the United States intended to take "all of Mexico" prompted Chester Lloyd Jones, among others, to respond to recommendations for some sort of force to compel Mexico to acquiesce to American demands to keep the Open Door policy. As mentioned above, Jones anticipated the language of globalization that appeared 70 years later by urging a policy of "economic interdependence" and jettisoning the language of conquest and words like "invasion." Jones was certainly not alone. Of U.S. policies in Mexico, Ernest Gruening also warned fellow Americans that "[we should] keep our hands off Mexico," and that by so doing follow a policy "at least consonant with our best national professions."[125] Ultimately, the United States followed the policy toward Mexico originally set down by Rosecrans in the immediate post–Civil War period and implemented consistently into the 1920s: Rather than armed intervention, the United States should engage in a policy of negotiation, but negotiation from a position of power focused on economic domination. The signing of the Bucareli accords in 1923 between the governments of Mexico and the United States effectively guaranteed the safety of existing U.S. investments in Mexico. Rather than a rollback of investments or at least a slowdown, American investments continued in the late 1920s and resumed a Díaz era presence. Americans overwhelmingly dominated oil, mining, cotton, bananas and other fruits and played a central role in finance at the end of the third decade.[126]

In addition to critics of intervention and annexation, many suggested that if the United States wished to maintain its dominant position in Mexico that it needed to reform the manner that Americans presented themselves. Efforts at eliminating American "insensitivity," coupled with opposition to territorial conquest and armed intervention, found expression in calls for reciprocity and equality between the two nations. The trend was captured by one writer who criticized what he saw as the inclination "to believe that difference from ourselves implies inferiority" and recommended "a little effort to see the good in a race we do not at present understand."[127]

Several policy moves by the State Department in the 1920s sought to deliver a "softer" image of the United States; they serve as examples of this new variation of the peaceful conquest, the anti-imperial peaceful conquest. The first is the appointment of the New York banker Dwight Morrow to the ambassadorship in Mexico City. The second is the tour of Mexico taken by Colonel Charles Lindbergh. Finally, there was the Good Neighbor Policy enacted by the Roosevelt administration. Each sought to put the United States in a position of friend and supporter of an independent, sovereign, and progressive Mexico (and Latin America) rather than a domineering, posturing power intent on unilaterally running roughshod over weaker nations.

Dwight Morrow became a particularly astute ambassador of "goodwill" charged with the "reconstruction of . . . unhappy relations with Latin America." He actively embraced the culture, particularly the folk art traditions, of Mexico and heartily entered into that nation's social and cultural life, a policy never attempted before by U.S. ministers.[128] Morrow's weekend sanctuary in Cuernavaca, named Casa Mañana (a romantic celebration of that which the word "mañana" affirmed in the minds of most Americans) stirred with the comings and goings of Mexico's cultural elite. Other activities complemented Morrow's active engagements of that cultural elite and the support of certain elements of Mexico's cultural nationalism. The Rockefeller Foundation's support for Mexico's famed artists, including Diego Rivera, and the funding of an institute for higher education in Mexico City; or Henry Ford's recruitment of a hundred

Mexican workers to labor in the Detroit Ford plant; and the Friends of the Mexicans conferences at Pomona College all delivered a new "softer" image of Americans and a respect for Mexico's cultural traditions.

Henry Ford made the good-will image an overriding objective, affirming that his program placed "Mexicans in a position to consider the Americans from a different viewpoint than that from which they have considered them heretofore, due to the fact that they have principally known them as exploiters."[129] Ford went beyond the usual formulas on Mexican labor and, in an optimistic tone, contended that Mexicans were just as intelligent as the "average American and show a great desire to work." In one brief statement, Mexicans were transformed from creatures of a lower order of intelligence that harbored a propensity to laziness to the equal of the "average" American.

One journalist reported, in the case of Colonel Lindbergh, that his visit "has done much to offset the misunderstanding resulting from our seeming indifference. It has proved that we value Mexican friendship and have friendship to offer in return . . . a gesture of good will which has been missing from our previous dealings with that country."[130] And the Friends of the Mexicans annual conferences brought Mexican officials and other guests to address issues of importance to Mexico. Pomona College also sponsored student exchanges and an Inter-American Institute to develop "mutually intelligent relations between American peoples."[131]

However, the Americanization of Mexico designed by Americans as the solution for the Mexican Problem as well as the original tenets of the peaceful conquest remained on course. The belief continued that nothing good was to be accomplished in Mexico until such character defects as excessive individualism and inability to work together were eliminated. As Samuel Guy Inman, an active proponent of good-will and a teacher at a missionary school in Mexico for ten years, stated in his book written from the perspective of American Protestant missionaries in Mexico, "Education in Mexico must, first of all, look to character." English classes, for example, at the Ford Motor Plant did more than offer bilingual proficiency. According to Henry Ford, the English classes and shop training emphasized the learning of "American ideals."[132] It was expected that the character education, which Protestant missionaries were actively implementing in Mexico, would combine "genuine patriotism [with] a passion for universal brotherhood." International politics then in place, sustained by "universal brotherhood" remained at the center of character education. Mexico and the Mexican people were expected to continue as a peaceful participant in the transnational "economic interdependence" that Chester

Jones and others touted as the most beneficial expression of U.S.-Mexican relations.

Meanwhile, the pacific conquest spelled out by Rosecrans, theorized by Conant, and implemented by Roosevelt and Root, among others, was neither abandoned nor weakened. Ever the realist, former consul general in Mexico City, George Agnew Chamberlain recommended that the United States focus on a single-minded objective, one that "presents Mexico with an alternative, a hard alternative but nevertheless a choice: economic control or military occupation. . . . there is no middle ground. If we stop short of economic control we will travel again and again mere byroads of peace."[133] The policy of economic control remained on course, briefly interrupted by the 1910 Revolution but reinvigorated in the postwar era. As the 1920s wound down to the Depression Era, the economic dominance of the United States had never been stronger. Oil, agriculture, mining, and finance all fell under the control of U.S. investors on a scale greater than that of the Porfirio Díaz period.[134] The peaceful conquest more than survived; it expanded simultaneously with a culturally anchored reform. Mexico remained an economic colony of the United States, more securely than during the "golden age" of Díaz.

CONCLUSION

American writing did no favors for the people of Mexico, although it defended or at least legitimized the presence of American capital and the social consequences that it brought in its wake. Although the published material spoke highly of the picturesque scenery and of the natural wonders sprinkled over the Mexican countryside, the people of Mexico were another matter. Writers delved into the history and racial stem of the Mexican population, determining that the vast majority of the population of Mexico was comprised of Indians and hybrids, the infamous mestizos. Everything else about Mexico slid down that racialized slippery slope. Mexicans were variously described as lazy, lascivious, nonindustrious, dishonest, indolent, imitative, childlike, and more. By debasing nearly all things Mexican except the truly wonderful scenery, writers consciously justified the peaceful conquest first discussed in the late 1860s, implemented in the 1870s, and institutionalized by 1900.

The gamut of writers then noticed features of Mexican culture and lifestyle that seemed similar to if not identical with the Oriental and, in the process, identified Mexico not with the West (or with Mexico) but with the Orient and all that the term "Orient" implied. Moreover, by comparing Mexico to India, Egypt, and Africa, among others, the British colonial system became a legitimizing agent for American political and economic ambitions in Mexico. The Oriental and the Mexican existed on a parallel cultural level, incapable of modernity and civilization on their own and requiring an outside force to pull them onto the modern stage.

Peaceful conquest was anything but a guaranteed endeavor; economic nationalism reared its dangerous head and together with Mexico's alleged cultural deviations from the supposed Anglo-Saxon norm something known as the "Mexican Problem" entered the discourse in the late 1910s. Among American elite circles, the Mexican Problem began to be discussed and expressed in the overriding objective: "What is required to keep Mexico within the economic orbit of the United States?" The problem was really Mexico's, a nation shorted by backward culture with elites incapable, unwilling, or unprepared to rule the country in correspondence with American imperatives. Overall, Mexico lacked the wherewithal to achieve higher levels of civilization. The solution that nearly every writer endorsed was the Americanization of Mexico, that is, escalating capital investments and increased presence of Americans who, it was said, offered examples of modern behavior, models for Mexicans to emulate.

In the final analysis, the Americanization envisioned by Americans encapsulated a kind of transnational sociological functionalism, that is, a political orientation that would preserve the economic domination of the United States. Even though the term "peaceful conquest" evolved into "economic interdependence," domination (i.e., conquest) never lost centrality in the political agenda of the United States, an agenda not only embraced by but also forcefully argued and defended by a myriad of writers.

In line with economic interdependence, Americans also launched a campaign to reform some of the more outrageous and insulting treatments of Mexico by tourists and writers. The images of Americans willing to learn the language and who admired the culture of Mexico became an ideal in the late 1920s, epitomized in the selection of Dwight Morrow to be the ambassador to Mexico. That sort of "human face" placed over U.S. foreign policy to win the "hearts and minds" of Mexico did nothing to change the prime objective of U.S. foreign policy toward Mexico. The peaceful conquest remained on course and if anything was strengthened by the "hearts and minds" emphasis that served as a weapon for preserving and expanding the imperial economic objective.

While the peaceful conquest proceeded without respite, social alterations in Mexico were occurring on an equally important scale. By 1900 large-scale migrations within Mexico, an unheard of phenomenon prior to 1870, had become a fixture, and by 1910 migration to the United States had become routine. The economic consequences of the invasion of U.S. capital elicited a massive population shift within Mexico that made its way into the United States. As Mexican immigrants crossed into the United States, the colonial representations written by Americans would now define immigrants as they settled into barrios across the United States.

This huge sum must remain more or less dormant until order shall prevail

FIGURE 1. "This huge sum must remain dormant." *Collier's Magazine* (July 1, 1916).

SMELTING WORKS, CANANEA CONSOLIDATED COPPER COMPANY, CANANEA, SONORA, MEXICO

FIGURE 2. Smelting works, Cananea. *Engineering and Mining Journal* 85 (April 4, 1908).

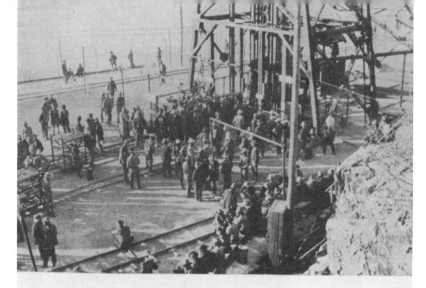

THE DAY SHIFT GOES DOWN
Loading Mexicans in mine cages to be dropped to their working places

FIGURE 3. At the Monte del Cobre mine. Ralph McA. Ingersoll, *In and under Mexico.*

FIGURE 4. Bringing ore from the mine. *Engineering and Mining Journal* 85 (June 25, 1908).

Bringing the ore from the mine.

Photograph by Frank H. Probert

EVERY LABORER IS SEARCHED BEFORE LEAVING THE PATIO OF THE MINES

The peon laborer in the mines has always received as wages only about the equivalent of "victuals and clothes"; and frijoles, tortillas, sombreros, shirts, trousers, and sandals, with a little mescal to wash down the food, represent about the sum total of food and raiment that the peon knows.

FIGURE 5. "Every laborer is searched." *National Geographic* 30, no. 1 (July 1916).

THE DIVIDING LINE

The path before the offices which separates the Mexican town below from the American Colony above

FIGURE 6. Monte del Cobre mine. Ingersoll, *In and under Mexico.*

El Dormitorio: THE BACHELOR'S QUARTERS, AND TYPICAL AMERICAN COMPANY HOUSES
Above is the Moving Tennis Court

FIGURE 7. Monte del Cobre mine. Ingersoll, *In and under Mexico.*

OF A SUNDAY MORNING AT THE DORMITORY

FIGURE 8. Monte del Cobre mine. Ingersoll, *In and under Mexico.*

LOVE IN A COTTAGE

Photograph by Bain

Although there is not a nail or a screw nor yet a pane of glass or a touch of paint in their house, and although everything that enters into its construction is nothing more than the salvage of the streets, this lazy peon and his hard-worked wife are perhaps as content with their lot as the owner of the best house in America.

FIGURE 9. "Love in a cottage." *National Geographic* 30, no. 1 (July 1916).

STUDYING ENGLISH IN Y. M. C. A., CHIHUAHUA

FIGURE 10. Studying English in the YMCA in Chihuahua. George B. Winton, *Mexico To-Day: Social, Political, and Religious Conditions.*

FIGURE 11. Company housing for Mexican laborers and families at a southern California citrus ranch. *California Citrograph.*

FIGURE 12. Company housing for Mexican laborers and families at a southern California citrus ranch. *California Citrograph.*

FIGURE 13.
"Amelia—a Mexican
girl of average
intelligence and
pleasing personality."
Pearl Idelia Ellis,
*Americanization
through Homemaking.*

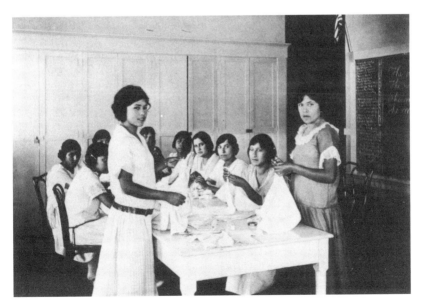

FIGURE 14. "Educate for the Home and better Homes will evolve." Merton Earle Hill, "The Development of an Americanization Program" (Master's thesis, University of Southern California, 1928).

FIGURE 15. A sewing class of Mexican girls. Ellis, *Americanization through Homemaking.*

FIGURE 16. Domestic science classes in Los Angeles City Schools. *Your Children and Their Schools* (Los Angeles Board of Education, 1937).

FIGURE 17. "In a development school [for the 'educationally mentally retarded'] the emphasis is not upon academic subjects but rather upon the child himself with his complex urges for expression and need for development." *Your Children and Their Schools.*

FIGURE 18. "Ducks and drakes—When a child enters a development school [for 'educationally mentally retarded'] he is received in a friendly manner ..." *Your Children and Their Schools.*

One of the Earlier Adult Classes.
Mexicans of the Lucas Ranch learning to read and write English, 1920.

FIGURE 19. Americanizing men. Merton Earle Hill, *The Development of an American-ization Program.*

Number 26

Such an Americanization program as has been set up
will produce young women like those shown in the
picture. One of the Mexican Chaffey Girl Scout
Troops at the girls' "Estate."

FIGURE 20. Americanizing women. Hill, "The Development of an Americanization Program" (Master's thesis, University of Southern California, 1928).

4. THE PEACEFUL CONQUEST AND MEXICAN MIGRATION WITHIN MEXICO AND TO THE UNITED STATES

The rapid increase [of Mexican immigration] within the last decade has resulted from the expansion of industry both in Mexico and in the United States. In this country the industrial development of the Southwest has opened up wider fields of employment for unskilled laborers in transportation, agriculture, mining, and smelting. A similar expansion in northern Mexico has drawn many Mexican laborers from the farms of other sections of the country farther removed from the border, and it is an easy matter to go from the mines and section gangs of northern Mexico to the more remunerative employment to be had in similar industries of the southwestern United States. Thus the movement from the more remote districts of Mexico to the newly developed industries of the North has become largely a stage in a more general movement to the United States. Entrance into this country is not difficult, for employment agencies in normal times have stood ready to advance board, lodging, and transportation to a place where work is to be had, and the immigration officials have usually deemed no Mexican likely to become a public charge.

Samuel Bryan, *Survey* (1912)

INTRODUCTION

When Stanford University economist Samuel Bryan wrote the above lines, the immigrant Mexican population was well on its way to earning the status of a new minority in the United States.[1] An estimated three-quarters of a million to one and a half million Mexicans immigrated legally and otherwise to the United States between 1900 and 1930. It has been said that migrants equaled 10 percent of the total population of Mexico. One observer noted that a population equal to that of the Mexican states of Sonora, Coahuila, Chihuahua, and Nuevo León, plus the territory of Baja California, had migrated to the United States during those three decades.[2] A series of upward migratory flows from Mexico entered the United States and moved from the border to the West and Midwest, into the very heart of the largest capitalist industrial enterprises: agriculture, railroads, automobiles, and steel. Rather than becoming a marginal and peripheral minority, the new immigrant community immediately integrated into the institutional framework of the United States to become a fundamental component of large-scale capitalist production in the maturing imperial nation. Their integration into enterprises operated by American capital certainly was not new for the immigrants. Mexican labor in Mexico had already become part of the industrial working class, on terms defined by American capital. Those working-class experiences were not left behind but followed migrants as they entered the United States and were absorbed into the American working class.

The Spanish-speaking population that had been in the United States before 1900, comprised of residents of the former Mexican territories and their descendants, had already been overwhelmed by aggressive American institutions and practices or was left to assume the status of an isolated regional minority, as in New Mexico. In California, the *californios* had practically disappeared as a dynamic social entity, with only scattered descendants of the once elite hacendado class still clinging to their historic past. In the post-1848 Mexican-American War period, the Southwest underwent a revolutionary transformation, changing from a self-subsistent Mexican feudal economy to United States–based corporate capitalism. In the process, the old Mexican territory was firmly annexed, then integrated into the fundamental political, economic, and social institutions of the United States. The American state fulfilled a long-held objective, one that the leaders of the anticolonial revolutionary struggle had hoped to someday realize, that is, to expand to the Pacific Coast. As the nation lengthened across the continent, the national institutional framework followed.[3]

No sooner had the institutional transformations propelled by the 1848 annexation begun to take root than the United States endured the Civil War, the second armed conflict for the unification of the nation. Shortly after the fratricidal cannons quieted and the reconstruction of the nation proceeded, the United States launched the peaceful conquest of Mexico. Then, Cuba, the Caribbean, Central America, and South America fell subject to the same economic objectives. More than the peaceful conquest of Mexico occurred as a consequence of U.S. imperial policy. That very same imperial foreign policy (examined in Chapter 1) also explains the mass migrations that first appeared within Mexico with the advent of railroad, mining, and oil capital and then crossed into the United States. Given this historical context, the key to explaining the migration, as well as the incorporation and subsequent political, economic, and social experience of the twentieth-century Mexican immigrant community, can be found in the economic expansionism—U.S. imperialism—that subjected Mexico to foreign domination. From this perspective, the Mexican-American War and subsequent annexation of the northern half of Mexico's territory fails to explain those factors that shaped the historical experience of the Mexican immigrant community during the twentieth century. Certainly, that war cannot explain the migration and ensuing settlement patterns. Explaining the origins of the Mexican immigrant community requires that the economic conquest by the United States be placed at the center.

MIGRATION AND THE ECONOMIC EMPIRE

Contrary to Samuel Bryan's explanation of three decades of Mexican migration (and the historical record), most studies of Mexican migration emphasize the Mexican Revolution of 1910 as the critical factor causing the migration, a theoretical model that is often simply titled "push-pull." The theory is rather simple. This privileged explanation for the migration during the 1900–1930 period in Chicano historiography and in most historical accounts of Mexican migration assumes that the 1910 civil war "pushed" people to migrate and that economic development in the United States "pulled" people northward. As applied to the literature, it goes like this: Mexico underwent a violent civil war which, combined with poverty and unemployment, caused people to be uprooted from their social anchors and placed them on a potential migratory path; hence, a push. Simultaneously, the United States' Southwest underwent economic modernization in response to new railroads and federal irrigation projects, which led to labor-intensive agricultural expansion and a long-term, insatiable demand for labor. Other areas of the economy also led to a demand for cheap labor, for example, the Arizona mining centers and road construction. As the Mexican population sought to escape the Revolution of 1910 and poverty and their combined effects, a simultaneous northward pull drew them directly into the United States.

Notice that the push in Mexico operated independently of the pull from the United States in this model, which has been in place in academic and public policy circles for the whole the twentieth century and continues to the present. The theory implicitly contends that Mexico and the United States are independent sovereign nations, and as such the U.S. policy of economic expansion into Mexico—i.e., the peaceful conquest—does not figure into the equation. However, if we examine closely the social consequences of American capital on the entire social face of the Mexican nation, we shall see (as did Samuel Bryan) that migration begins not with the 1910 revolution but rather with the stimulus of the same railroad, mining, and oil corporations operating in Mexico *and* in the United States. By employing this theoretical approach, which incorporates the economic conquest of Mexico, the push from Mexico and the pull from the United States are joined to become one single process, rather than two separate movements—or, put another way, push and pull are one and the same. Just as American capital fashioned the development of industrial enterprises within Mexico, the same capital propelled migration within Mexico and eventually that migratory flow entered the United States.[4]

MIGRATION WITHIN MEXICO: THE FIRST PHASE OF MIGRATION TO THE UNITED STATES

For several centuries under Spanish rule and into the national period, Mexico's demographic pattern remained virtually unchanged. The vast majority of the population resided in the central plateau region, with the northern and southern states rather sparsely populated. After 1848 the northern tier of states—Sonora, Chihuahua, Durango, and Coahuila—and Baja California were practically depopulated until the turn of the century. Most people settled in or around a few large estates, small-scale mining operations, and indigenous communities. That pattern obtained throughout the Spanish colonial period and the first half-century of the national period. The social impact of American capital permanently altered that centuries-old demographic pattern, an alteration that simultaneously satisfied the labor requirements of the new enterprises.

Railroads

The advent of railroad construction in the early 1880s brought in its wake an internal demand for labor that could only be satisfied by recruiting within Mexico. On an annual basis, from 30,000 to 40,000 workers were required to cut through mountainsides, build bridges, and lay and maintain the tracks. However, sizable stretches of road passed through the sparsely populated northern states, while the available laboring popula-

tion resided in the central states. The only means to obtain adequate labor was to send recruiters into the settled areas with promises of wages in
hard currency and free transportation to the work site. Soon worker settlements appeared in the new construction zones, and as the roads were
completed permanent rural boxcar camps and town settlements housed
maintenance crews. Mexico's population began to move northward as
railroad towns like Torreón began to spring up, as well as railroad worker
camps in isolated areas all along the lines. One traveler's description of a
construction camp, about 15 miles above Chihuahua City, informs us of
the experiences of those early laborers on the railroads. He wrote:

> On a side track stood a boarding train, but many of the men were liv-
> ing in tents, and all about us the smoke of their fires rose in the clear,
> dry air, which brought out the very seams and fissures of the mountain
> peaks along the distant horizon. Most of the contractors had their own
> "outfit," a kitchen and storage tent with simple utensils, tents for them-
> selves, containing rude bunks or occasionally cots, and sometimes tents
> for their men.[5]

More than the relocation of labor was involved, as the roads offered
more transport efficiency and, for those exporting agricultural goods, a less
expensive form of moving produce to market. This in turn undermined an
older form of mass transport, the *arrieros* or mulepackers, which at one
time had numbered as many as 60,000 workers and had been, ever since the
early colonial period, the backbone of the transport system. Thousands of
arrieros were put out of work by railroads, and the men then entered the
ranks of the new American enterprises or joined the unemployed. In addition, skilled artisans of all sorts—e.g., weavers, tanners, soapmakers, and
wagon drivers—were similarly affected by the new forms of small-scale
manufacturing stimulated by United States capital and imports. These displaced workers entered the ranks of a growing surplus labor pool en masse.
While railroads were busy reshaping the Mexican economy, they created a
mass of unemployed workers, and the same railroads benefited by tapping
into that surplus and hiring thousands for their labor force.

But much more than the uncertain fate that faced *arrieros* and other
tradesmen loomed large with the coming of the rails. Railroads were usually planned and built along routes that traversed lands held by free peasant villages, particularly in the central plateau region. The effect was to
raise the potential value of the plots, generally held communally and, based
on tradition, passed from one generation to the next. Along these rail
paths, large landlords realized that with rail transport, lands used nearly

exclusively for subsistence crops would be subject to a substantial increase in value; that is, the lands could easily be used for the production of cash crops that required shipment to distant markets. Consequently, wealthy landlords persuaded the Díaz administration to enact a series of federal land laws that declared that all lands required valid proof of legal ownership. Many peasants lacked legal documentation, and so vast expanses of peasant lands were "denounced," that is, charged with invalid titles and placed on the market. The laws' sole objective was to remove peasants from their traditional farmlands, thereby opening the way for rich landowners to appropriate the titles and utilize the lands for cash crops.

Not surprisingly, expropriations tended to follow the paths of planned or already constructed rail lines. Along such paths, peasants violently opposed the expropriations but to no avail, and the resulting mass migrations created the first large-scale alteration of the demographic pattern.[6] In the process, more than 300,000 peasants, unable to prove their titles, were removed from their traditional farmlands, the largest demographic alteration in Mexico's history.[7] The legal maneuver, however, did not change the feudal character of the countryside; peasant labor continued on the former peasant lands, now transformed into hacienda lands.

The motive for the egregious land grab was entirely monetary and intended to make use of the new transportation facilities for exporting agricultural goods. Put another way, on the very same holdings, the subsistence agriculture of the peasants gave way to the cash crop agriculture of hacendados. More than the transfer of lands was at stake. The disguised theft, or expropriation, allowed the forcible, albeit legal, transfer of free peasant holdings to elite landlords, the very same elites who opened the door to foreign capital. The newly dispatched peasants migrated from their villages to surrounding towns and cities, and in particular they settled in Mexico City, where, unemployed and homeless, they formed one half of the city's population.[8] At the center of Mexico, then, they became a surplus labor supply that could be tapped into by the railroads and the second wave of U.S. investors, the mining companies.

The spectacular and dramatic mass migration of peasant families did not escape the eye of interested observers. In his 1908 study of Mexican labor for the U.S. Department of Labor, Victor Clark noted, "Entire villages have migrated to other parts of Mexico, where employment has been found in the mines or on the railways." Specifically, in relation to the railroads Clark found, "Along the northern portion of their routes resident labor is so scarce that workers are brought from the south as section hands and for new construction."[9] The only point that Clark left unsaid was that the railroads were at root of the de-peasanting of the land—the very same entities that came to employ that displaced labor force.

Mining and Smelting Operations

Railroads contributed more than new transportation facilities; they also made it possible for mining companies to enter into Mexico on a large scale. It may be said that Mexico's railways served a dual purpose: a system for importing mine and smelter machinery into Mexico and for exporting ores and processed metals to the United States. On the Mexican Central, for example, in 1908 no less than 48 percent of its cargo related either directly or indirectly to mining and smelting.[10] As mentioned in Chapter 1, nearly three hundred American mining enterprises controlled mining in Mexico, most of them spread out over the northern states of Coahuila, Sonora, Durango, and Chihuahua. Again, before the advent of mining, these areas were nearly depopulated, but with the opening up of operations, a population shift occurred equal to that which moved out of peasant villages on the central plateau. Over 300,000 persons migrated permanently from the central region to the northern band of states that contained mining sites, railroad camps, and boom towns specializing in trade linked with the new economic forces. Across the mining regions, new towns sprang up overnight to house the labor supply, which numbered approximately 130,000 to 140,000 at its peak.

One mining engineer observed in 1906 that the "increase in number of mining operations in recent years has been so great as to make the securing of an adequate supply of labor a difficult problem." Consequently, recruiters swarmed into the central regions to import labor for the north. The results were spectacular. Cananea grew from a small desert cluster of huts to a bustling community of 25,000 in a matter of a few years, employing nearly 6,000 regular miners. The same engineer noted that within eight years, Cananea underwent a rapid transition. The one-time hamlet populated by "warring prospectors" became a vibrant citylike settlement noted for "most of the comforts of civilization."[11] Likewise, Batopilas grew from a village of a few hundred to a community of 5,000 and its mines employed 1,500 workers. Across the mining states, new towns appeared as soon as a mine opened, while older mining communities like Batopilas expanded dramatically. Mining company towns with names like Santa Eulalia, Concordia, Nacozari, Navojoa, and Esperanzas and smelting operations at Chihuahua, Monterey, and Aguascalientes, among others, spiraled overnight into thriving communities. The Río

Plata mine in western Chihuahua exemplified a widespread settlement pattern in the mining districts, as the manager for the American-owned Mexican Chemical Company in Chihuahua noted:

> The camp is picturesquely situated in the cañon between the mine and mill. The buildings, numbering five and substantially built of adobe, comprise a large boarding house, store, warehouse, assay office and officer's quarters. There is also a settlement of 400 Mexicans nearby.[12]

In addition to the labor employed to construct and maintain railroads and to work the mines, older towns and cities were suddenly re-formed in the wake of the new kinds of businesses brought forth by rails, mines, and petroleum. Towns like Torreón, which was once an unimportant clutch of ranches, became a central point on the rail map with a population of 43,000. Nogales, Gómez Palacio, Guaymas, Tampico, and Nuevo Laredo all experienced a similar significant growth stimulated by the new foreign-inspired industries.

The demographic consequences of the peaceful conquest were etched permanently into the pattern of the Mexican nation. For the first time in its history, the northern section of the nation was steadily gaining in population, not due to any independently induced economic dynamic but owing entirely to the action of foreign capital. Internal migration originated with the influence of foreign capital and formed the first stage of a migration that ultimately extended to the United States and ended by serving the very same capital. Put another way, what began in Mexico terminated in the United States. Victor Clark noted that the movement of Mexican labor brought it within a few miles of the American border through labor policies implemented by U.S. capital. "Thus there is a constant movement of labor inside of Mexico itself," he recorded, "to supply the growing demands of the less-developed States, and this supply is ultimately absorbed by the still more exigent demand . . . of the border States and Territories of the United States."[13] Clark also referred to a "considerable diffusion of mining labor across the border from northern Chihuahua and Sonora." Certainly, Mexican labor in American-owned mines worked for the same employers on both sides of the border.[14]

Again, Mexican migration was not comprised of two independently functioning stages as is often argued; rather, the movement of labor was then, and remains today, one single process from Mexico to the United States. Beginning in the early twentieth century, that single migratory flow produced the Mexican immigrant community as one discrete ethnic minority in the United States. In the final analysis, the U.S. economic empire, Mexican migration, and the ethnic Mexican community were inseparable and interrelated social phenomena. Again, the observation of Victor Clark testifies to the single migratory process:

> Like the railways, the mines have had to import labor from the south; and they have as steadily lost labor to the United States. The representative of one group of mining properties in the State of Chihuahua said that within a year he had brought to that vicinity approximately 8,000 mine laborers from Zacatecas and the older mining districts of central Mexico, and that not far from 80 percent of these had left, a part going to New Mexico and the remainder to Arizona.[15]

Clark also interviewed a railway agent who lamented that "his company had brought north about 1,500 laborers . . . within a year, and that practically all of them ultimately crossed over into Texas." The reason for the departure of recruits is not hard to find. Representatives for employment agencies working under contract with American corporations entered into the interior of Mexico to actively recruit labor, and these recruiters were complemented by an army of labor agencies stationed at El Paso. Once labor had migrated north, labor agents then recruited the Mexican labor supply into a continued migratory flow that terminated in the United States.

Clark's description of a typical recruiting mission demonstrates the blurring between recruiting for work within Mexico and recruiting for work in the United States. "Recruited laborers," wrote Clark, "whether destined for northern Mexico or for the United States, travel in parties, under a boss or 'cabo' who holds the tickets. One is told of locked car doors and armed guards on the platforms of trains to prevent desertions en route."[16] Clark made note of the single migratory process that he observed, and using language similar to that of Samuel Bryan, he argued that the migration consisted of "two main stages." His careful examination emphasized the point:

> The progress of the laborer from his home state in interior Mexico to his place of work in the United States is therefore in two main stages; first, as recruit he is taken, or as a free immigrant he works his way, to the border. At this point he falls into the hands of the labor agent, who passes him along his final destination.[17]

Note that Clark mentioned several immigration methods, all stemming from the actions of American capital. First, there were recruiting agents who removed workers from one site to another within Mexico. Second, some migrants worked their way to the border (presumably working for

American enterprises, the only employer of importance that could offer laborers the means to work their way to the border). And finally, labor agents near or on the border. Each factor propelled the migrant northward in Mexico and ultimately across the border.

The entire migratory experience in Mexico was replicated in the United States. After the railways, oil, and mining companies had altered the demography and social relations of Mexico, these same economic forces altered the demography and social relations of the Southwest and of the Mexican side of the border as well. Among the border's larger communities—Ciudad Juárez, Nogales, Nuevo Laredo, Mexicali, and Matamoros—existing populations rose significantly as the migrations moved north. For some agricultural regions on the U.S. side—the Imperial Valley, for example—these populations served as a sizable commuter labor pool, a temporary supply of short-term or day migrants tailored to the exigencies of the harvest seasons.

CROSSING THE BORDER

Beginning around 1907, the rate of migration from Mexico increased significantly, with some 26,000 persons officially admitted, and by 1910, before the onset of the violent period of the Mexican Revolution, approximately 75,000 Mexicans were crossing annually into the United States.[18] This pace was maintained until the years 1913–1916, the most violent period of the revolution, which caused a sharp downturn in migration. After the violence of the revolution subsided, the earlier upward movement was resumed and in the 1920s took on the characteristics of a massive population relocation. Over the decade, nearly one-half million persons migrated from Mexico, many without registering for legal papers, and entered into a large-scale social process that resulted in the establishment of a Mexican immigrant community as a permanent ethnic minority in the United States.

Entry into the United States took several forms, and recruiting agencies were a fairly well known institution that awaited the migrant. As mentioned earlier, many migrants were recruited in Mexico and transported into the United States. Others crossed on their own initiative, after having been transported north by recruiters working for American mining and rail operations in Mexico. Still others were recruited at the border, while some remained on the Mexican side, waiting to enter the United States when the harvest season arrived. Each method of entering the workforce in the United States was part of an experience that began in Mexico. Not all migrants entered in the manner described here; some were contracted to work via wartime federal labor laws that enabled the importation of 70,000 Mexican workers between 1917 and 1921 to work in agriculture.

El Paso served as the main entry point and site of departure for those going west, north, and east. In the first decade of the century, at least six labor agencies plied the newly arrived with offers of jobs on railroad construction crews. Some 2,000 workers per month were furnished to railroads between 1907 and 1908 by agencies that charged workers a one dollar fee. One agency, which charged a six dollar fee, placed 13,000 Mexicans and earned a tidy profit of sixty-five thousand dollars.[19] An open border kept the flow of labor moving (and companies skimming wages from their workers), as the 1911 report of the U.S. Senate Immigration Commission indicated.

> At El Paso the Mexicans have been permitted to enter this country freely when without money if employment was to be obtained through these agencies. In some instances the agents act as supply companies, the railroad companies protecting their bills, and charge no commission but rely on the profits from selling goods at comparatively high prices, while in other cases they charge an employment fee of $1, which, together with the charge made for subsistence of laborers while in El Paso and en route to the place of work, is deducted by the railway companies from the earnings of these laborers.[20]

As the report found, not all migrants sought out the labor agencies. Some went directly to the rail offices and hired on to work for practically room and board. Several migrants who worked for railroads in 1918 reported wages of one dollar per day, with room and board in a boxcar costing them a dollar per day.[21] Certainly, the ever-present company store that charged inflated prices accompanied the boarders in boxcars and earned sizable profits. Quite possibly many migrants had already experienced the American company store in Mexico (and possibly the hacienda's store, the *tienda de raya*) and were aware of the unavoidable costs that such a store carried for the employee. On the other hand, with expectations of landing a job, many migrants eluded the agencies and followed family members or close friends to incipient immigrant settlements developed around places of work. But work was limited to a few branches of the economy, so the vast majority of migrants found work with the railroads, in agriculture, or in the mining camps of Arizona, New Mexico, and Colorado. In the mining camps of Arizona, Mexicans comprised over 40 percent of the labor supply in 1925.[22]

The railways performed multiple tasks related to labor recruitment. First, they engaged in recruiting labor in Mexico and moving labor within Mexico northward to the border. Second, railroads acted as the chief distributor of Mexican labor to various work sites in the United States. As Clark noted:

> The reasons that make El Paso the most important distributing point for Mexican immigration are its direct railway communication with the swarming States of Mexico; the presence across the border, in the State of Chihuahua, of large mines and smelters, which, in supplying their own needs, assist the southern laborer to the frontier; and the direct railway communication that the city enjoys with such chief labor-absorbing areas of the United States as the prairie grain and cotton region, the Colorado and the Territorial mining fields and California.

Here again, Clark underscored the unitary migratory movement involving railways and mining in Mexico. At that time, railroads were the first major employers of Mexican labor, and between 1900 and 1930 "Mexicans constituted two-thirds of the track labor forces in the Southwest."[23] The chief engineer for the Santa Fe system claimed, "Ninety percent of all our track men from the [West] Coast to Chicago are Mexicans."[24] One 1926 study of California railroads found that nearly four out of ten Mexican workers were employed by the railroads, more than double those who worked in agriculture. Across the Southwest, as many as 48,000 Mexican track workers, totaling 75 percent of the labor force, worked during the construction season. Railways in turn served to channel the flow of migrants along an emerging economic pattern centered in agriculture and thus the establishment of settlements in a rural and urban configuration.

INTEGRATION AND SETTLEMENT PATTERNS

Migration within the United States followed a multistage pattern, a pattern first observed in Mexico. Migrants initially arrived at the Mexican side of the border, and many settled there. Hundreds of thousands, however, crossed into the United States and settled either permanently or temporarily in a community until a job offer or attractive prospect was in hand. Most left El Paso and made several more stops before settling permanently in one community, often working their way across the country to a final destination point. Rarely did they go directly from their place of origin in Mexico to a more or less final place of residence in the United States. As in Mexico, migration continued the multistage process, and for the migrant moving from work site to work site, the process was an unbroken sequence, a single migration. We have, then, a migration engendered by American capitalist enterprises that began in Mexico, continued within the United States, and concluded with the gradual (and unending) formation and re-formation of the Mexican ethnic community.

Paul S. Taylor noted that one of the economic divisions with a keen interest in Mexican immigrant labor was large-scale agriculturists. With constantly expanding production, Mexican migrant labor proved a godsend. The great increases in all areas of agricultural production—cotton, sugar beets, citrus, truck crops—were as formidable as the flow of migrants across the border. Citrus expanded in California from practically nothing in 1880 to nearly 300,000 acres in 1930. California's Imperial Valley was transformed from a desert in 1900 to a vast system of agriculture and cattle raising that covered 500,000 acres in 1930. The famous San Joaquin Valley contained little or no cotton in 1910 but by 1925 grew 260,000 acres of cotton, requiring a harvest force of 18,000 migrants. Across the United States, a total of 750,000 acres of sugar beets were being farmed by the 1930s, up from 135,000 acres in 1900. In Colorado alone, the area dedicated to sugar beets jumped from 150,000 acres in 1924 to 250,000 acres two years later.[25] In 1921 a social critic observed the prevalence of Mexican labor in sugar beets. He wrote:

> You may travel from the far western beet fields of Southern California to the northern beet fields of Idaho or the eastern beet sections of Michigan and everywhere you will find Mexicans working patiently and efficiently in the beet fields.[26]

In each of these examples, production was dominated by what came to be known as agribusiness, that economic sector comprised of corporate agricultural interests, banks, and ginning companies like Anderson Clayton and marketing corporations like Sunkist. Labor, on the other hand, came to be almost entirely Mexican labor, the cheapest available and primarily hand labor. The ever observant Carey McWilliams noted that between 1900 and 1940, "Mexican labor constituted sixty percent of the common labor in the mines of the Southwest and from sixty to ninety percent of the section and extra gangs employed on eighteen western railroads."[27] Each economic branch that depended on Mexican immigrants was highly labor intensive. The overwhelming presence of Mexican labor in agriculture maintained over the century.

Just as in Mexico, migrants traveled with their families, and employers in the United States reacted and adjusted to this condition.[28] Across the Southwest and Midwest, Mexican settlements comprised of nuclear and often extended families appear concurrent with migration. Within a span of two or three years, what were once communities without a single Mexican face contained a thriving Mexican contingent. At El Paso, next to the American Smelter and Refining Company, smelter workers formed a colonia they named Ismelda (a Hispanization of "smelter"), one of three barrios in the city. In Arizona copper-mining towns—for example, Bisbee, Globe, and Morenci—the Mexican community was established on company property according to the dictates of mining corporations such as Phelps Dodge and Anaconda. At Kansas City, a railroad maintenance worker camp sprang up overnight, a process paralleled by the formation of temporary boxcar camps, which lined the roads from Los Angeles to Oklahoma. One can only imagine what contemporary observers witnessed. Paul S. Taylor, an eminent University of California economist and specialist on Mexican immigration, provided later generations of students of Mexican immigration with troves of information and this image of railroad camps. "The converted box-cars which shelter railway extragangs, tell their own tale," he wrote, "so too the dismounted box-car, which is being replaced along the right of way in the Southwest by rectangular concrete hollow tile houses which accommodate several families, each allotted two rooms."[29]

Agricultural communities formed in the cotton, fruit, and vegetable fields of California, Arizona, and Texas. In California's San Joaquin Valley, Imperial Valley, and the great agricultural center in Southern California, colonias were formed in quick succession between 1910 and 1930. In the citrus-growing region of Southern California, a squatter camp created in the early 1920s by citrus pickers and their families named La Jolla was transformed into a colonia as pickers began to build their own homes and construct a permanent community. One housing tract for Mexican citrus pickers was named Campo Colorado by the residents because of the red-shingled roofs; it was one of two dozen such housing tracts developed by the Southern California Fruit Growers Exchange, later known as Sunkist. At the Leffingwell Ranch in Whittier, California, the company constructed housing specifically for Mexican laborers, which separated them from a contingent of Japanese and Filipino workers and the American office personnel.

The phenomenon of company towns and privately developed colonias repeated itself throughout the region. In California alone, over two hundred Mexican colonias, with populations numbering a few hundred in Colonia Juarez in Orange County to the 35,000 living in East Los Angeles, dotted the landscape from the central to the southern sections of the state. Along the border, in a strip 150 miles wide from Brownsville, Texas, to Los Angeles, 85 percent of immigrants reconstructed their culture and community and in the process evolved a new ethnicity.

But what is most fascinating about the process of migrants entering the economy and social institutions of the United States is the repetition of the company town pattern. First experienced in Mexico by those working for American companies, this totally novel form of housing and community life also became the bailiwick of Mexican laborers and their families in the United States. The similarities in many respects between the housing of American companies in Mexico and those in the United States are startling. Rows of wooden and adobe one- or two-room houses lining a dirt path, unpainted and rather forlorn, are strikingly similar in both settings. No other ethnic community in the United States experienced the company town to the extent that the Mexican immigrant community did.

As in Mexico, companies realized the value of housing for recruiting labor, as well as for keeping it (often referred to as "stabilizing labor") and politically controlling it.[30] Company towns afforded, in the case of citrus growers and railroad corporations, a closed locale in which to instruct their workers as to the political culture appropriate to relations between worker and employer. And just as important, housing anchored the labor supply, which was then available to act as a recruiting force during periods of economic upswings, and countered the persistent turnover of the labor supply, wooed by promises of higher wages or better working conditions in other branches of the economy.

The offer of housing sweetened the deal in attracting workers, but housing was a necessary part of the employment scheme, given that most workers came with families. Consequently, company towns seemed to appear overnight. Southern Arizona's copper mines employed at least 3,000 Mexican miners "from across the border" by 1904, but that increased to 16,000 twelve years later.[31] Shortly thereafter, Clifton came to be known as a "Mexican camp" although, as in Mexico, "the more responsible positions of engineers, shift-bosses and timber-men" were all held by Americans.[32] Railroad boxcar camps were particularly numerous, causing one railroad manager to observe that "groups of houses dot the desert from here [El Paso] to Los Angeles."[33] In Los Angeles County, at least thirty such camps comprised but a few of the "row houses" that once encircled the city of that name and that survived into 1950.[34] Eastward from El

Paso, boxcar camps dotted the landscape all the way to Kansas City. In the sugar beet fields of Colorado, companies like Holly, Spreckels, and the Great Western Sugar Company provided free housing for their laborers, but the housing was of poor quality, in varying stages of dilapidation. Houses of adobe or rough boards, shacks "crudely patched and repaired", tents, and refurbished barns provided shelter over the season and some-times became permanent abodes. It was said of the companies that their interest in providing housing, such as it was, was intended "as a means of building up a permanent labor supply" and that the establishment of these colonies was "a means to an end."[35]

Within the span of a few decades of spectacular growth, the citrus in-dustry in California became the second-leading industry (oil filling the top spot) and the source of 60 percent of the nation's supply and 20 per-cent of the world's supply of this fruit by 1940. The officials of the labor-intensive industry went to great lengths to develop a housing policy aimed specifically at attracting Mexican labor and keeping it tied to the local grower association (and in the process lessen dependence on Japa-nese labor). Associations furnished one-bedroom houses that had no run-ning water or electricity, often no more than planks for walls, and that commonly were rented for around seven dollars per month, which was deducted from the paycheck. From these beginnings, immigrants fash-ioned a community and reconstructed their culture in an environment that was not particularly friendly to Mexicans.[36]

By 1920 an ethnic transition had taken place in the citrus labor force. Japanese and Chinese workers had practically been eliminated from the citrus groves, and by 1940 at least 90 percent of the 35,000 pickers and packinghouse workers were Mexican men and women. In addition to the significance of Mexican immigrants comprising the bulk of the picking and packing force, the citrus industry's housing projects were considered significant; they became models for other lines of industry to emulate. Self-styled "model camps" were featured in the industry's professional journal, *The California Citrograph*, complete with design, layout, architec-ture, and cost benefits to grower associations interested in efficient meth-ods of labor management. What is most interesting is that the same ref-erence to model camps and proper conditions for housing miners is found in the literature on mining in Mexico.

In the journal *The Mexican Review*, for example, a headline in the Feb-ruary 1918 issue announced "A Model Mining Camp" in El Oro mining district. The article mentioned some of the improvements intended to create a more efficient workforce, such as a theater, church, and hospital, "for their benefit and amusement." According to the author of the article, "There have never been any strikes or other troubles in this camp."[37] Now compare that remark to a statement appearing in a *California Citrograph* editorial titled "The Well Housed Employee," published in the same year. The author suggested that "the Mexican laborer who has a comfortable little cottage in which he may maintain his family, is the contented man, and is less likely to be attracted by the blandishments of another 25 cents a day."[38] The citrus industry institutionalized such thinking; the 1925 annual report by the Placentia (California) Orange Growers Association parroted the same argument:

> The Mexican camp each year proves of great benefit to the Association. At the beginning of the season it assures a supply of men who have had the experience with our methods of picking and standards required by the Association. . . . Aside from this feature, it serves to prevent labor troubles since the large percentage of contented employees exerts a beneficial influence upon the floating labor which each year must be employed to fill the crews.[39]

The head of the Industrial Relations Department for the Southern California Citrus Growers Association added that "the sole" object of housing was "a satisfactory supply of labor who will work at the lowest possible cost."[40] The several examples of company-sponsored housing exemplified a form of social engineering, with its prime objective being the maintenance of a flexible labor supply concurrent with a need to politically control labor.[41] One should also add one more element found in American company housing in Mexico that appeared in company housing for Mexican labor in the United States: a paternalistic mind-set that considered Mexican laborers in need of close supervision at work and in their community (discussed in Chapter 6).

Gender, Family, and Child Labor

One difference between the experiences of Mexican labor in Mexico and in the United States lies in the different roles assigned to children, women, and men as laborers in the two countries. In Mexico the vast majority of workers in American-owned industries were hired men, single if possible, married if necessary; occasionally children and women were hired as ore sorters. Rarely was the topic of married men as workers or families as labor a topic of conversation in the literature in reference to Mexico. However, across the border the distinction and comparison of the labor performed by singles versus families, youths versus adults, and of women versus men becomes an important matter.

Some industries, particularly certain forms of agricultural production, cotton and sugar beets being two major examples, relied on family labor nearly exclusively and shunned men without families in tow. In cotton and sugar beets, women and children were regarded as subordinate to the head of the family, and only one wage was paid to the entire family. Such a form of wage payment was common in the cotton fields of Arizona, Texas, and the San Joaquin Valley, and in the sugar beet industry of Colorado and Michigan. Hiring and contracting was done on the basis of family, although employers dealt exclusively with the head male.

Sugar-refining corporations commonly contracted with independent farmers to grow sugar beets, but beginning in 1920 contracts commonly stipulated the hiring of Mexican families exclusively and larger families were at a premium.[42] A study conducted by the National Child Labor Committee found that

> it becomes the company's concern to secure for the farmer such a supply of cheap labor as will encourage him to raise beets at the contract price. This the company finds it possible to do by resorting to a family system of labor, that is, by securing fathers with large families of children. The general practice is for the sugar companies to send out in the spring of each year their labor recruiting agents, who will go into Texas, New Mexico, and to the Mexican border, where through local employment agencies they recruit a sufficient number of families, especially those with large numbers of children.[43]

One study of child labor in the beet fields found that nearly 50 percent of all children under the age of sixteen and 22 percent of those under ten worked in the fields.[44] Similar figures were found in other lines of agricultural work. The practice of family labor was especially harmful to the children, because they were generally refused entrance to schools or were not free to attend during the picking seasons or could attend a strictly limited number of days of school.

In Texas nearly half of all Spanish-surnamed children were not enrolled in school due to family labor as late as 1945. One researcher described a scene that was doubtlessly repeated in many agricultural centers of the Southwest:

> In the Lower Rio Grande Valley children in busses on their way to school often passed other children in trucks on their way to the fields. Many children worked and grew up in the valley with little or no edu-

cation, because they were poor, because it was customary to use children for field labor, and because of lack of enforcement of the State compulsory-attendance laws.[45]

In Southern California, school districts amended the school schedule during the nut harvest season to allow Mexican children to accompany their parents and assist in the picking chores, a schedule designed exclusively for the Mexican community.

A variation on the theme of family labor appeared in the emphasis given to hiring men with families by the railroad and the citrus industries. Not that the labor of wives or children was important to the productive processes; instead, the motive was the expected submission of the male to the company's standards. These employers applied a yardstick often utilized by certain industries, that men with families tended to be less belligerent, more malleable, dependable, and docile, and therefore less likely to strike for wage increases or better working conditions. As a general rule in the railroads, if a family man was available, the job would go to him in preference to a single man. What is evident here is the manner in which family was defined, manipulated, organized, and reorganized to correspond to the company's perceived needs.

Other forms of production or sectors within a single line of work relied on women and played a role in shaping the possibility of women becoming independent breadwinners. The dependence on women as laundry workers, particularly mangle operators, as cannery workers in the fruit and seafood industries, and as packers in the citrus packinghouses is an example of the way that economic forces shaped gender and family relations among Mexican immigrants.[46] In these industries women learned a culture of the workplace and a sense of self-worth that stands in contrast to their role on the cotton ranches of Texas and California, where their sense of self-work was severely restrained. Further, although men in the citrus industry were used exclusively as pickers and their teenage sons were discouraged from picking full-time, young daughters of veteran packers were often hired to work in the packinghouses.

Another parallel in the employment pattern of women in Mexico and the United States that stands out was the use of women as *mozas* for American residents in Mexico and as domestics, nannies, house cleaners, hotel workers, and cooks for Americans in the United States. One study found that in El Paso, the U.S. Department of Labor Employment Bureau placed over 1,300 Mexican women, as compared to 6 American women, to work as domestics in November 1919. Again, here is an example of the role that gender played on both sides of the border, conditioned by the economic forces.[47] Men found that the former categories of *cargador* and *mozo* were in less demand across the border. The same bureau that sent out 1,300 women could find employment for only 176 Mexican men. Despite the variation, the stereotyped role of *mozo* clung to women immigrants across the border.[48]

Other means besides company housing were used for tying the laborer to a single job. Bonuses determined by productivity were awarded at the end of the season and were commonly used to keep workers for the entire harvest or construction project. The total labor cost for the season was determined with the bonus in mind; thus, for all intents and purposes, the bonus was a portion of the wages earned by the worker and deliberately retained by the employer until the end of the harvest. The railroad, citrus, and sugar beet industries commonly used this system to induce their laborers not to desert to more lucrative employment.

Nevertheless, competition among enterprises relying on Mexican labor increased to the point of widespread labor stealing by employers. Desertions plagued companies on an ongoing basis, at times reaching as high as 50 percent in agriculture and mining. Railroads were particularly susceptible to bouts of desertion and thus often encouraged their workers to recruit, offering them rewards for getting relatives and friends to apply. And in Texas, agricultural interests lobbied and persuaded the state legislature to pass the Texas Emigrant Law of 1929, which made it a crime for agents from out of state to recruit labor in Texas without proper licensing.

Despite this law, stealing labor from Texas to work in the Colorado beet fields continued. Recruiting agencies resorted to extraordinary means to lure workers away. Practices more or less similar to those of *enganchadores* in Mexico, who were known to lock recruits in trains to keep them from jumping to a contractor or another recruiter, were not uncommon. Contractors who stole labor from Texas and transported their hidden cargo in covered trucks to out-of-state work sites used such lockdowns routinely.[49] In addition, the contract labor system used extensively by mining, oil, and railroad concerns in Mexico found its parallel in the United States.

As in Mexico, methods for securing labor in the United States varied, with some companies hiring individuals and others using the contract system.[50] In both locales, wages were either piece rate or hourly, or a combination of both. Mining operations in Mexico often paid on a piecework basis, though at times they paid on an hourly basis. In California, citrus ranchers preferred the piece rate combined with a bonus and an hourly rate. Agribusiness and railroads in the United States often contracted with a single "boss," usually a Mexican with contacts within the immigrant community, who assembled a crew to work for a set price and period of time.

Migratory agricultural laborers were often secured via this sort of system. In Texas alone, some 400,000 cotton pickers followed "the big swing" to pick as the bolls matured in stages across the cotton belt. Carey McWilliams believed that up to 60 percent of cotton workers were routed through contractors who transported families to a work site. Known as the *jefe*, the contractor "speaks English, knows the routes, deals with the employer, and organizes the expedition."[51] These workers generally traveled from a fixed abode, but migration forced them to live in tents, barns, and shacks, and not infrequently beside irrigation ditches. Contractors were known to renege on wages and to keep a portion of promised wages until the contracted work was completed, a practice similar to the bonuses used in the citrus industry that fixed workers to the job. Employers generally negotiated with the contractor and had little or no dealings with the individual employee.[52]

Finally, it should also be noted that in both Mexico and the United States, the conceptualization of a Mexican wage and Mexican work followed migrants wherever they went. In Mexico, miners and railroad workers generally earned one-half the amount paid to Americans for the same work. In the Arizona mines, Mexicans were relegated to certain unskilled tasks and generally earned wages lower than were paid to American labor. The term "Mexican work," a standard in the lexicon of employers, meant unskilled, cheap, arduous labor that Americans generally refused to undertake because it was so ill compensated. Mexican immigrants became the backbone of the labor supply in the Southwest's labor-intensive industries—railroads, sugar beets, cotton, citrus, and truck crops. In addition, Mexican labor began working in laundries in the cities, and in the Midwest took positions in Michigan's steel industry and the auto plants in Detroit.[53] In the United States as in Mexico, Americans were the administrators of the corporate enterprise and controlled general company policies, which included the organization of labor, wages, types of laborers, work experiences, and company housing.

URBAN SETTLEMENTS

As far east as Chicago and as far west as Los Angeles, from San Antonio to San Diego, Phoenix to Kansas City, large Mexican immigrant settlements could be found by 1925. However, the urban settlement pattern may be a bit misleading, as the urbanized Mexican was often a part-time to full-time worker in rural production. Los Angeles County in 1930 was ringed by areas of agricultural production, being one of the major agricultural counties in the United States. Frequently, Mexican labor from the city of Los Angeles and its surrounding colonias worked in agriculture, as did the people of the four barrios in urban Santa Ana, California, the county seat of neighboring Orange County. In the latter example, virtually all who worked did so in agriculture, either in citrus, other fruits, or vegetables. Furthermore, in the case of East Los Angeles and the many surrounding colonias in the county, regular migratory treks to seasonal harvest areas to pick cotton, fruits, and vegetables were not uncommon. Some small colonias practically emptied during harvests, as did the colonias of towns like San Gabriel, Montebello, and Whittier, where residents frequently left for a short stint at cotton, fruit, or some other crop usually reliant on family labor. This pattern was not unknown in other areas of the Southwest, in particular San Antonio, where it was said that agriculture played a bigger economic role in the barrios than did urban-type industries.

Still, Mexican immigrants were not completely absorbed into rural, nonindustrial labor. Many men worked on construction crews and as maintenance men for urban railway systems. In Southern California, an interurban rail system constructed twenty-two boxcar camps. Railway worker settlements could be found in such nonrural suburban towns as Pasadena, Alhambra, and Tajuata (located just outside Los Angeles and later known as Watts). Women were particularly evident in laundries in Los Angeles and El Paso, in citrus and other fruit packinghouses, and in the fish canneries of San Diego and San Pedro (California).

SEGREGATION: THE MODE OF INTEGRATION

As in Mexico, American capital in the United States dictated a segregated residential pattern that divided Mexicans from Americans and other nationalities. Already Mexican labor was set apart and assigned work assumed to "fit" peculiarly Mexican abilities. The stigma of "Mexican work" followed Mexicans into the United States. This was particularly true in company towns. In the case of the Arizona mining corporations and the citrus associations of Southern California, strict segregation by nationality was enforced. Beyond the confines of company-built housing, company towns—that is, towns dependent on a single line of work—generally followed the practice of establishing Mexican residential zones as separate areas within the larger community, usually across the tracks or some other visible demarcation line. California was especially known for this practice. Other means, such as the frequent use of restrictive covenants, also served to divide minority from nonminority.

In cities throughout California, Mexican immigrants who wished to be homeowners were obliged to purchase lots and build their homes in zones restricted to Mexicans, and in the process the people developed their own cultural ethos, with churches, theaters, businesses, saloons, and sports activities that undergirded a consciousness of community. But a pattern of Hispanicized English words, a practice first manifest in Mexico, also emerged, more fully developed than in Mexico. And so we see words like *parquin* for "parking," *marqueta* for "market," *bils* (pronounced "beels") for "bills," *troque* for "truck," *garach* for "garage," and many more.

In restaurants, theaters, public parks, and public schools, there were varying degrees of segregation. Despite residential segregation and other restrictions that set Mexicans apart from the majority, however, the integration of the Mexican immigrant into the processes of large-scale capitalist production was never in doubt. Rather than being marginal to the economy and thereby to the society, Mexican immigrants were vitally integrated into basic economic institutions. Because of their economic entrenchment, residential segregation was a form of integration, in that it involved a public policy applied to the Mexican immigrant community that deeply affected the lives of the colonia residents and greatly impacted the geographic placement of their communities.

One could argue that segregation effectively "mainstreamed" Mexican immigrants by making them subject to the political policy-making institutions. Although the distribution of colonias across the various states was not based on the wishes of immigrants, who would then have been fashioning their communities independently, still their integration into the economy cannot be denied. Undoubtedly, the flow of migrants and the placement of colonias followed economic matrices basic to corporate capitalist enterprises. The U.S. economy, formed about large-scale enterprises such as Union Pacific, Southern Pacific, Atchison Topeka and Santa Fe, Phelps Dodge, American Smelting and Refining Company, Sunkist, Anderson Clayton, Great Western Sugar Company, Bank of America, U.S. Steel, Ford Motors, and others, incorporated Mexican labor into the core of its operations. Mexicans were indeed as mainstreamed as the very capitalist enterprises that competed for their labor and sheltered them in boxcar camps, company housing, and restricted neighborhoods "across the tracks."

It is no wonder, then, that the industries employing Mexican labor lobbied for the contract worker agreement of 1917, successfully opposed with all their might the inclusion of a quota on Mexico in the 1924 Immigration Restriction Act, and lobbied for the Texas Emigrant Law of 1929. For all practical purposes, the border remained a fiction throughout the three decades covered in this analysis. Whenever necessary, Immigration Service authorities simply looked the other way, allowing workers to move freely across the border. An Open Door policy was traditionally observed for labor during the various harvest seasons in California's Imperial Valley, "America's Winter Garden," which depended upon daily commuter labor from Mexicali across the border.

CONCLUSION

A new minority was born out of the peaceful conquest that subordinated Mexico to the economic power of the United States. Mexican elites collaborated on the economic expansionary policies designed by American corporate capital and implemented by the U.S. State Department. American capital in control of Mexico's railroads, mining, and oil brought about a historical shift in the centuries-old demographic pattern, redistributing the Mexican population to points north and eventually acting to drive the flow across the border.[54] From northern settlements within Mexico, American capital continued to pull labor northward into the United States. Out of this general economic force propelling migration, a new ethnic minority evolved in the United States.

A common interpretation of the ethnic Mexican experience isolates the process of becoming an ethnic minority to cultural factors within the borders of the United States. However, in the case of Mexican immigrants, the social and economic processes of becoming an ethnic Mexican appear first in Mexico, with the incipient development being completed later in the United States. For example, the labor policies that Mexicans experienced working for American oil, mining, and railroad industries in Mexico were the same as those they encountered in the United States. Mexicans on both sides of the border experienced company towns, company stores, residential segregation dividing Mexicans from Americans, a contract labor system, railroad and mining labor (often for the same corporation), domestic work, Hispanicized English words, the Mexican wage, and working for American employers.

Often the response to Mexican immigrants is described as one of marginalization and segregation; however, the segregation experienced by Mexican immigrants was in fact a form of integration and mainstreaming. Integration and segregation were, in reality, one and the same. Mexican immigrants worked at the very core of society, in the largest and most powerful American economic institutions, and were essential to that core. Paul S. Taylor offered this illustration of the integration of the immigrants into American society:

> The Mexicans are here—from California to Pennsylvania, from Texas to Minnesota. They are scattered in isolated sections of from two to five families; they are established in colonies in the agricultural West and Southwest which form, in places, from one to two thirds of the local population. They have penetrated the heart of industrial America; in the Calumet steel region on the southern shore of Lake Michigan they are numbered in thousands; in eastern industrial centers by hundreds. And they have made Los Angeles the second-largest Mexican city in the world.[55]

Mexicans performed the work reserved for the unskilled, and they were relegated to that class of labor regardless of the knowledge and abilities that they brought to the workplace. Nonetheless, Mexican workers were thoroughly integrated into the productive system, even if subject to work and residential segregation. Bryan placed the value of Mexican immigrant labor in perspective. "Mexicans have proved to be efficient laborers in certain industries," reported Bryan, "and have afforded a cheap and elastic labor supply for the southwestern United States." Never were Mexican immigrants excluded from or marginalized in the policies designed and enforced by the economic, political, and legal institutions of the United States.

By the first decade of the twentieth century, the newly arrived immigrant group—the latest to enter the United States en masse—began an evolutionary process of becoming a distinct ethnic minority. Over the course of the twentieth century, that migration and integration pattern has remained constant. The following chapter will examine the cultural images and definitions of Mexican immigrants that were borrowed from those constructed by American authors writing about Mexico. In short, the Mexican Problem (not merely Mexican immigrants) migrated into northern Mexico, across the border, and, without slowing, filtered into the economic, social, and cultural institutions of the United States.

5. THE TRANSNATIONAL MEXICAN PROBLEM

"That Mexican" whom we have so long contemplated from north of the Rio Grande, has therefore come to live with us. With his inherited ignorance, his superstition, his habits of poor housing, his weakness to some diseases, and his resistance to others, with his abiding love of beauty, he has come to pour his blood into the veins of our national life. "That Mexican" no longer lives in Mexico; he lives in the United States. The "Mexican problem" therefore is no longer one of politics; it is one of people. It reaches from Gopher Prairie to Guatemala.

Robert N. McLean, *That Mexican! As He Really Is, North and South of the Rio Grande* (1928)

INTRODUCTION

Originality certainly was not uppermost in the minds of those who wrote on the emerging ethnic group then settling across the United States, as the quote from Robert N. McLean's 1928 study testifies. *That Mexican! As He Really Is, North and South of the Rio Grande* exhibited the general thinking of Americans who wrote about Mexican immigrants. McLean did not explain Mexican immigrants to his readers by beginning his story at the border; instead, he began with the peoples living in Mexican villages that emptied as their residents moved north. One of the book's reviewers, James Batten, history professor at Pomona College (the site of the Friends of the Mexicans conferences), noted that McLean "knows Mexico and the Mexicans on both sides of the border, and his Juan García is a typical Mexican peon. The Mexican cannot be understood without a knowledge of his background of history, racial culture, religious belief and material philosophy. Dr. McLean makes these factors clear. . . ."[1] The book's mythical protagonist, Juan García, lived on both sides of the border, and thus to understand him as an immigrant, one must first comprehend him in his native environment. On balance, McLean, like many writers on the Mexican immigrant community, replicated what had already been written about Mexico by Americans, and thus the Mexican Problem in its entirety moved across the border with Juan García. This general perspective found acceptance among many observers and entered into the lexicon of those concerned with the social, political, and economic impact of a million or more Mexican migrants on the United States.

The body of literature on Mexico proved a boon to those who, for various reasons, chose to probe, analyze, and explain to the American public precisely who these newcomers from Mexico were and how to deal successfully with them. Officials charged with public policy matters, as well as Protestant religious leaders, as in the case of McLean and his colleagues, who found Catholicism a contributor to the Mexican problem, were particularly interested in information regarding Mexican immigrants. Consequently, it should come as no surprise that the first cohort of writers on Mexican immigrants were primarily interested in social questions, including morality, housing, health care, delinquency, nutrition, education, and of course Americanization. Invariably, the matters of race and culture associated with the Mexican Problem cut across virtually every study and analysis. For sure, the term "Brown Brother," used by several writers in reference to migrants, was never meant to imply brotherhood; on the contrary, its use implied a kind of paternalistic racial whimsy.[2] Yet few were motivated to call for the migrants' wholesale removal despite their burgeoning presence, which was growing each day and spreading east, west, and north. The Mexican workers' value to the economy of the Southwest was writ too large for the restriction scenario to prevail.

Writers repeated in detail the definitions that the literature on Mexico used to explain Mexico and Mexicans to the American public. The template included the historical and racial background, Orientalism, peonism, and all that those qualities ascribed to Mexicans in Mexico and that were repeated in the literature on Mexican immigrants. Naturally, with such a negative set of attributes the Mexican immigrant could present only liabilities rather than any positive contributions to American society. However, as we shall see in Chapter 6, the solution to the Mexican Problem "in our midst" was in the main similar, if not identical, to the solution for the Mexican Problem in Mexico: Americanization. And as in Mexico, Americanization meant, above all, remaining in your place. Here we examine the representations of Mexican immigrants that carried forward an imperial tradition, a tradition that first appeared with the construction of American railroads in Mexico. That mindset established a justification for legal formulas that enabled the application of a host of discriminatory private and public policies to the Mexican immigrant. These policies, whether deliberately or not, glued the migrant community to the lowest rungs of the American working class.

It needs to be pointed out that the images generated by American writers and immediately adopted into the common parlance of the United States were not carried over from the period following the Mexican-American War. Words like "greaser," for example, that were common mid-nineteenth-century usages in relation to annexation and the incorporation of the Mexican populations were discarded in favor of the language of economic empire. The dependence that those writing on Mexican immigrants had on the works on Mexico written by American authors after the 1880s was impressive. They did not simply extract casual references from the works; rather, they appropriated the literature wholesale for their studies. We begin with a brief overview of the familiarity with the literature on Mexico that experts (and would-be experts) on Mexican immigrants exhibited in their works.

RECYCLING THE CONVENTIONAL

Over the course of the first phase of twentieth-century Mexican migration, writers on immigrants, whether university professors fashioning a new perspective or graduate students working on a thesis, consulted, cited, and eventually depended on the literature on Mexico for insights into the immigrant population. The imperial images that they constructed for reasons far removed from Mexican immigration turned inward and established a domestic intellectual foundation for explaining the newest immigrants to America's shores. The body of literature on Mexico was assumed to represent not only the latest information regarding Mexican immigrants but the most accurate and defining interpretations of Mexican culture and peoples. The literature then became a guide for public policy makers seeking to understand Mexican immigrants and thereby fashion appropriate public policy.

Only a few examples are required to effectively demonstrate the general reliance on the literature. We begin with a review of a leading figure in sociological studies on Mexican immigrants, Emory Bogardus. Bogardus studied under the famous specialist on urban immigrants Robert Park (who with Richard Burgess founded of the famed University of Chicago School of Sociology), and served on the faculty at the University of Southern California until his death in the late twentieth century. Bogardus assumed his faculty position in the 1910s, quickly published two general theoretical surveys and soon became chair of the sociology department. Mexican migration had by then become a major social phenomenon, and his training made him particularly suited to specializing in the study of Mexican immigrants. Within a few years, Bogardus had published a number of books and articles on Mexicans and become *the* expert on Mexicans in California.

Bogardus first approached the discussion of Mexican immigrants in his *Essentials of Americanization* (1919), a volume devoted to questions related to the political allegiance of immigrants during World War I. Bogardus devoted a general chapter to each immigrant group that settled in the United States. Because Mexican immigrants were still somewhat outside the critical issues surrounding immigration to the United States, Mexicans were not considered until the sixteenth chapter, which covered but five pages. The length is rather beside the point, for in his suggested readings for those interested in delving deeper, Bogardus offered no less than eight books written on Mexico exclusively, all of which should by now be familiar to the reader. Authors cited in previous chapters of this work such as C. Reginald Enock,[3] Frederick Starr,[4] E. D. Trowbridge,[5] Nevin O. Winter,[6] and George G. Winton[7] were among the authors offered by Bogardus for further reference.

Bogardus followed *Essentials of Americanization* with a short bibliography, *The Mexican Immigrant: An Annotated Bibliography* (1929) written specifically for the specialist in the field of what was then referred to as Race Relations. The author divided the work into three sections, "Culture Backgrounds," "Studies [of Mexicans] in the United States," and "Interracial Adjustments." The first two categories are of interest to this study. By "Culture Backgrounds," Bogardus meant the culture of Mexico. Bogardus contended that an "understanding of the Mexican immigrant rests directly on knowing his culture traits." He then proceeded to list thirty-seven books and fifty articles, all of them written on Mexico by many of the same authors covered in this study and far more than he listed in his *Essentials of Americanization.* Of the thirty-seven books, twenty-three are addressed in this study (a number of the publications are irrelevant to this study, such as one published in 1848 and another dealing with divorce laws in Mexico). A few names should refresh the reader's memory: Wallace Thompson,[8] Robert McLean,[9] Reau Campbell,[10] Susan Hale,[11] Alden B. Case,[12] Percy F. Martin,[13] and Edward A. Ross.[14] Each work received a short description and evaluation. Thompson's *Mexican Mind,* an open embrace of imperial racism, was merely noted as "An analysis of the Mexican mode of thinking, their racial characteristics, habits of thought and of action." In the articles section, publications by Frederick Simpich, John Dewey, William Showalter, and George B. Winton were acknowledged as authoritative accounts. Of Simpich's "The Little Brown Brother Treks North," Bogardus merely noted, "If Mexican immigrants and others are restricted, Americans shall need to do more manual labor or produce less."[15]

The bibliography then proceeded to identify those works on Mexicans in the United States; here only three books were listed, but ninety-nine articles, master's theses, and doctoral dissertations followed. The three books are important to this study, and individuals linked with Protestant missionary organizations operating in Mexico authored each of them. Vernon McCombs' *From over the Border* was published by the Council of Women for Home Missions; Robert N. McLean's *That Mexican!* included a chapter on the Catholic Church and an open avowal of the Mexican's need to convert to a more authentic Christianity. (McLean was also an associate of the Homes Missions Council.) Finally, Jay S. Stowell's *The Near Side of the Mexican Question* held court and found the Catholic Church guilty of corruption, among other things. In turn, each of these works suggested further readings, and who is it that McCombs and McLean suggested? Here only a short list of by now familiar names demonstrates the crossover that characterized the writing on Mexican immigrants. McCombs listed, among others, Edward A. Ross, E. D. Trowbridge, George B. Winton, and Robert N. McLean. McLean returned the favor and listed Vernon McCombs in addition to Wallace Thompson, Clarence W. Barron,[16] Hubert Howe Bancroft,[17] and Jay Stowell, among others.

Bogardus achieved considerable respect for what many considered authoritative studies and reports on Mexicans by the time his work *The Mexican in the United States* appeared in 1934. His status grew beyond regional recognition as he became a nationally respected authority on Mexican immigrants. Consequently, his latest work earned the attention of all those interested in general issues related to the Mexican community and was read seriously. Fifteen years earlier, Bogardus had offered a first bibliography on Mexican immigrants; his second appeared in 1929 and included an annotated bibliography. His 1934 work presented a larger annotated bibliographic section, which in many ways repeated the earlier works but added newer titles, all of which were included because they were "deemed the most important" works available. Here Bogardus included far more works on Mexico than in his earlier work, and many of the titles will be familiar to the reader. Authors like George H. Blakelee,[18] Robert Glass Cleland,[19] Edward M. Conley,[20] Lewis Spence,[21] and of course the ever strident voice of Wallace Thompson were represented. Each received a short description, and Thompson's *Mexican Mind* received yet one more comment from Bogardus. On this occasion, Bogardus wrote, "An analysis of the Mexican's mode of thinking, his habits of thought and of action, and of his racial characteristics."[22]

In the usual academic fashion, Bogardus anticipated that his suggestions for further reading would "become a part of common knowledge." Certainly, undergraduate and graduate students would have been intrigued upon reading a description like that offered for Wallace Thompson, and the evidence illustrates that many were. Like many of his contemporaries, Bogardus failed to recognize that the information on Mexican immigrants communicated through the works that he recommended for further reading had entered into the realm of "common knowledge" long before he began to study the Mexican immigrant community. One might say that he was preaching to a rapt choir.

WIDENING THE DISCOURSE

Citing the literature on Mexico served to authenticate the writer's reliability and became a widespread practice, particularly in education (discussed in greater detail in Chapter 6). A large number of master's theses were part of the literature on Mexican immigrants, and these generally depended on the sources listed by Bogardus and others. Two examples serve to make the point. A University of Southern California graduate's thesis[23] cited Wallace Thompson, Edward A. Ross, Harry Carr,[24] and Ernest Gruening[25] along with Jay S. Stowell. A second thesis[26] listed Ernest Gruening, E. D. Trowbridge, Wallace Thompson, and George B. Winton[27] in addition to works by McLean, McCombs, and Stowell. These two examples were not the exception, as we shall see in this and the next chapter; the reliance on specialists on Mexico became the rule. As a final example, an early advocate of educational opportunities for the children of Mexican immigrants, Herschel Manuel, cited Wallace Thompson's *Mexican Mind* in his pioneering study published in 1930, *The Education of Mexican and Spanish-Speaking Children in Texas*.

INTRODUCING MEXICAN IMMIGRANTS: THE HISTORICAL AND RACIAL BACKGROUND

The growing number of Mexicans in the United States was not the only important issue discussed; also considered was the historical origin of the Mexican community. Vernon McCombs warned his readers that the "present immigration of Mexicans into the United States cannot be fully understood unless we also take into consideration some important facts in the history of Mexico." Few disagreed with McCombs. Practically every writer on Mexican immigrants during the period studied here followed the model suggested by McCombs. A graduate student at the University of Texas learned his lessons well and repeated:

> In order . . . to understand the Spanish-speaking people and to analyze more correctly, to get their trend of thought so as that it may be directed, and to get their temperament so that the work may be made to harmonize with it, it will be helpful to investigate this background.[28]

This approach explains why authors like Bogardus included references to the sizable body of works on Mexico for analyzing the contemporary Mexican immigrant. As if practicing formula writing, authors invariably referred to Mexico's history and cultural ethos allegedly to elicit deeper insights into the hidden humanity of Mexicans in the United States. The narratives repeated information that authors on Mexico had discussed ever since the 1880s.

A brief look at several authors demonstrates the use of Mexico's history to construct a mythical being: the average Mexican immigrant. In his chapter entitled "Backgrounds," McCombs covered the Pre-Columbian period with brief historical descriptions of the Toltecs, Aztecs, Chichimecs, and the leader of the peoples who were defeated by the Spaniards, Montezuma. The period was summed up with a short phrase: it was a "fascinating panorama." Our author then followed the Pre-Columbian era with the coming of the "energetic Spaniards representing the mingled blood of the Moors, the Romans and the Iberian *conquistadores*" and the birth of Spanish colonialism. McCombs then skipped over to the national period and the rise of Díaz and the post-1910 presidents who followed Díaz.

Robert McLean delved deeper into the history of Mexico's indigenous peoples, noting that they evolved politically into a "monarchical government" and that they created land systems described as "frankly socialistic." He also noted that their religion centered around high priests, superstition, and human sacrifices, and that their agricultural practices were surprisingly successful and provided for the society's well-being. Like so many of the authors writing on Mexico, McLean excoriated the Spaniards, whom he described as a class of "buccaneers" who practiced "cruelty and deceit . . . extortion and cupidity . . . with a chief interest in gold." Before long the ignoble conquerors parceled out the choice lands among themselves, dividing as well the Indians who dwelled upon those lands to serve as bound labor. New Spain, argued McLean, became a nation of serfs. The Black Legend played well in the United States, or so it seemed.

The exploitation by the Spaniards did more than result in the domination of the indigenous peoples; the conquest also led to the mixture of the two peoples into the mestizo. Three groups of people eventually came to populate the Spanish colony: Spaniards, Indians, and mestizos. The latter comprised the offspring of the first two. In his 1919 work, *Essentials of Americanization*, Bogardus noted the form that reproduction took after the conquest. He wrote:

> Of Mexico's population of 10,000,000, it is estimated that 19 per cent are white (Spanish), 43 per cent are mixed bloods (Spanish and Indian with Negro admixture), and 38 per cent are native Indians. The process of amalgamation—mixture of races—is gradually taking place. . . . the Indians are not dying out as an isolated race, but are contributing their qualities to a new Mexican race of Spanish and Indian origins. But a mixed race, living at the same time and the same locality as the parent races always confronts a hard struggle. Recognition is reluctantly given to it; taunts and cries of shame are heaped upon it. Mexican immigration to the United States is composed largely of these mixed bloods.[29]

McLean went further than Bogardus and found little in the amalgamation that foretold anything other than tragedy. Consider his take on *mestizaje*: "The third of Mexico's mortal ills is found in the great divergence of her races." Although McLean found the ills of Mexico related to its peoples, the real problem was not due to "blood" but rather to the divergence of climates and altitudes, which enervated or energized according to geological and meteorological factors. Nonetheless, racial mixture combined with locality constituted a reality that demanded study in order to understand the Mexican immigrant.[30]

Naturally, the mapping of the historical record in order to explain the immigrant's immediate circumstances and his impact on American society entered into the public policy realm and academic fields without hesitation. Not content to diverge from the common approach, the State of California commissioned a study of Mexican immigrants residing there in 1930 and began the narrative with a discussion of the racial composition of Mexico. The study cited information taken from U.S. House of Representatives hearings on immigration, which described Mexico's population and its historical and cultural formation in the most convoluted fashion.[31]

As early as 1912, graduate students elaborated on the mixed-blood theme. In his thesis on housing in the Los Angeles Mexican community,

John E. Kienle made note of Mexico's "racial lines" on the third page and finished with a quote from C. Reginald Enock's *Mexico: Its Ancient and Modern Civilisation.*[32]

> There are three classes of Mexicans. The one, which is regarded as the highest in rank, is of the European or Spanish descent. The next is the Creole, which is the amalgamation of the European and the native, and the third is the Indian, or pure blooded Indians. In Mexico there is a blending of peoples. . . . the "mixed white and aboriginal race from which the principal human element of the country shade off indefinably into the peon class."[33]

Kienle was not the last aspiring academic to open a discussion on Mexican immigrants with a reference to hybridity, the key that many felt explained the unique Mexican character. And he was certainly not the last to quote from a recognized authority. In her 1934 master's thesis on a Mexican citrus worker community in Southern California, Jessie Hayden referred continually to Wallace Thompson's *Mexican Mind* for substantiating statements. Hayden made note of the racial inheritance, one that Thompson continually repeated, with this line: "The primary strain of blood, the Indian, brought to the mixture and to the consequent cultural conflict many psychological elements as well as racial heritages which appear in Mexican life."[34]

Another master's thesis, "Adult Mexican Education in the United States," by Grace E. Reeves, covered the identical material with slightly different language.[35] The Mexican, contended Reeves, "is a composite of two ethnic groups: Spaniards and Indians," and she detailed the proportions of "blood lines" flowing through Mexico. Europeans accounted for 20 percent, "full-blooded Indians" reached 40 percent, and the "mixed" numbered 40 percent. But then, such an accounting should be expected from a student who cited the works of authors like Robert McLean, Ernest Gruening, Chester Lloyd Jones, George Creel, Edward A. Ross, Lewis Spence, and the specialist in the field of Mexican immigrants, Emory Bogardus.

THE NATIONAL PERIOD AND THE PEACEFUL CONQUEST

Having established the "blood lines," narratives then proceeded to a general discussion of the national period, which traveled along the following paths. After several centuries of Spanish cruelty and misgovernment, Mexico gained its independence and began a series of never-ending civil wars, which finally came to an end with the triumph of the Liberals and Juárez over the French-installed emperor Maximilian. After Juárez's death, Mexico came under the thirty-year reign of the Liberal Porfirio Díaz, a dictatorial period that Jay Stowell described in soft, positive terms similar to the favorable language used by authors on Mexico. That Díaz "established a stable government" seemed to be the most important of Díaz's accomplishments; but Díaz went beyond that and "negotiated foreign treaties; extended educational facilities; established credit for Mexico; built railroads, harbor facilities and other public improvements; and did much to regulate the internal affairs of the Republic."[36] If read carefully, we note that Stowell expressed no misgivings over any of Díaz's policies and reiterated the thinking of those who helped shape and maintain the peaceful conquest. Perhaps we should also mention the praise for Díaz that McCombs offered; the latter felt that the dictator was one of the "great Mexican deliverers."[37]

Robert McLean veered somewhat from the approach taken by his colleagues and critiqued what he contended was American abuse in the form of greedy capitalists, insensitive tourists, and a haughty U.S. foreign policy. McLean argued that both Mexico and the United States could benefit from a relationship in which the United States was more generous with Mexico, one that took the edge off of an oft-times contentious U.S. "superiority complex." And what did McLean suggest? In anticipation of the Inter-American hemispheric unity policy that followed World War II, McLean called for a new relationship with all of Latin America by initiating more "humane" treatment of Mexican immigrants. McLean offered the example of the managers of the Tagus Ranch, a large agribusiness owned by the Los Angeles Times, and explained their worker-friendly policy.

> But just as there are employers who think of "that Mexican" only as one of the raw materials of production, so there are those who are thoughtful of his welfare. Near Tulare, California, is a ranch called "Tagus," where seven thousand acres of fertile soil furnish employment for permanent as well as casual laborers. There is no labor contractor; but serving as "labor manager" is a bilingual young American intelligent enough to realize that contentment and well-being are factors in production. The permanent camp, located in a grove, is lighted by electricity, and is composed of neat white cottages, arranged in streets, and covered with vines and flowers.[38]

The prescription for harmony between the United States and Latin America began with welfare capitalism at home, a policy that the Tagus Ranch found profitable as well. The policy ostensibly created a contented labor force, a condition that McLean praised for having brought about class harmony. "There is no labor trouble," concluded McLean, and for him this proved the need for reformed attitudes and employer practices toward Mexican immigrants.

But there was more than class harmony and, according to McLean, U.S. interests in Mexico might also benefit, for the "Juan García who returns to Mexico from such a camp will tell about a much different America from the one who lived in the neighboring contract camp." McLean did not stop there but recommended other policies, such as people-to-people programs and student exchanges, which had the potential to raise the level of goodwill between the two countries. McLean certainly anticipated future foreign policy designs; some of what he suggested did appear with the appointment of Dwight Morrow. Finally, McLean opted for the continuation of the peaceful conquest—in his words, "respect for Mexico's sovereignty, in the spirit of cooperation and goodwill; sympathy for her struggle to endow her people with land . . . the way of a neighbor; it is the path of peace."[39] Such a prescription for reforming U.S. foreign policy as well as private investor policy within Mexico posed no challenge to the open door to American investments.

THE MEXICAN PROBLEM IN THE UNITED STATES

The eminent social critic and civil rights activist Carey McWilliams noted the prevalence of references to the Mexican Problem in the literature on Mexican immigrants but was unaware that the term originated in studies of Mexico authored by Americans and that it was related to U.S. economic expansionism. Sometimes the word "question" took the place of "problem," as in an article on Mexican migration by Charles Thompson, who noted that the issue was of relevance to those charged with public policy. "The question of Mexican immigration," he wrote, has gathered the attention "of social workers, of educational and religious leaders, of commercial, industrial and agricultural groups, and of statesmen."[40]

In his oft-cited work and precursor to Chicano Studies, *North from Mexico: The Spanish-Speaking of the United States* (1949), McWilliams titled his eleventh chapter "The Mexican Problem" and opened it with this indictment:

> In the vast library of books and documents about ethnic and minority problems in the United States, one of the largest sections is devoted to "the Mexican Problem." There is a curious consistency about the documents in this section. For one thing, the singular is always used. Pre-

sumably, also, no problem existed, singular or plural, prior to 1920. *Reader's Guide* lists fifty-one articles on the "Mexican Problem" from 1920 to 1930, by comparison with nineteen articles on the same subject for the previous decade. When these articles are examined, it will be found that "the problem" apparently consists in the sum total of the voluminous statistics on Mexican delinquency, poor housing, low wages, illiteracy, and rates of diseases. In other words, "the Mexican Problem" has been defined in terms of the social consequences of Mexican immigration.

Obviously, McWilliams was not aware of the imperial origins of the phrase "the Mexican Problem." More than domestic discussions developed the term; again, we need to examine the transnational nature of the Mexican Problem.[41]

At midcentury, perhaps the most widely discussed issue connected intimately with Mexican migrants was the word "problem" with the qualifier "Mexican" affixed. The expression appeared in numerous works, including the work by Robert N. McLean cited above. McLean was not the first to use it. Rumblings that Mexican immigrants collectively comprised a unique complex of social problems appeared with the first systematic academic study of Mexican immigrants, *Essentials of Americanization* (1919) by the distinguished sociologist Emory Bogardus.

Of importance is not the placement of the topic in the book (seventeenth chapter) or its length (five pages), but rather the first sentence of the opening paragraph to the chapter. It spoke to the issue at hand. "In the Southwestern states," he declared, "'the Mexican problem' has developed with rapidity since 1900." Bogardus then offered one key to understanding the nature of the 'problem,' stating, "The Mexican immigrants represent the peon, or the mixed and least developed classes of Mexico."[42] The professor was certainly not alone. The omnipresent Frederick Simpich stated what most students of the Mexican Problem probably already accepted. In his article "The Little Brown Brother Treks North," Simpich summarized what many had by then taken for granted.

> But the undeniable fact that we do differ so widely from the Mexicans in race, in political and social habits and standards, and in history, traditions, and thinking processes, makes the settlement of the problem immensely difficult.[43]

The "problem" appeared in a variety of presentations. A Southern California school superintendent, Merton E. Hill (later selected to direct the office of admissions for the University of California), introduced his widely cited study (based on his doctoral dissertation) with a paragraph titled "The Problem." Hill introduced the reader to the heart of the "problem," stating, "One of the most momentous problems confronting the great Southwest today, is the assimilation of the Spanish-Speaking peoples that are coming in ever increasing numbers into that land formerly owned by Mexico." A few pages later, Hill returned to the Mexican as problem and narrowed it to the local region with this warning: "The greatest problem confronting Southern California to-day is that of dealing with the Mexican element."[44]

Not a few felt similar if not identical concerns. In his master of science thesis, Charles Carpenter cast a dark future for Los Angeles stemming from Mexican settlement. "This large Mexican population," he wrote, "is causing a serious social as well as economic problem in the counties of Southern California."[45] However, the in-migration was a response to labor demand, which spawned social problems, according to settlement house worker Elizabeth Fuller. She noted that the industrial development of Los Angeles "attracted [Mexicans] to it yearly and the housing of these people becomes a current problem."[46]

Authorities in Texas were similarly alarmed. In a paper delivered at the sixth annual convention of the Southwestern Political and Science Association, William Garnett of Texas A&M College declared, "The problems associated with the Mexican invasion of the State are . . . the most pressing race questions now confronting Texas."[47] In his 1930 study of the education of Mexican children in Texas, Herschel Manuel pointed out that his "interest in the Mexican Problem is that of the observer" and not that of a specialist. He nonetheless authored a substantial review of the educational experiences of Mexican children in Texas, examining and analyzing those that he considered to "present difficulties which together may be called 'the Mexican Problem.'"[48] Graduate school training emphasized the point. A Texas schoolteacher completed his master's thesis at the University of Texas titled "Problem of the Elimination of Mexican Pupils from School." The author illustrated his argument with a quotation from the study sponsored by the University of Texas, "A Report on the Illiteracy in Texas," alleging that "the illiterate Mexican child presents by far the most difficult human problem confronting elementary education in Texas today."[49]

Writers seemed to fall into line when dealing with the southwestern Mexican Problem, as did Charles Thompson (cited above), who claimed that "Mexicans are coming faster than they can be absorbed" and that the "problem is complicated by the migratory habits of the Mexican."[50]

Wherever the Mexican immigrant and his or her family traveled, they were easily identified not only by their appearance but also by a constantly increasing list of publications. A mass of books, articles, theses, and dissertations indicted them for undermining such American institutions as the educational system and quite possibly for placing the sacred American way of life at risk.[51]

Ultimately, the "Problem" crossed borders and affected the two countries. In the spirit that motivated many of his contemporaries, Jay Stowell contended that "we can as little permanently confine people and social problems within political areas as we can control water with a basket; they will not stay put. Mexico's problems and Mexico's achievements become ours by the very law of propinquity. . . . We are man and wife by common law marriage, and no international divorce court can ever issue a decree which will separate our interests."[52] Indeed, the ties binding the United States and Mexico were, "indissoluble" and "interdependent," as George Creel and Chester Lloyd Jones announced, respectively. McCombs addressed the same matter from a different vantage point and advised that "the Mexican Problem . . . is one from which we cannot run away."[53] It existed in both Mexico and in the United States, or so claimed an aspiring school administrator who gave notice in his master's thesis that "The Mexican Problem . . . exists wherever there are Mexicans."[54] Robert McLean's reasoning, noting that the "Mexican Problem" inhabited the lands from Guatemala to Gopher Prairie, was not novel at all.

The Core of the Mexican Problem within the United States: Orientalism and Peonism

Packaging Mexican migrants as Orientals, a prima facie indication of an empire mindset, disturbed no one's sensibilities, or so it seemed. Referring to Mexican immigrants as a version of Orientals, or at least an approximation of them, appeared every so often and never prompted a disclaimer; it appeared to many to be self-evident. In the examples taken from writers on Mexican immigrants, Mexicans were more frequently compared with Orientals than identified as Orientals. The editor of the *San Francisco Chronicle* and member of the University of California Board of Regents, Chester H. Rowell, affirmed in a special issue of the *Survey* on Mexican immigrants that the "Chinese coolie is the ideal human mule. He will turn less food into more work, with less trouble, than any domestic animal. . . . He can be rented wholesale." More important, in his opinion, Mexican peons were not up to the level of the Chinese, for although the Mexican proved to be as "racially alien as the Chinese coolie," he was "not so good a workman." And to add to his argument, Crowell claimed, "The Mexican peon is not a 'white' man. He is an Indian . . . a selection downward, from the bottom of Mexican life, to fill a place below the bottom of our own."[55] Whether viewed as Indian, peon, or Oriental, no Mexican in either the United States or in Mexico could ever expect more from life than that which awaited biological deviants from the Anglo-American norm.

Sometimes the linkage to the Oriental was made in a subtle fashion, but most often it was ham-handed. Frederick Simpich, one-time U.S. consul at Nogales, Sonora, contributed his opinion in an article titled, in the style of the day, "The Little Brown Brother Treks North." During an era of tense debate about whether to place a quota on immigration from Mexico, the former consul observed that more information was necessary before a rational decision could be made. His reasoning suggests the popular (and official) American perspective on Mexicans in both Mexico and the United States:

> But there is far more to this question of reducing Mexican immigration than its mere effect on our cheap labor supply. Who are these peons? What is their physical and mental condition? Are they any better, or worse, than the Orientals . . . ?"[56]

Some found pronounced similarities between the two groups but not a biological identity. Vernon McCombs declared that Mexicans' affinity to politeness was similar to Orientals' and surely indicated an ethnic relationship greater than coincidence.

> There is a marked talent among these people for diplomacy and adaptability to delicate situations. With minds accustomed to drawing the most courtly and fine shades of meaning in spoken or written speech, they possess winning powers which are the despair of the average American. Here they resemble the Oriental, to whom many regard them as ethnically related.[57]

Mirroring the literature on Mexico, authors dealing with Mexican immigration segued from a focus on the Oriental to one on the peon. Overall, the discourse on Mexicans as Orientals gathered less attention than the interest allotted to Mexicans as peons.

Given the notable recourse to peonism to explain Mexican immigrants, the matter deserves attention here. That the Mexican came from the peon sector of Mexican society earned general agreement, as well as a substantial discussion as to what this meant for explaining the immigrant. Anthropologist J. E. Pearce, of the University of Texas, was asked to comment on the Mexican immigrant by Herschel Manuel as the latter gathered materials for his book *The Education of Mexican and Spanish-Speaking Children in Texas*. Pearce obliged. "The immigration from Mexico" contended Pearce, "into Texas is, for the most part, from the peon elements of the northern portions of the central plateau and of the northern coastal plain of Mexico. Probably three-fourths of the immigrants are of pure blood Indian origin."[58] The anthropologist retraced a well-worn path and posed no challenging ideas. And so Jay Stowell was on strong grounds when he observed that the "multitudes" of Mexican immigrants were "simple Mexican peons."[59] Stowell's contemporary Frederick Simpich repeated the familiar assertion, stating, "Today the hordes crossing the Rio Grande, as well as those who are already here, are largely from the impoverished peon class."[60]

That Mexico's immigrants came from the peon "classes of Mexico" seemed to define with some precision just who these newcomers were and surfaced with every discussion of Mexican immigrants. One article, titled according to convention "The Mexican Peon in Texas" and appearing in a 1920 edition of *The Survey*, explored related themes. The piece opened, "There are two classes of peons in Texas, those who intend to make the state their home and those who come only for the cotton-picking season and return as soon as it is over."[61] Californians reached a similar if not identical conclusion. An educator writing for the journal *Sociology and Social Research* asked readers to recognize that the "larger percent of the Mexican population of Southern California represents the peon class."[62] In his study of education in a Southern California rural community, Merton Hill advised his readers that "when the term 'Mexican Peon' is used it should be understood that the type of Mexican who is a worker is meant."[63] After all was said and done, writers willingly admitted that they were discussing an immigrant group integrated into the American economy but that it was nonetheless a worrisome, indigestible mass which posed dire social and cultural consequences for the United States.

Authors held nothing back when it came to a dialogue on Mexican immigration, particularly when it came to exclusion or quotas. *Christian Science Monitor* correspondent Richard Lee Strout worried that Mexico's immigration was "not a problem of the future; the problem is now." He continued, "The Mexican peons are coming in more rapidly now than did the Asiatics when the Pacific Coast demanded, and secured, complete exclusion."[64] Comparing Asian migration to Mexican migration assumed an identity in that the two groups allegedly brought similar problems to the United States and therefore deserved identical legislative fates.

Others were content to express images that portrayed Mexicans as a strange variety of the human being, with behavioral characteristics comparable to those of some insect. Frederick Simpich seemed to relish the opportunity for such descriptions. In a journalistic piece for the *National Geographic* (1920), the author addressed border Mexicans who crossed into the United States for temporary stays. "Mexicans are restless," he claimed, and

> the peons like to ride. Whenever they have saved money from a few days' work, they swarm up and down these lines to border towns, carrying women, children, birdcages, blanket rolls, and family utensils, running to and fro apparently as aimless as the inhabitants of a disturbed ant-hill.[65]

In case the reader failed to get the picture, Simpich followed the above description with another, very similar one. "Like the natives of Nogales, Agua Prieta, and Naco," he told readers, "most of the peons of Juárez make a living by working in the adjacent American border town—swarming to the American side, carrying babies and bundles." Simpich's description of one of the border towns and its people speaks to the nature of the discourse on peons. "Drab, dusty Agua Prieta, with its sleepy peons and sad-eyed burros" seemed to sum up his view of the border as a whole.[66] Authors held little back in their opprobrium; the discourse cast its net wide.

Dissecting the Mexican Problem

A connection could now be made with behavior patterns, including social as well as economic conditions associated with the "peon classes of Mexico." Sociologist Emory Bogardus, for example, counseled his readers that in order to explain "the family life and conditions" of the "mass of Mexican immigrants," it "was necessary first of all to consider the Mexican immigrants in light of the family culture traits of the peon classes of Mexico."[67] Few questioned Bogardus' summation; certainly graduate students were in no position to deny the experts their opinions. In her master's thesis, "Methods of Teaching Mexicans," Betty Gould emphasized the social effects embodied in the peons, in her opinion a particular type of Mexican. "The majority of Mexicans in our public schools," she complained, "are not representative of the better class of Mexicans. They represent, rather, the very lowest type, the day laborer, or the peon." Gould then pointed out the larger social consequence of these peons: "Their standards of living are very low as a visit to a Mexican home will readily show."[68] Bogardus' and Gould's observations were only the tip of a very deep iceberg.

Writers left no stone unturned when it came to examining the behavioral characteristics that separated Mexicans from Anglo-America. It seemed that every possible human behavior observed within the Mexican community was scrutinized, analyzed, compared to those of other ethnicities, and ultimately evaluated for possible change or retention. However, the script that they elaborated had been written long before the likes of Gould, Bogardus, and Walker began their "objective" sociological ruminations. They created a discourse guided by a mindset that assumed the existence of a very tangible Mexican Problem and set out to define precisely why it constituted a "problem" for the United States. Upon defining the "stuff" of the "problem," a series of unanimously endorsed ethnic-specific remedies inevitably moved forward.

American conceptualization of Mexican immigrants and of Mexicans in general crystallized into a decided slice of American culture. Victor Clark observed that the "wants of the Mexican peon are hardly more complex than those of the original Indian from whom he is descended."[69] Analysts who followed Clark generally considered the Mexican immigrant a cultural and biological being far removed from the vast majority of Americans (blacks and Asians excluded). As one student wrote, "Mexican ideals are very different from our own."[70] Another echoed, "Many Mexican traits are exactly opposite to those of the Anglo Saxon and in a sense hard for the uninitiated to understand."[71]

Samuel Bryan's 1912 overview retraced the path that others had taken before him and that many others were to follow. His grim report skewered the immigrants, who were described as an "undesirable class of residents," for practicing a culture that "gives rise to serious problems." Among their attributes, Bryan listed "lack of ambition," "largely illiterate," "no political interest," "clannish," and "low standards of living." Bryan concluded, "Although the Mexicans have proved to be efficient laborers . . . the evils to the community at large . . . overbalance their desirable qualities."[72]

Nearly two decades later, Herschel Manuel noted a trend among writers of describing Mexicans as a distinct variety of human being with a litany of "alleged traits," which he listed. They read as if written by Wallace Thompson (who was cited by Manuel):

1. Imitativeness.
2. Conservatism.
3. Respect for authority.
4. Appreciation for friendship.
5. Skill with finger work.
6. Love of music.
7. Strength of home ties.
8. Adherence to custom.
9. Patriarchal organization of family.
10. Sensitiveness to praise or blame.
11. Ignorance and superstition (in lower classes).
12. Respect for church.
13. Apathy.
14. A disparity between words and deeds.
15. Honor and dignity.[73]

Note that there are both positive and negative qualities in Manuel's list (as in Clark's and Bryan's listings); both poles were, in essence, elements that contributed to making the Mexican different and a problem. However, the lists seriously undercounted the distinguishing qualities that appeared throughout the literature. We can add a substantial number of alleged negative qualities; for example, laziness, a mañana attitude, irresponsibility, immorality, propensity to alcohol consumption, violent behavior, criminality, low intellectual abilities, fatalism, and more. On the other hand, authors asserted that Mexicans were courteous to a fault, that they shared their last meal with strangers, and that they loved flowers and color. We examine in detail these and other ascriptions below.

Manuel's list began with imitativeness, a trait that many authors linked to Mexicans in general. Accordingly, being of an imitative nature, Mexican immigrants supposedly lacked creativity and tended to follow rather than lead. A settlement house worker wrote that for a Mexican, the lack of ability to lead and the propensity to imitate were somewhat parallel deviations from the accepted norm. "It is very much easier for him to follow, to imitate," she declared, "than it is for him to lead, to command, to originate. His Latin temperament explains this."[74] Bogardus added that the "Mexican immigrant . . . is submissive to authority. He has learned 'to follow, obey, to imitate.'"[75] Under the heading "The Mexican Mind" another wrote that

Apathy seems to be the characteristic which is most outstanding and which drags upon the wheels of progress toward better standards of thinking and living. The Mexican is imitative. He can copy and reproduce but he does not have the ability to assimilate ideas and skills. He is not original and seems to have one idea at a time. The fact that he is willing to shirk communal responsibilities makes it easy for him to recognize and accept authority.[76]

Not surprisingly, the writer cited (and very nearly plagiarized) Wallace Thompson's *Mexican Mind*. (We shall see in the next chapter that she was not alone in borrowing freely from Thompson.) Using such an appraisal led one student of Mexican immigrants to write, "As Mexicans are great imitators they should be provided with suitable examples to imitate."[77] Note the word "suitable." Undoubtedly, the writer considered the average peon an inappropriate model to emulate; rather, the ideal was the Anglo-American norm. Given the problem at hand, imitation could be employed in anticipation that cultural reform, a moving away from Mexican cultural traditions, would be forthcoming. One could call it an exercise in imitation in order to eliminate imitation.

A trait commonly attributed to all Mexicans (and to all Latin Americans) that has endured in the minds of Americans to the present contends that the mañana approach to life governs behavior and social relations. No other cultural trait affixed itself to Mexico as did the mañana complex. The mañana attitude implied a willingness to put work or a responsibility off until tomorrow, or that tomorrow will solve today's problems so no need to hurry. Under the heading "Mañana Attitude of Mexicans," one schoolteacher described the complex from the prevalent American point of view. "The Mexican will do what he has to do today," he averred. "Preparedness for the future is the least of his worries. . . . Pool halls, playing or watching baseball and general loafing are his glory."[78]

Naturally, the ascription only made sense relative to what was considered the American norm. Consequently, as an educator wrote,

The Mexican immigrant is not touched by the American urge to be doing something all the time. He is content to sit by the hour in the sun or even to lean against any convenient building or fence. Patience is one of his virtues. Often when his work is dependent upon the weather he will wait in good humor for hours.[79]

"Mañana" also meant that the Mexicans' sense of time differed radically from that which defined American behavior. Bogardus suggested that Mexicans "live so largely in the present that time has no meaning for them.

With them time is not commercialized as with us. Their wants are not aroused as ours, consequently, they do not drive themselves as we drive ourselves." Bogardus finished his discussion of mañana by stating that it "is fatal in the United States. Not everything can be put off until tomorrow; tomorrow does not always or usually take care of itself."[80] So, Mexicans tend to procrastinate and wait until tomorrow to take care of what should have been taken care of today. Meanwhile, progress passes them by.

The mañana attitude was often interwoven with another equally fatal characteristic: indolence or laziness. For example, one academic wrote that "the Mexican is naturally indolent, and his tendency to 'never do today what can be put off until some other time' is one of the outstanding problems with which the school is confronted."[81] The average Mexican's reluctance to engage in work, or laziness, seemed axiomatic to many analysts of the Mexican immigrants' cultural character. The same academic cited above declared that Mexicans were "naturally inclined to be lazy" and later added, "It is common to consider the Mexican's natural lack of ambition as laziness."[82] Laziness might be presented as "shiftlessness," as Bogardus touted in a 1919 work. "The Mexican laborer," he claimed, "is often shiftless and thriftless."[83] Sometimes "laziness" might translate into "unambitious" or having a "lack of initiative."[84] Each term meant the same thing.

Popular writers picked up the terminology and all that it implied. A writer of the political commentary journal the *Nation* remarked that for the Mexican (and the Mexican immigrant), the "desire to better one's economic position seems to lose its force in the up-side down world south of the Rio Grande. The Indian-Mexican enjoys savoring life (with rest and leisure), and the American enjoys crowding it. . . . But, they (the Mexicans) look happy. They are reposeful and contented. Of course they are happy. What becomes of progress, if you are happy and contented with what you have?"[85] In an article appearing in the *Survey*, the author advised readers that Mexicans "lack ideals and purpose . . . [and] take life and everything it offers casually. . . . they seem not quite awake.[86] Another researcher writing in *Sociology and Social Research* used slightly different phrasing: "The Mexican wants labor only when he wants it, in amounts and intensity to suit his poetic soul and his malnourished body."[87] In a second article, the same author offered a somewhat revised thesis, arguing:

> The Mexican dislikes work. Work is work; joy is joy. The two are not the same. There is joy in play, in music, in color, in rest, in the dance, but not in work. There is no such thing as the joy of working at difficult tasks. One does disagreeable work for money, not for joy.[88]

Finally, at the 1920 National Conference on Social Welfare, an audience listened to a panelist comment, "Much has been said about the laziness of the peon. It must be remembered that his wants are very simple and if he can make ends meet by working five days instead of six he is going to do so and rest an extra day."[89]

The cataloging of Mexican cultural traits seemed to come in waves or clusters; once the first allegation was issued, more observations flowed in systematic fashion. Bogardus was not unique among social scientists when he wrote that the Mexican "has not been trained in assuming responsibility. He has not much of this world's goods to become responsible. He has not been taught to save; he has little or nothing to save. Thrift has not entered his vocabulary. Poverty has been his natural lot." One much lauded trait purported to have penetrated into the deepest heart of their nature was an ability to do artistic handwork, particularly folk art, and to create music. Bogardus made no departure from the conventional when he claimed, "Art is a kind of religion to the Mexican. He has natural tendencies of an artistic nature. Whether seated under a tree, or leaning on a hoe and talking with his compatriots matters little, for in either case he is in himself a picture." Later, the famed sociologist added, "The Mexican is vitally interested in handicrafts. He is nimble and artistic with his fingers, not only on the guitar but in making simple works of art."[90]

Mexicans were depicted in contrasting and contradictory ways. On the one hand, Mexicans were criticized for a decided bent to imitate, but, on the other hand, they were hailed for their artistic originality.[91] Such were the learned discourses of the day that the U.S. empire spawned in reference to Mexicans and Mexican immigrants. Contradiction seemed to permeate the studies: employers lobbied vigorously against an immigration quota, claiming that their harvests and rail construction plans would be undermined, but the published "findings" claimed that Mexicans were lazy, unambitious, irresponsible, shiftless, thriftless, and so on. Why did this mindset brimming with contradictions and inconsistencies fail to impress the serious social scientist? Perhaps the answer rests in the very contradictions themselves. On the one hand, the Mexican laborer was an inferior human type; but, on the other, this very deviation made him a worthy and valuable laborer. Victor Clark, for example, in his 1908 study of Mexican laborers in the United States offered this potpourri of characteristics that distinguished Mexicans from Americans on both sides of the border.

The Mexican laborer is unambitious, listless, physically weak, irregular, and indolent. On the other hand, he is docile, patient, usually orderly in camp, fairly intelligent under competent supervision, obedient, and cheap. If he were active and ambitious, he would be less tractable and would cost more. His strongest point is his willingness to work for a low wage.[92]

He intimated that if Mexicans were "active and ambitious" they would be less desirable. Clark also commented that employers "in Mexico and the United States, noted similar qualities." And by defining Mexicans in a wholesale negative fashion, employers easily concocted a justification and an argument for paying Mexicans wages far below prevailing rates and restricting them to particular sites within the productive system for as long as necessary. Perhaps another part of the answer can be found in the strength of the unquestioned belief in the superiority of the American nation among the American republics. Blessed with a God-given right to expand economically, the United States thereby held a responsibility to civilize not only Mexico and all of Latin America but Mexican immigrants as well.

Defining the Mexican as a member of an inferior species from an inferior nation served to justify the empire and class domination at home. Writers invariably argued that Mexico required the continued tutelage (i.e., Americanization) of the United States, "the elder statesman among the American republics." Simultaneously, authors on Mexican immigrants read these publications and participated actively in that imperial refrain but anchored their meanings within the framework of Mexican immigration, integration of Mexican immigrants into the productive system, and the expansion of Mexican settlements. The Mexican immigrant merely presented one more challenge to the imperial civilizing mission of the United States.

The above traits purporting to define the Mexican immigrant mirrored the definitions emanating from American writers in their studies of Mexico. The one trait that stood out above all others as critical to distinguishing Americans (minus American Indians, Asians, and blacks) from Mexicans was an inherent childlike nature. In the minds of observers of the American economic conquest, childlike behavior patterns identified and distinguished the Mexican peon. Bogardus was not alone in suggesting that the Mexican "is somewhat like a small child brought up in a paternalistic home, who goes about the place freely, picking up and enjoying whatever touches his fancy."[93] In other words, the fabled tendency of Mexicans to steal stemmed from an environmentally produced infantilism. Another writer had a nearly identical perspective of Mexicans in the community of Watts, near Los Angeles, describing them as "child-like, timid, carefree people."[94] Later, the same author quoted from Edward A. Ross' study of Mexico: "He is as easily led as a child, and the master who understands him and means right, generally has no difficulties in managing him."[95] A Pasadena, California, settlement house worker followed the thought pattern and argued, "The one trait of his nature which is foreign to our temperament is his submission to existing conditions. He is child-like and can generally be directed into constructive activities for his own advancement."[96]

Organizations advocating better treatment of the Mexican immigrants embraced the "Mexican as child" theme, as did those who supported a quota on Mexican immigration. Vera Sturges, secretary of the Non-English Speaking Women section of the Young Women's Christian Association, reiterated the child theme. She counseled her readers to judge the Mexican immigrants in light of their true nature,

> for they are in general submissive, quiet, serious, and peaceful. Even now they do not think for themselves, are easily led, need restraint, and are hard to stop when once started—characteristics which are the logical outgrowths of slavery working through given qualities. Intellectually they are children. They are apt along mechanical and agricultural lines, but the most part undeveloped. Like other primitive people they do not consider the value of their lives nor that of anybody else, but they cannot honestly be termed bloodthirsty and warlike.[97]

CONCLUSION

Before the term "Mexican Problem" was freely applied to the immigrant Mexican community, it had already become a common identifier for all Mexicans in the minds of many Americans. As Mexicans migrated to the United States and settled into barrios across the Southwest and Midwest, the term was fixed upon them. All that the term implied defined Mexicans—how they thought, behaved, and lived. As in case of the term's usage in Mexico, it seemed that no stone was left unturned in discovering its behavioral applications in the United States. When it came to dissecting the nature of the Mexican immigrant, everything from sexual practices to housekeeping attracted a commentary and critique.[98]

However, there was a silver lining in the dark clouds that hung over the growing colonia system across the Southwest and parts of the Midwest. On the bright side, it was said that Mexicans were good with their hands, were graced with artistic abilities, loved good music, enjoyed family life, shared their wealth with their neighbors, and took life one day at a time. Some marveled that they were not bogged down by the materialistic machine age and congratulated them for that.

The U.S. interpretation of the Mexican Problem varied little from its common usage in Mexico. After all was said and done, the literature repeated that "Mexicans are not like us," and this constituted, on the one hand, the Mexican Problem and, on the other, advantages to be exploited by corporate employers. Clark, for example, noted, "Cotton picking suits the Mexican for several reasons: It requires nimble fingers rather than physical strength. . . . it employs his whole family; he can follow it from place to place . . . which seems to suit the half-subdued nomadic instinct of a part of the Mexican race."[99] Whatever the advantages, that alleged difference set the stage for state-administered attempts at resolving the formidable dangers posed by "them" without altering their economic integration and standing in the class order. Invariably, writers prescribed a long-time heavy dose of Americanization.

6. EMPIRE, DOMESTIC POLICY, AND THE EDUCATION OF MEXICAN IMMIGRANTS

The Mexican as an individual presents many problems to the school. He represents a race that has long been under conquest and political despotism. His background represents unfortunate racial experiences and lack of culture. The irresponsibility of the Mexican child can probably be traced to the fact that a generation ago, his ancestors were peons. The child comes from parents who have not learned modern civilization. They can not jump from one civilization to another overnight. As a usual thing, Mexican customs and habits are carried on in all Mexican homes, an almost unfailing characteristic of which is their patriotism to their own country, as demonstrated by their rigid observance of all Mexican holidays. Their unwillingness to speak the English language in their homes is a serious handicap to the child in school who is attempting to learn to speak English. The Mexican is naturally indolent, and his tendency to "never do today what can be put off until some other time" is one of the outstanding problems with which the school is confronted. With few exceptions, almost every person interviewed mentioned the problem of tardiness, resulting from the "mañana complex." Too, the Mexicans lack the ability to adapt themselves to unusual situations.

Betty Gould, "Methods of Teaching Mexicans," master's thesis (1932)

INTRODUCTION

The threads connecting books on Mexico with studies on how best to socialize the children and adults of the new immigrant community were firmly woven together. The quote taken from the Gould thesis indicted the Mexican community in ways that most writers on Mexico would have found reasonable, perhaps even understated. Indeed, Gould said nothing out of the ordinary, nothing that her mentors and graduate colleagues would have contested. The Mexican, she said, "presents many problems of the schools." Again, the Mexican Problem, and all that it implied, not only anchored her thesis, but the discourse within the American educational establishment as well.

The purpose of this chapter is to demonstrate the clear links between the culture of empire and the domestic public policy applied to the Mexican immigrant community. We shall see that empire encompassed both the imperial nation and the nations dominated by that imperial power as well. The Mexican immigrant community, the social consequence of imperial economic expansionism, entered a society in the process of shaping itself into an imperial power, domestically and transnationally. Domestically, the United States had moved away from its former democratic moorings (such as they were) and begun an era of corporate control of the American political system, meaning a top-down system of bureaucratic management. The nation's corporate-influenced public policy took many forms among which were racially inspired school segregation and the use of IQ testing to predict educational outcomes and track students into permanent curricular tracks. IQ tests were also used a means of politically socializing society's children; we have known for some time that the preservation of the class position and occupational character of a community was a major outcome of intelligence testing.

Unfortunately, most studies of the ethnic Mexican experience tend to ignore the imperial dimensions of migration and the consequent formation of immigrant communities across the Southwest and Midwest. Certainly, empire and the domestic public and private policy applied to such communities has never been given much serious attention either, much less focused discussion. Previous discussions of the Chicano educational experience have virtually neglected the role of empire in shaping educational policy. Most studies (my dissertation and book on Chicano education included) remain tethered to a national or regional focus.[1] Moreover, practically all works on Chicano educational history focus on race as the critical factor in shaping that education. As the reader is well aware by now, this study brings the United States empire into the historical discourse. Here we are concerned with the educational experiences of the Mexican community and the intimate connections between an expanding economic empire, the culture of empire, and the shaping of domestic policy applied to the Mexican immigrant community. Although the focus is on education, the discussion is applicable to law enforcement, the justice system, and other areas of public policy.

This chapter will elaborate on an educational program that was designed exclusively for the Mexican community and aimed, for the most part, at forcing de-Mexicanization (or Americanization) within a segregated setting by emphasizing industrial or vocational training for Mexican children. The consequences for the Mexican child were enormous; the class position of the immigrant community was to be maintained through the school, a state institution designed to reproduce, politically and economically, the working class for American corporate capital. Immigrant children were not the only target of Americanization; adults and especially women were also singled out for Americanization, with the expectation that women would become agents of a larger community Americanization.

However, educators were never concerned with changing the economic conditions of the Mexican community; rather, education aimed at eliminating the core of the much-discussed Mexican Problem. First, the Mexicanness of immigrants needed to be eliminated. Once done, the true academic potential of the students would be exposed and learning might take place effectively. Americanization, however, did not alter the curriculum, which for the most part emphasized the industrial arts and thereby reproduced the class standing of the Mexican community. Nor did segregation deny the integration of the community into the economic mainstream of the United States. Segregation provided one method for the integration of the Mexican community into the public educational systems. As Mexicans were segregated, their integration into the political and economic institutions of the United States moved forward and grew deeper. The segregation of the Mexican immigrants, whether economic, residential, or educational, ensured that they would circulate actively within the very core of the nation's economic, social, and political institutions. An emphasis on marginality—that is, reading the history of the Mexican community as if it were a social or economic existence on the margins of society, outside the mainstream—fails to explain, much less describe, the experience of the Mexican community. Segregation was nothing less than the form that integration assumed.

EDUCATORS AND THE CULTURE OF EMPIRE

The educational establishment, including teachers, administrators, superintendents, and boards of education, perplexed at the sudden arrival of so many immigrants from Mexico, searched for strategies to socialize their newest minions. In tandem with the expansion of the American schooling system to implement a state-mandated policy of compulsory education for all children—a substantial problem in itself—schools faced the matter of including the children of Mexican immigrants. The questions that school educators and policy makers raised revolved around shaping the most efficacious approach for socializing these newcomers. The educational world searched for answers, and they found them in the substantial trove of information in the literature on Mexico, which they used freely and with the intention of applying the lessons learned. Educators, following the example of the academicians, assumed that Mexican children and their parents together posed a Mexican Problem for the schools to resolve. The education of the Mexican child would be designed for the archetypal Mexican portrayed in the literature.

Dozens of theses and dissertations written at schools of education and social work, in addition to a handful of professional research endeavors, not only discussed the Mexican Problem at length, but also quoted from and cited the works on Mexico as well.[2] Those few who did not cite or refer to the literature nonetheless described a "typical" Mexican that harmonized with the vision of writers who quoted widely from the literature. We shall see that the Mexican Problem permeated the literature and contributed to shaping an educational program aimed exclusively at the Mexican community. A few examples tell the story.

In her master's thesis written at the University of Southern California School of Education, Helen Walker referred to the works of Eva Frank, Edward A. Ross, Frederick Simpich, Wallace Thompson (two books), Jay Stowell, and George Creel.[3] Anna Lofstedt's 1922 thesis cited C. Reginald Enock, John K. Goodrich, Helen Marston, Lewis Spence, Frederick Starr, Wallace Thompson, E. D. Trowbridge, Nevin O. Winter and George B. Winton.[4] In her thesis for the sociology department at the University of Southern California, Mary Lanigan cited Ernest Gruening, Robert McLean, Wallace Thompson, Edward Trowbridge, George Creel, George B. Winton, Vernon McCombs, and Jay Stowell.[5] In his thesis on test scores by Mexican children, George Curtiss Gillette utilized the works of Helen Marston, Ernest Gruening, Vernon M. McCombs, Robert N. McLean, Edward A. Ross, Jay S. Stowell, and Wallace Thompson (two).[6] In addition to quoting extensively from two books by Wallace Thompson, Laura Lyon cited Robert McLean, Jay S. Stowell, and Vernon McCombs in her thesis on the education of Mexican girls.[7] Of all the authors, Wallace Thomson appeared the favorite among prospective school administrators as they shaped their theses into policy proposals. Of the nearly two dozen theses and dissertations that cited works on Mexico, no less than twelve cited Thompson. Indeed, the frequency with which Thompson was cited indicates his authoritative standing in the field of education. In addition to wholesale references to Thomson, several appeared to have plagiarized from him.

Given their dependency on works on Mexico, educators followed the same rubric as the writers on Mexico. The Arizona Department of Education advised its teaching corps that "the teacher of Mexican groups will need not only to know the immediate background and home life experiences of the Mexican pupils under her supervision but also will need to know the history and the cultural development of the race as a whole."[8] The Arizona prescription mirrored a general approach to understanding the Mexican child. A Stanton, Texas, school principal recommended that educators study the Mexican immigrants' background in order to have a sense of their needs. "In order to understand the Spanish-speaking people," he advised,

> and to analyze them more correctly, to get to their trend of thought so that it may be directed, and to get their temperament so that the work may be made to harmonize with it, it will be helpful to investigate their background. Since the Spanish-speaking people as they exist today are generally a combination or an amalgamation of two peoples, of two races, the Indians and the Spaniards, it is well to know the part that each race has contributed to the formation of this group of people.[9]

The thesis by a longtime Southern California teacher in Mexican immigrant communities, Jessie Hayden, provides an example of the wholesale borrowing from Wallace Thompson's *The Mexican Mind*. In her work on an experiment in education for the local Mexican community, references to Thompson pepper the work. One such reference provides a clear instance of plagiarism. In her thesis she wrote:

> There is an outstanding characteristic of the Mexican, apathy, which remains an infirmity of the will; forever the promise of the mañana— the great things of the morrow. It is this apathy of the will which drags upon the wheels of such progress as might exist. The yoke of this custom also lies upon the Mexicans every where with a weight which is impossible to explain to the American or the European. The harness of the past ages seems to bind the Mexican from the cradle to the grave, and waits for his children and his children's children.[10]

Now compare Hayden's passage to Thompson's own words:

> But for all this altruism and this concentration upon self as well, there is apathy. Forever the lack of ambition for aught save idleness; forever the promise of "*mañana*" and the great things of the morrow,—these drag upon the wheels of such progress as might be . . . an infirmity of

the will, an inability to stir out of that helpless drifting. . . . Apathy remains, outstanding as a characteristic of Mexico.[11]

Apparently, no one bothered to check Hayden's sources and the blunder
went unnoticed, but the message that Mexicans comprised an apathetic
lot sounded clearly. Moreover, those earning their advanced degrees and
entering into the ranks of polished educators and aspiring administrators
articulated the Mexican identity that Thompson and his cohort constructed. At times, students of Mexican immigrants seemingly plagiarized
in a rather unconscious fashion. An educator writing on homemaking
courses for Mexican girls nearly matched Thomson's words without citation, noting that the

> Mexican temperament . . . hampers educational and social progress
> among these people. Apathy seems to be the characteristic which is
> most outstanding and which drags upon the wheels of progress toward
> better standards of thinking and living. The Mexican is imitative. He
> can copy and reproduce but he does not have the ability to assimilate
> ideas and skills.[12]

Ideas spawned by Thompson and his cohort spread widely and strongly
influenced a generation of educators, social workers, and academics who
studied Mexican immigrants with the express objective of recommending
specific educational policies for their subjects. As one teacher pointed out,
"Methods should be used that are especially adapted to the personality of
the Mexican child."[13] Southwestern educational practices coincided at
many levels with the imperial images of Mexicans prominently displayed
in the literature on Mexico. The cultural constructs regarding Mexican
immigrants were self-evident to such an extent that their incorporation
sometimes required no citation whatever.[14] In a school district publication directed at administrators and teachers, an assistant supervisor in the
Los Angeles School District defined the Mexican Problem as one stemming from "the influx of immigrants from the Republic south of us." He
further explained what in all probability appeared to his contemporaries
to be an obvious postulate:

> The infusion of Spanish blood into Aztec and Maya veins has Latinized
> later generations since the sixteenth century. The mixture of the two is
> fundamentally responsible for the carefree, if not indolent, characteris-
> tic of the race. . . . The lofty spirit of independence of both races explains
> the composure of the present day Mexican under circumstances and
> conditions which would appall the Anglo-Saxon or American subject.[15]

Such facile assertions, of enormous proportions (and consequences), seemed appropriate when educational practices relevant to the Mexican immigrant community were on the public policy agenda.

THE EMERGING THEORY AND PRACTICE OF STATE-MANDATED EDUCATION

Simultaneous with an economic expansion of the United States via the export of surplus capital and goods, the corporate economy evolved steadily, which had far-reaching social and cultural effects. In addition, the representations of Mexicans constructed by American writers in general coincided with domestic theories and practices concerning race, particularly genetic theories propounding inherited intelligence along racial lines. In addition, the American system of socialization and the predominant political culture also underwent substantial change and by the late nineteenth century jelled into a reformed schooling and cultural pattern. From a system of education based largely in small, rural communities in the early nineteenth century, the educational structure evolved into a program of compulsory schools educating large masses of students at the end of the century.

Education took on new functions; in the early nineteenth century the apprentice system served to train lawyers, merchants, artisans, and other independent professionals for the agricultural and commercial capitalist order. However, with the growth of capitalism from a regionally dispersed agrarian economic order to a large-scale national industrial system based on monopolistic and oligopolistic enterprises, the older schooling system simply was not adequate to handle the needs of the rapidly changing corporate-centered society. The newer system could handle the training of just about every professional and nonprofessional occupation. In this movement toward a professional and nonprofessional training system, the public school occupied a central position.

The schooling system did more than prepare society's children for the new industrial occupations; the new enterprise also inculcated a corresponding political ideology. The old political precepts, rooted in classical political economy, that helped guide youth into adulthood under the earlier system became irrelevant in the new corporate industrial order. The notion that hard work, industriousness, and education would surely result in success (which meant becoming a capitalist) seemed out of place in an industrial order in which the production of commodities depended on the hard labor of a working class whose members, barring exceptions, would never reach the capitalist class. Production in the industrial era depended on the labor of a permanent working class, a class that had no other relation to capital than that of wageworker. Indeed, in the post–Civil War era, the industrial working class increased substantially, numbering over 5 million. The vast majority worked for the major industrial corporations and became the dominant workers for railroads, oil, steel, and mining. These in turn merged with the giants of finance and industry headed by the likes of J. P. Morgan, Jay Gould, and Andrew Carnegie.

Organic Social Theory

Meanwhile, as the classical competitive economy faded, small forms of production fell under the power of the new corporate behemoths. As the old capitalist order gave way to the new, a political cultural change evolved as well. The old notions that hard work equaled success (the Horatio Alger myth) and that success meant the acquisition of capital succumbed to a re-formed perspective on the role of the individual in society. The conception of the social order in modern societies as one within which individuals freely sought out their destiny by dint of industriousness (the "rags to riches" myth) conflicted with the new social relations representative of the corporate order. Under large-scale capitalist production, commodities were formed by low-wage labor working twelve-hour days and living in tenement districts near industrial enterprises. In keeping with this momentous alteration, hard work did not automatically reward success and a rise into the capitalist class, once the hallmark of the American credo. On the contrary, hard work and industriousness in a factory, railroad, or steel mill seldom led to entering the capitalist class; rather, it led to remaining in the working class.

Other conditions, for sure, argued for the need for cultural reforms that coincided with the corporate order. As the industrial working class grew to major proportions, it also became conscious of itself as a discrete class with self-interests and a political agenda that did not always harmonize—indeed, it more often conflicted—with the interests of large-scale capital. Shortly after the Civil War, the American working class began to organize nationally, and with that organization came strikes—sometimes citywide strikes and at other times nationwide strikes—and a violent period of class warfare ensued that extended into the twentieth century. As U.S. corporations expanded into Mexico, a class war manifested at various times against the very same capital within the United States. Interestingly, the working class used the political credo that had prevailed in the earlier precorporate era. Workers' organizations claimed that labor performed the hard work, constituted the prime factor in production and the source of capital's prodigious profits, and yet received little more than poverty. Industriousness, they claimed, was not being rewarded; instead, those who did not labor reaped the profits. This social relation, workers claimed, contradicted the laws of nature which governed all societies and that upheld labor to be the source of all wealth.

The threat of a revolt and even a revolution from below, in the form of theoretical challenges and practices, prompted the development of new paradigms for explaining the evolution and development of societies. Here the emerging field of sociology, led by Edward Alsworth Ross among others, took the forefront in explorations examining new formulas to explain the logic of social development and change.[16] In essence, the new theoretical design moved away from the classical emphasis on a Spencerian unfettered competition (and even competition between classes) to an emphasis on cooperation, particularly between classes. The new paradigm, termed Organic Theory, reasoned that the role of all members of all modern industrial societies was to act cooperatively and thereby realize the common welfare. More, social classes (or the existence of wealth and poverty in a single social order) per se were not the main obstacle to the optimal functioning of society. Instead, faulty cultural conceptions, in particular the Marxist theoretical emphasis on class struggle as the motor of social change, which certain sectors of the working class embraced, propelled social breakdown, anarchy, and decomposition rather than a transition to a better society. Constructing alternatives to the calamitous possibilities associated with Marxism became the order of the day in academia and in corporate boardrooms.

Sociologists theorized that the adherence by every member of society to a common set of rules that guided public and private behavior provided the key to realizing an organically unified society. A common political culture, including a common language but more important common political belief systems, inevitably bound all members of society into a single, unified whole, working toward a common objective. The opposite cultural pattern, marked in particular by linguistic variability, allegedly led to the kind of class warfare that marked the rise of corporate industrial capitalism in the late nineteenth century.

The Concept of Intelligence

The classical principle that the social class structure and the distribution of capital reflect the varying degrees of industriousness practiced by its members, a conception rooted in the Enlightenment, contradicted the corporate social order.[17] Consequently, the contention that hard work invariably led to success was replaced by a an emphasis on factors beyond the control of individuals in the social order. Instead of a social order that organized itself on the basis of individuals independently seeking their own interest or advantage, a theory of consciousness was created that underscored the role of the intelligence with which humans were naturally but unequally endowed. This theory claimed that the ability to think abstractly determined why some people were workers (physical laborers) and others were capitalists (intellectual laborers). The new cultural ethos explained that the capitalist social structure was nothing more than a reflection of the distribution of intelligence in society; in fact, there was not even a capitalist logic to the order, as a social order in which the rules of capitalism predominated merely reflected the untrammeled expression of nature.

Pioneers in the field of psychology, particularly William James, the "Father of American Psychology," theorized that the social and economic distinctions in society merely reflected the varying distribution of intelligence. And in fact, James theorized that the vast economic and political differences observed in the United States in the late nineteenth century, the great wealth centered in a diminishing class of corporate capitalists alongside the poverty of the expanding working class, mirrored the vast differences in naturally ordained intelligence.[18] The theoretician James and the developer of the IQ test, Lewis Terman, argued that the "smart ones" simply rose to the top because nature ordained such to be the case.[19] Moreover, national political leaders also had superior intellectual abilities, which explained their rise to positions of leadership. The old explanation of democracy, that the people governed through their peers, evolved into a political theory of elite governance by the select few, a theory that implicitly ratified the governance by those ensconced in the higher socioeconomic ranks.

The theoretical conceptions elaborated by William James and Lewis Terman, as well as those of Edward Alsworth Ross, dovetailed; from their disciplinary vantage points each labored to promote an organic, seamless social order within the United States. Such a conceptualization implied that the existing capitalist order was a construction of the sum total of intelligence in society and that social distinctions had little relation to any internal logic of capitalism. Political disorder, that is, class warfare, emanated from a dysfunctional cultural system. However, since political order did not arise through its own efforts, realizing the organic society required continual and vigorous state intervention—social engineering if you will—into the social process.

Schooling for an Organic Society

Emanating from the reformation of the productive system and its corresponding political culture, a state-run system for training youths for this new order came into place, that is, the public schools geared up to provide compulsory, free education for the young en masse. School systems across the nation incorporated a stress upon teaching a set of common cultural norms that were expected to bind all members of society into an organic whole. Americanization for immigrants, many of whom were of the working class, served as one tool to reach this goal. Secondly, schools employed a bureaucratized version of mass testing, together with tracking and curriculum differentiation, as the most important means to effectively train students for the new industrial order. In essence, the new system of socialization would prepare students to enter the varied occupations in the corporate order, placing them in a specific curricular track according to each individual's "naturally" endowed intelligence as measured by the IQ test. In the process, the class order was reproduced and an organically unified society unfettered by breakdowns caused by cultural differentiation was anticipated. In addition, a systematic allocation of individuals to sites along the corporate economic order commensurate with their measured intelligence was intended to create a more efficient society.

As they settled into their new communities, Mexican immigrants experienced a reformed educational system adapted to economic and political conditions originating from a corporate capitalist order. This emerging twentieth-century educational system, managed by the very same state enforcing the imperial open door for American capital in Mexico, the Philippines, the Caribbean, and all of Latin America, greeted Mexican immigrants as they emerged as an ethnic minority. Mexican immigrants thus experienced empire in both its transnational and domestic arenas.

EDUCATIONAL POLICIES AND PRACTICES AND THE MEXICAN IMMIGRANT COMMUNITY

Education in the United States has been historically thought of as a window of opportunity that allows those in the lower echelons of society to escape from the ranks of "less fortunate." The myth has endured despite theoretical designs and policies that deliberately functioned to prevent such an outcome during much of the twentieth century and that still function today. During the period under discussion, Mexican children were segregated by fiat and immersed at school in both Americanization and industrial training programs, which effectively precluded social change and the storied escape (known as "upward mobility" or the American Dream) from poverty or the working class, or both. Across the Southwest, school districts mandated a school policy for the Mexican community that differed in important respects from the policy for the dominant Anglo American community. Segregation in the case of the Mexican child did not originate entirely in the racial practices that stemmed from the "separate but equal" doctrine; we must also keep in mind the imperial culture then in the process of development and its broad impact on schooling policy.

Educators in district after district repeated the sad refrain that the Mexican child was different from the Anglo American child and therefore their separation into two educational programs was required. It was said that Mexicans came from a cultural system at odds with the prevailing norms and practices of American schools. Again, the litany of cultural faults came into public discussion: Mexicans were apathetic, lazy, indolent, prone to delinquency and alcoholism, lacked industry and initiative, and so on. And of course, that Mexicans were childlike was thrown in for good measure.[20] Herschel Manuel commented that the inferiority of Mexicans "was so pronounced and so much a part of general knowledge in the state [Texas] that it seems superfluous to cite evidence that it exists."[21] A Southern California elementary school teacher's list ran for pages; here a shortened version provides a glimpse of the era:

> The Mexican loves personal attention and it has a great effect upon his thought processes. Often he will respond if shown attention, when without it nothing would move him. Suspicion is a trait that seems to exist even with relation to his own people and is a result of his own cunning and generations of intellectual dishonesty. The Mexican does not look upon lying and stealing as grievous crimes; he is deceitful and regards the ethical side of religion lightly. . . . The emotional phases are largely animal-like,—fear, self-assertion, sex, and greed. To the Mexican, honor is an outstanding virtue, but it is not the honor of honesty and truth but rather that of prestige and prowess. He will lie and steal, if need be, to maintain his "honor."[22]

Later, the author quoted Robert McLean to the effect that Mexicans "lack a conscience . . . no love for right." And true to form, Mexicans were good with their hands, loved color, and were artistically and musically inclined.

SEGREGATION OF MEXICAN CHILDREN

The segregation of Mexican children seemed a universally accepted method for educating the Mexican community and was rarely challenged by the dominant community.[23] Writing in 1931, one student observed, "Segregation . . . is now an accepted practice essential to the rapid progress of the Mexican child."[24] Consequently, before anything of value could be worked out for the carriers of the Mexican Problem, only a segregated program would ensure satisfactory results. Segregation, it was said, was in the best interests of the Mexican community, as well as that of the Anglo American community. In the final analysis, academic work simply was not a part of the Mexican persona.

In his master's thesis, Charles Carpenter (who ten years later appeared as a Southern California school district superintendent) wrote that the vast differences between the two communities in culture and intelligence, as well as the need of Americanization for Mexicans, indicated that a separate environment was of mutual value. The logic of this assertion seemed to him, at least, self-evident. He summarized his research for and against segregation with these short phrases:

> Considering the above facts, (1) because of the great social differences of the two races, (2) because of the much higher percentage of contagious diseases, (3) because of a higher percent of undesirable behavior characteristics, (4) because of much slower progress in school, and (5) because of their much lower moral standard, it would seem best that:
>
> 1. Whenever numbers permit, Mexican children be segregated. . . .
> 2. A special course of study be prepared to meet the needs of Mexican children.[25]

Carpenter's ideas were not entirely of his making; he relied on two works by Wallace Thompson and those of Vernon McCombs, Robert McLean, and Ernest Gruening.

A University of Texas specialist in rural research published a study on illiteracy in the state that made a similar case for segregation. He cautioned, "There is but one choice in the matter of educating these unfortunate children and that is to put the "dirty" ones into separate schools till they learn how to "clean up" and become eligible to better society."[26] In general, segregation was more often rationalized upon a cultural basis rather than racialized argument, but the outcome varied little. One Southern California school superintendent argued that "pupils should not be put in Mexican classes because they are Mexicans; they should be put there because they can profit most by the instruction offered in such classes."[27] Another school administrator implied that the objective of segregated schooling was not separation but a cultural change, the adaptation to American life and the final resolution to the Mexican Problem. He concluded:

> When the Mexican child enters school he has to start from "scratch" so to speak. His home and social background is nearly zero. The only language he has heard is Spanish nor did the conversation of his parents or brothers and sisters impart to him many of those everyday facts that the American child has known since he could understand anything.
>
> An appreciation of the conditions under which the Mexican child lives his first five or six years of life is therefore essential for a proper understanding of the "Mexican Problem."[28]

In the segregated schools the resources, physical structures, and quality of teachers differed significantly from the schools designed for Anglo children. Even the accounting system for Mexican schools in a district was separated from the general financial bookkeeping. Mexican schools were managed through separate ledgers and administrative practices—meaning inferior buildings, second-hand classroom resources, inadequately trained teachers, and lower standards in every category of school administration. The general practice of boards of education was to send novice teachers and those about to retire to Mexican schools; a novice who displayed talent in the classroom would be promoted to an Anglo school in the district. Placement in a Mexican school was seldom a sought-after assignment and teachers at a Mexican school suffered from a sense of inferiority; the short-term objective of many was advancement to an Anglo school. Manuel observed an "exodus" from Mexican schools throughout South Texas schools; he considered a Mexican school "a training school from which the most capable teachers may be drawn to other schools." He added that "a large number are untrained and unskilled for this work."[29] One teacher stood out from the crowd when she criticized California's segregated schools for "poor buildings . . . the poorest teachers of the force . . . and as little spent in money and effort as can be."[30] Segregation meant inferiority and discrimination all along the line of the schooling process.[31]

Traditionally, segregation was meant to instruct the child in proper methods of behavior, meaning learning to think and act like the mythical model American. For this, schools generally separated children in smaller districts into what were commonly called "Americanization rooms." In districts with larger Mexican populations, separate rooms evolved into separate schools, generally with the proviso that at the seventh or eighth grade level Mexican children would be integrated with Anglo children. However, this usually did not take place as planned. Districts tended to keep Mexican children in Mexican schools till high school, and some Mexican schools virtually ended the education of Mexican children in the tenth grade. The Americanization effort in the early grades was retained in the segregated schools, with many children held back until they became somewhat proficient in English. Grade retardation affected many children, and it was common for students to drop out by the eighth grade, in order to seek work or join their parents in the fields.

In agricultural regions only the lucky children attended segregated school, as many school districts simply refused to enroll Mexican children. This was especially true of Texas cotton districts and in Colorado beet fields. As mentioned above, as late as 1945 only one-half of Mexican elementary school age children were enrolled and attending school in Texas. This did not happen because parents refused to send their children to school; rather, compulsory school laws were not enforced and quite often Anglo schools refused to admit Mexican children. The rational for nonenforcement usually emphasized that the children would drop out anyway, so why enroll them? However, the reasoning had more to do with family labor and the unpaid labor of children than pedagogical considerations. According to one study, had the attendance laws been enforced in Texas, "planted crops would have been deserted by the hundreds." Further, "the fields would have grown up in weeds."[32] School districts in regions where the labor of children contributed to the prosperity of the area simply refused admittance for Mexican children, or they simply looked the other way when children worked in the fields during the school day.

Although California rural districts were subsidized by the state to open migrant schools, these in fact functioned mainly to baby-sit children for half of the school day, at which time they joined their parents or other relatives in the fields. Teachers in the migrant schools were ill trained or not trained at all, resources were scant, and massive overcrowding was the rule.[33] Many districts modified the school day for Mexican schools so that the labor of children would be available for certain harvests. In Orange County, California, for example, Mexican schools cut the hours to half a day during the walnut-picking season, so that children might work with their parents. Within the segregated environment, several practices created an atmosphere of severe discrimination. Americanization based largely on the Mexican Problem syndrome, combined with IQ testing, tracking, and industrial education, provided the key factors that comprised the educational program for Mexican children in the segregated setting. Each of these will be examined below.

AMERICANIZATION

The Los Angeles superintendent of schools, Susan Dorsey, lamented the Mexican Problem in the district's midst. In a 1923 meeting with district principals, Dorsey urged a campaign for resolving the problem:

> It is unfortunate and unfair for Los Angeles, the third-largest Mexican city in the world, to bear the burdens of taking care educationally of this enormous group. We do have to bear a spiritual burden quite disproportionate to the return from having this great number of aliens in our midst. This burden comes to us merely because we are near the border.

Later she would add, "We have these Mexican [immigrants] to live with, and if we can Americanize them, we can live with them."[34] No other objective loomed as large as the charge to Americanize Mexican immigrants and their children; school district after school district took up the burden of cleansing society of a potential cultural malady. As we look back on her statement, we see that she frankly delegated to her subordinates a program aimed at nothing less than the Americanization of the Mexican immigrant community. In a similar vein, Emory Bogardus warned his readers, just few years before Dorsey addressed the district principals, that "no Americanization program is complete which does not include the Mexican immigrant problem."[35] And by "Americanization," administrators and teachers intended the inculcation of "those ideals, customs, methods of living, skills and knowledge that have come to be accepted as representative of the best in American life."[36] Clearly, Mexicans were considered as lacking in that regard.

Eliminating the Mexican Problem, in the minds of most educators, above all else required the removal of the Spanish language, which would result in monolingual English-speaking children. Consequently, language instruction was central to virtually all Americanization programs, which meant the elimination of Spanish through a gradual increase in the exclusive use of English. Herschel Manuel quoted from a study on instruction of Mexican children in Texas, which claimed that "the first great problem in the work of Americanizing these children" was the teaching of English. Once the conversion to monolingual English speaking was complete, the subject underwent a wholesale and wholesome personality change:

The child whose vernacular is English has already acquired much of the culture of the American. Consciously, he is an American, and other Americans are his people, and his friends. He lives in an American atmosphere. Whatever goes on in his home and among his associates is American in tone and content. Not so the other [the non-English speaker]. His home reflects the culture, ideals, customs, thought and attitudes of another race and another people.[37]

The objective, the elimination of the Mexican Problem via English, required immersion classes and exacting methods of instruction. Thus, the first two years in the segregated schools were passed in Americanization rooms, but the remainder of the schooling experience continued the stress on Americanization. One teacher contended that Americanization via learning English was more than the teaching of an academic subject or the "requirements for the grade . . . it means teaching them how to live as well."[38]

Nothing of lasting value could be expected until the Mexican child acted, spoke, and thought like an American child. In the classroom and on the playground, if a student was caught speaking Spanish, punishment in some form was sure to follow. The child who learned to speak English not only fluently but also without accent earned extra praise and rewards. The child who failed to learn English or who spoke with a heavy accent constituted the laggard. Rewards and punishments followed the level of Americanization, as in one school district that held special picnics for those who were not cited for speaking Spanish on the school grounds. At the Harlingen Mexican School (Harlingen, Texas), the principal reported that only those children who spoke English consistently were eligible to join the English Club; the club enjoyed its own separate daily recess and an exclusive picnic every six weeks.[39] Other schools awarded badges that proclaimed "English Speaker" designed to motivate students along the path of English achievement and cultural enlightenment.

Just as language was assumed to be the key to Americanization in public schools, Protestant denominations decided that conversion to Protestantism and its ideals was the solution to the Mexican Problem. In cities across the Southwest, Protestant missions implemented their own version of Americanization, a process that had its origins in Mexico. Protestant leaders defined the Mexican Problem in religious terms, yet they critiqued the very same traits that the secular Americanizers critiqued, such as immorality, deceit, imitation, indolence, fatalism, thievery, and the like.[40] Indeed, not a few sociologists found the religion of Mexico incompatible with American ideals. One researcher noted that the Mexican im-

migrant has "been taught submission by the Church in Mexico, and patience and obedience by three generations of peonage there. Therefore,
the democratic form of government in the United States does not especially appeal to him."[41]

Conversion to Protestantism assumed a place alongside the public
schools' emphasis on language conversion. Like his Protestant missionary
colleagues, Jay Stowell defined the work of Protestant organizations such
as the Young Men's Christian Association in the barrios as "pure Americanization work done in the spirit of Christian service."[42] Stowell respected the presence of the Catholic Church enough to recognize its
dominance within the Mexican immigrant population. However, that institution's shortcomings inevitably influenced its followers. As Stowell
put it, it would be best for the

> Roman Catholic Church to frankly acknowledge her shortcomings in
> the past and embark upon an educational campaign to substitute a reli-
> gion of enlightenment for a religion of superstition; a religion of right-
> eousness for a religion of formality; a religion of service for one of moral
> and financial exploitation; a religion of Americanism for a religion of
> un-Americanism. . . . If she refuses someone else must do the job.[43]

Naturally, the Mexicans' Catholic religion made them unwitting agents of
un-Americanism and a negative influence in society.

Consequently, by the 1920s forty Protestant mission schools operated
in the border states from Texas to California, all bent on converting
and Americanizing Mexicans. Eighteen of these schools were boarding
schools, eight for girls, seven for boys, and three coeducational. Five of
the boarding schools were in major immigrant centers—Los Angeles, El
Paso, Tucson, Albuquerque, and Laredo. In addition, nearly four hundred Protestant centers of various kinds throughout the United States but
concentrated in the Southwest "carried on an active campaign of proselytizing."[44] Such activism by the Protestant churches, affirmed Stowell,
would bring about "higher ideals of life and conduct, a more wholesome
interpretation of God and of Jesus Christ, and an attitude of unadulter-
ated Americanism."[45] The same missionaries who praised railroads in
Mexico for their Americanizing influence somehow disregarded industrial influences in the United States as potential Americanization agents.
The missionaries' focus moved from a conversion of Mexico to Protestantism through the peaceful conquest to a religious conquest of Mexicans in the United States and their conversion to Protestantism, the religion of true Americans and the source of Americanization.

Protestant missionaries and the public schooling system also focused on adults who, like their children, were treated to emphatic doses of Americanization. Women in particular were subjected to added attention by school districts in California. Here settlement houses in urban and rural centers run by school districts and Protestant organizations such as the YMCA and YWCA emphasized the development of American conventions in the home, including the use of English, as well as customs related to child-rearing, cooking, housekeeping, gardening, and sexual mores. Women were particularly encouraged to attend afternoon classes in settlement houses and community centers, in the hope that they would become agents of community-wide Americanization via the home.[46] Men, on the other hand, were taught English skills that would make them more effective employees. In Southern California, Americanization teachers sought to inspire women to develop American housekeeping customs by having them visit a typical American home, and encouraged imitation of "good housekeeping" via prizes for homes most representative of the acceptable styles.[47] One teacher recommended that as one means of achieving lasting Americanization, students should be motivated to want neat surroundings:

> The lack of neat surroundings is one of the first facts that one notices in a Mexican settlement. Such a lack is considered by Americans as being decidedly undesirable. Consequently, the teacher in the school must attempt to instill in the Mexican child a love and desire for neat surroundings.
>
> Current magazines contain many pictures of neat homes and gardens. Such pictures may well be mounted on colored paper and displayed often. The children will always admire such pictures, and unconsciously improve their own conditions through this admiration.[48]

Whether Americanization focused on adults or children and was sponsored by public or religious agencies, the program was always based on the need to eliminate the Mexican Problem, that is, to reconstruct the culture of Mexican immigrants along the lines of the American norm, in order for them to socialize effectively in the organic society.

INTELLIGENCE TESTING AND TRACKING

The general agreement that Mexicans, in particular Mexican children, required a curricular program adjusted to their performance on IQ tests underscored the discussion on the educational programs best suited to Mexican children. Mexican children not only scored lower on intelligence tests but were also the subject of no less than fifty intelligence studies between 1912 and 1950. Half of the researchers blamed the genetic endowment of the community, while the remainder blamed the culture of the child. Some warned that the results were inconclusive and therefore recommended that the reader regard the conclusions with a healthy skepticism. Yet a well-grounded critique of the ability of any measurement to gauge the ability of a child to think abstractly was never published; all seemed mesmerized by the potential of science to devise a method for measuring something called IQ.

Some researchers carried out studies testing the influence of language, home environment and migration, yet the results were inconclusive. The matter seemed to rest on political bias rather than on hard data. If the bias leaned toward genetics, the researcher favored vocational or industrial education for Mexican children; if the researcher leaned toward a cultural bias, she/he prescribed the same vocational or industrial education. Either way, testing results indicated that the Mexican child was different and that this difference dictated a specific curricular program. Based on the widespread discussion of test outcomes, Chaffey (California) Unified School District superintendent Merton Hill explained that "pupils of Mexican peon parentage do not progress as well in the schools as do the American pupils, and . . . they cannot be expected normally to be more than 58% as successful in pursuing academic courses."[49] In tests administered in Los Angeles by the school district in the 1920s, Mexican children were found to score on average at 90, some 10 points below the norm.

In the modernized school system, the IQ test played a central role in assigning children to specific tracks and courses. In districts from Los Angeles to El Paso, a new bureaucracy characteristic of the modern school, the counseling center, moved to the center of the educational process. In the East Donna (Texas) school district, intelligence tests were administered to "all children annually under the guidance of the research director . . . who gives a generous portion of his time to the Mexican child," or so reported one observer. In the San Antonio school district, a school administrator noted that on the basis of the "distribution of intelligence," a curriculum matching that distribution was an absolute necessity. She found that, on the basis of standardized tests, "individual groupings of children have resulted most favorably in meeting individual needs."[50] The Needles (California) district superintendent summarized many educators' perspective. As he reported, there were three main problems in educating Mexican children. The first was language.

The second of these difficulties is the parentage of the children. Almost all of their parents are of the peon class and their standard of living is far below that of the average American family; their customs are much different from American customs; and probably most important of all, their intelligence as a whole is inferior to the average American intelligence.[51]

Peonism was buttressed by the lamentable scores made by Mexican children on intelligence tests. Our school superintendent was no voice in the wilderness. According to a University of Texas professor, "The average Mexican child was found to be fourteen months below the normal mental age development for white children. . . . Mexicans as a group possessed about 85 per cent of the intelligence of a similar group of white children." The research project also demonstrated that as the children grew older, the gap widened.[52] Science, or at least an exercise claiming to be science, had imprisoned Mexican children in an educational straitjacket. On the basis of test scores, tracking students into superior, normal, subnormal, and educationally mentally retarded classes became the norm, but for Mexican children, the majority was forced into curricular tracks least likely to lead to employment beyond the working class.

In Los Angeles, the Division of Research systematically reviewed student IQs across the district in order to identify individual abilities and then group students into curricular tracks corresponding to their intellectual levels. At least one half of all Mexican children qualified for slow-learner instruction and no less than 27 percent of all children branded educationally mentally retarded were Mexican, although Mexicans constituted only 13 percent of the total district population. In the mining town of Miami, Arizona, where large numbers of Mexican miners were imported to work, the school superintendent initiated a testing program aimed specifically at identifying the intellectual levels of Mexican students. On the basis a "mentality survey," he concluded:

> The consistent lagging of the Mexican groups behind other class-groups indicated the necessity of a specialized curriculum for these children, especially since it was evident that scarcely any of them ever reached high school.[53]

The scenario repeated itself in district after district.

VOCATIONAL EDUCATION

Writers on Mexico had long before made the point that Mexicans' ability to work with their hands distinguished them from other races. The "good with their hands" assertion found reinforcement in the rising dependency on IQ test scores for organizing the schooling enterprise. And just as writers on Mexico suggested that the educational programs aimed at American blacks seemed logical for Mexican peons, educators in the United States saw similar benefits in the old boot strap philosophy for the education of Mexican immigrants. The assistant superintendent of the Los Angeles schools likened the philosophy of Booker T. Washington's Tuskegee Institute to the program for "foreign people" in Los Angeles. In many ways, the training at Tuskegee and the training given at schools for Mexican children were parallel. The Los Angeles administrator was not alone in suggesting the model recommended for American blacks. Chaffey (California) school superintendent Merton Hill also recommended the implementation of the educational policy commonly recommended for the American black community. Hill observed:

> Comparisons between the Mexicans and negro pupils show that teachers consider them approximately on the same level. This is of value, for information regarding the development of negro education should prove useful in the development of Mexican education; as industrial education for negroes has proven most successful so should it prove for Mexican pupils.[54]

Schools across the Southwest uniformly emphasized vocational or industrial education for Mexican children as preparation for employment appropriate to the lower intellectual abilities they were assumed to have. Not only did school districts embrace vocational education for Mexican children, U.S. Office of Education publications affirmed that vocational education was particularly appropriate for Mexican children.[55]

Frequently, schools sidestepped IQ testing by placing Mexican children in what was considered "appropriate coursework" based on past performance of the children. As one Southern California elementary school principal noted, "The Mexican children's experiences have been so limited and their requirements so simple that it is extremely difficult to bring them to feel a need for learning." He therefore elaborated a program that emphasized "cooking for girls and woodshop for boys," which he thought would "satisfy a real need."[56] Note that the vocational coursework divided the work of boys and girls; this was done consistently across the board. A survey of thirty-two school districts across the Southwest that segregated Mexican children found a generalized emphasis on nonacademic coursework for Mexican children. The author of the survey reported:

> On several important points, the majority seem to be agreed. Segregation, of beginners at least, is now an accepted practice essential to the

most rapid progress of the Mexican child. The use of courses of study fitted to the needs and ability of the Mexican children is another requisite just as widely acclaimed. The introduction of manual and domestic arts at a lower level than is now practiced is the wish of a large majority who want the Mexican child to have the advantage of these courses before the early drop-out prevents them from receiving this important instruction.

The researcher (who, by the way, cited two of Wallace Thompson's books) added that where such practices have been instituted, "much progress has been made . . . in the solution of the Mexican problem."[57]

Arizona school administrators were advised by the State Department of Education to invest the Mexican child with vocational courses in the early grades. The reasoning was rather simple and straightforward, without recourse to mental tests. Vera Chase, professor of education at Arizona State Teachers College, advised the state's teachers that "a large part of the group will, under present conditions, engage in unskilled or semi-skilled labor." She recommended that, "because of the tendency to marry young, vocational training should be introduced early and homemaking should be an important part of the elementary course for both boys and girls."[58] An Arizona school principal applied just such an approach in his district. He cautioned teachers to recognize that "the overwhelming majority can never go beyond the eighth grade" and therefore required a substantially altered schooling program. He then offered a solution.

> The vocational school, such as is now located at Lowell School, is a step toward meeting the needs of those boys who cannot continue their education. The manual training and home economics departments are also striving to give the children training directly applicable to their own life situations. What we need is more such vocational schools with varied activities for both boys and girls to train them to do better the things they will very likely do any way out of life. Very few of them will reach the white-collared job. . . .[59]

Such approaches were not novel; schools throughout Southern California utilized the same method for Mexican children. In the Los Angeles schools, the district canvassed employers for information about the kinds of jobs open to Mexicans and on this basis established special courses training for the available occupations. Laundries employed Mexican women, so schools made an effort to train the "sub-normal" to operate ironing machines.[60] According to one report, Los Angeles provided schools for the educationally mentally retarded that enrolled all children scoring below 70 on their IQ tests; here vocational courses were the lone curricular track. One administrator wrote:

> Several employers have told us that a dull girl makes a very much better operator on a mangle that a normal girl. The job is purely routine and is irksome to persons of average intelligence, while the sub-normal seems to get actual satisfaction out of such a task. Fitting the person to the job reduces the "turnover" in industry and is, of course, desirable from an economic point of view.[61]

In some school districts, schools emphasized training young girls for domestic work in anticipation that either they would be raising families of their own or that, because of their low intellectual abilities, they would be employed in domestic service. One teacher wrote of her experience in teaching Mexican children: "Many girls will very likely find employment as house-servants. They should be taught something about cleaning, table setting, and serving." In her classroom, she prepared girls for a domestic vocation by having them "set the table with paper dishes, knives, and forks."[62] Domestic work and the social status inhering in this role, then, followed the women as they crossed the border into the United States.

Vocational coursework, it was argued, matched the abilities, cultural predisposition, and needs of the Mexican children. One teacher recommended that courses for Mexican youths should, among other things, "provide for much handwork." She based her observation on the widespread belief that "Mexicans for centuries have been hand workers. In this kind of work they can feel success and with it, happiness."[63] So deeply ingrained was the emphasis on handwork that not a few districts referred to their junior high and high schools for Mexican students as the industrial schools of the district. San Antonio's Lanier Junior High was just such a school. The San Antonio district *Bulletin* noted that "motor minded ability seems to be a social characteristic with all the Latin peoples," and, not surprisingly, the Lanier Mexican school stressed this stereotype. The junior high offered "home making, and industrial activities," meaning "sewing, cooking and art work for girls; machine shop practice, auto repair, auto painting, top making, and sheet metal work, plain bench and cabinet work in wood and a department in which type-setting and job printing are taught for boys."[64]

But some thought that although Mexicans might have a natural predisposition for handwork, the problem of educating them went deeper than merely providing industrial training. One teacher wrote that since "the child is naturally inclined to be lazy, and almost all Mexicans are, he cannot see why he should bother with his [school] work."[65] Variations on the cultural predisposition thesis excluded academic work, as the author of an article in *Texas Outlook* argued. She contended that the "English-speaking child finds academic standards everywhere the ruling standards. Whereas the Spanish-speaking child isolated in the little Mexican community finds everything to the contrary." Only one curricular option, the "standards of the work-a-day world," made any sense for Mexican child. Under such inexorable limitations outlined by the two studies, only basic vocational coursework made any sense.[66]

Educators always believed that in providing schools that emphasized vocational coursework, a public service was performed for the Mexican community. By fitting the school to the child, it was contended, success rather than failure faced the Mexican child—and not just personal success, but success that the community could readily benefit from. The school superintendent at Miami, Arizona, made this approach one of the main features of his district. He spoke for many school administrators in his appraisal of his district's program for Mexican children. "When it is recalled," he wrote,

> that the children of the Mexican laborers in the mines of the district almost invariably drop out after the sixth year to take up unskilled manual labor or to set up homes of their own, it will be readily appreciated that the schools owe it to these children to provide them with definite training in this direction in place of condemning them to failure, discouragement, and early elimination by confining their school training to the traditional course of study looking toward high school entrance and graduation.[67]

In this very same spirit, the principal at the San Fernando School for Mexican Children, near Los Angeles, petitioned the school district to officially change the name of the school to the San Fernando Mexican Industrial School. He argued that with the name change a greater emphasis could be given to courses that could "better fit the boys and girls to meet the problems of life in the future years." Girls were to be given "extensive sewing, knitting, crocheting, drawn work, rug weaving and pottery. They will be taught personal hygiene, home-making, care of the sick. With the aid of a nursery they will learn the care of little children. The boys will given more advance agriculture and shop work of various kinds."[68]

Interestingly, the Protestant schools stressed vocational work as well. At the Kingsville Texas-Mexican Institute, half of the day was spent on academic subjects in the schoolroom. For the remainder of the day, girls were taught "various household arts," and the boys were instructed on a "well-equipped farm." Jay Stowell mentioned that at the Protestant schools, many "have wood-working or other manual training." As at the Lanier Junior High in San Antonio, the Lydia Patterson Institute in El Paso offered vocational courses—printing, carpentry, tailoring, shoe repairing, and auto shop. When it came to the Mexican Problem, Americanization, and vocational education, officials guiding the Protestant schools walked the same path as those directing the public schools.

REFORMING THE EDUCATIONAL PRESCRIPTION

A minority of educators who critiqued the main recommendations for solving the Mexican Problem contended that, among other things, segregation retarded rather than promoted Americanization. These voices contended that by mixing with Anglo American children, Mexican children would learn by imitating those who had already learned appropriate cultural practices. However, practically none of the critics ever suggested that Americanization was unwarranted or that vocational education was unnecessary. The main themes of the few reformers dealt with the efficacy of IQ exams for a child whose language and cultural background were different from those for whom the tests were developed. Here the challenge was not to the validity of IQ testing; instead, the criticism was aimed at the wholesale acceptance of the test scores for purposes of predicting the school performance of Mexican children. Herschel Manuel maintained that the tests were inconclusive. He urged that the results be interpreted with caution and that educators, rather than stampeding to employ the tests for tracking, await further research in the matter. He also went a step further to argue that there were reasons to believe that the distribution of intelligence among Mexicans paralleled that of white children.

Manuel was almost alone in his critique of IQ tests and, together with George Sanchez, was one of the few to suggest that intelligence was equally distributed among Mexican children and white children. However, like Sanchez, Manuel did not challenge the potential of tests to measure intelligence; his only complaint was that culturally and linguistically different children were unfairly discriminated against. The best that Manuel could do was to raise doubts but not tackle the Mexican Problem head on. And so he wrote:

> (1) Much of the descriptive material in the field of racial psychology, including that of the Mexican, is to be taken with a great deal of caution.
> . . . .
> (4) The factors responsible for the generally unfavorable standing of the Mexican children in Texas schools are many, and much additional

work is needed to disentangle them. Among them are the following: (a) the lack of knowledge of the English language; (b) the low socio-economic status and cultural level of a large proportion of the population; (c) . . . inferior school opportunities; (d) possibly inferior heredity of a considerable number—the present writer thinks that this factor may be easily overestimated and alleged to be the critical factor in cases in which it is not; (e) unsuitability of our measuring instruments to reveal clearly the extent and nature and differences in racial groups.[69]

The matter of testing remained open to discussion; meanwhile, the overwhelming indictment of Mexicans as a problem for the schools stood its ground. Manuel presented little damaging criticism concerning reliance on the tests, and although Manuel can be credited with critiquing the generalized labeling of Mexican children as particularly gifted with their hands as a specious argument at best, the practice prevailed. Indeed, the Mexican Problem had become institutionalized and took on a life of its own, a deeply ingrained contention upheld by school administrators and academics as well. In many ways, the Mexican Problem foreshadowed the culturally deprived child thesis that surfaced in the late 1950s and which informed the Great Society policies of the late 1960s.

Critics of the educational policies directed at the Mexican immigrant community were few, and these were virtually ignored. From the early 1900s into the late 1960s, Mexican culture was considered a barrier to success in American society and was countered by the combination of IQ testing, tracking, and vocational education. In the minds of educators, Mexican culture explained the Mexican Problem. The only practice that became subject to substantive change was the use of the segregated Mexican school as a means to prepare Mexican children for an integrated schooling experience (which seldom occurred). Here the credit can be given to the Mexican parents who rose across the Southwest to challenge the constitutionality of segregation. *Mendez v. Westminster*, a 1946 California case, stands as one of the nation's first constitutional challenges to the racial segregation of a people on the basis of the "separate but equal" doctrine.[70] The community's courage in the face of the power of the state and tradition has been recognized. Unfortunately, the imperial political context within which the segregated and discriminatory practices appeared has not been appreciated.

Despite the advance, which was uneven across the Southwest as de facto segregation took the form once filled by de jure segregation, the curriculum content and the image of Mexican culture as antithetical to success in the United States continued to reverberate in the board of education meeting halls. Americanization remained a major objective, vocational education stood its ground, the assertion that Mexicans were "good with their hands" remained, their scores on IQ exams continued below those of the general population, and the dropout rates in high school improved but little. Anthropological theorists of the postwar era repeated the phrase that Mexican culture stood in contradiction to the basic values that prevailed across the United States. Margaret Mead, for example, contended that Mexicans "accepted schooling but not the 'Anglo' motivation for education—the higher standard of living, the better job. . . . They [Mexicans] choose and reject according to their system of values."[71] Mead was not the only anthropologist to place the responsibility for lack of achievement on the Mexican community. Florence Kluckhohn stressed the wide divide between a culture of achievement and a culture of failure, or the Mexican Problem. In a presentation before a meeting of social workers she argued:

> We cannot simultaneously expect the diversity of Mexican cultural orientations and expect Mexicans to become well enough assimilated for at least some sizable proportion of them to become successful Americans. Mexican orientations—in our system—assure very little for individuals except a lack of mobility and a general lower class status.[72]

One example from a doctoral dissertation written in 1942 exemplifies the general trend in the graduate student literature. In his University of Texas doctoral dissertation on the education of Mexicans in Texas, Perry M. Broom described some of the generalized behavior patterns of Mexicans: "Tendencies toward imitation, conservatism, submission to authority, and emotional instability all color the 'Mexican' personality."[73] Even as late as 1957, graduate students were citing Wallace Thompson. One thesis, "A Survey of the Problems Involved in the Americanization of the Mexican American," cited Thompson as an authority in a section titled "The Mexican Temperament." The author wrote, "Thompson indicated that the Mexican psychology of learning is not one of creative thinking but rather, of imitation."[74] The same author went on to discuss the "mañana spirit," which he described as "symbolic of the Mexican people. . . . a reluctance to hurry, apathy, and hopelessness." Another thesis on approaches to teaching Mexican adolescents, presented in the same year, emphasized that "most Mexicans who are now residing in California belonged to the lowest peon class in Mexico." This fixed a definition in the minds of the reader of the subject. The author then pointed out that educators generally believed the Mexican to be "lazy, greasy, rough, aggressive, crude and he lies, steals, and cheats." Furthermore, the propensity to steal originated in "differences in culture."[75] The same litany of cultural deficiencies first observed in the late nineteenth century had stood its ground to the middle of the twentieth century.

The same contentions that appeared in the graduate studies filtered into the popular media and public policy. Like the professional travelers who had preceded him by half a century or more, the editor of the *San Diego Union* (California), James Clifford Safley, wrote a series of articles on his travels through Mexico and published them in the *Union* in 1952. The editor traversed the same images that had long been fixed upon Mexico and Mexicans. "Latin temperaments," he wrote, "wax hot in conflict and are slow to cool in the ashes of defeat." But, once having established that the Latin temperament distinguished Mexicans from the reader, he then reviewed the sum total of distinctive characteristics. Mexicans were "courteous . . . patient, tolerant." Mexicans fell "into three racial groups—the creoles, the mestizos . . . and the Indians." Mestizos were a "new type of people, biologically and socially." More important, Mexico badly needed Americanization. Of one Mexican state governor's administration, Safley commented that "he would let them [citizens] loose from their lethargy and introduce them to American ways of accomplishments." Of another state without an Americanization process, the editor commented, "These folk seem to be content with their lot, for seldom do they strive to improve their condition."[76]

One last example of the unquestioned use of the Mexican Problem syndrome appeared during the anti-Mexican riots that occurred in Los Angeles in the early 1940s with the backing of the local police and news media. Los Angeles Police Captain Duran Ayres issued a report that repeated the ideas that rolled from the works of Thompson et al. Ayres was quoted as indicting Mexican youth and the Mexican community as a whole for behavioral aberrations rooted in the biological history. "The Caucasian," he intoned,

especially the Anglo-Saxon, when engaged in fighting, particularly among youths, resorts to fisticuffs and [they] may at times kick each other, which is considered unsportive: but this Mexican element considers all that to be a sign of weakness, and all he knows and feels is a desire to use a knife or some lethal weapon. In other words, his desire is to kill, or at least let blood. That is why it is difficult for the Anglo-Saxon to understand the psychology of the Indian or even the Latin, and it is just as difficult for the Indian or the Latin to understand the psychology of the Anglo-Saxon of those from northern Europe. When there is added to this inborn characteristic that has come down through the ages the use of liquor, then we certainly have crimes of violence.[77]

All of these factors are critical to explaining the rise of the Chicano school reform movement of the 1960s. In the perspective of the civil rights activists of the time, the Mexican Problem that Carey McWilliams had critiqued, and its supposed panacea—Americanization, testing, and vocational education—were an institutionalized form of discrimination. In the minds of Chicano generation activists, these practices were the real culprits behind the achievement differential separating the dominant society from ethnic Mexicans. Despite the anger and concerted action to create fundamental educational reforms, the basic educational problems that faced the Mexican immigrant community in the 1960s remained to the end of the twentieth century and the beginning of the twenty-first.

CONCLUSION

Mexican immigrants experienced the U.S. empire in two of its major settings: in an economic colony as their country became economically a part of the U.S. empire, and at the imperial center when they entered the United States. As migrants crossed into the United States, the imperial perspective on Mexicans, constructed by a host of American writers, entered into public policy discourses and assisted in informing public policy makers about the character of the Mexican immigrants and methods to socialize that community. Policy concerning the education of immigrants was further influenced by the fact that the United States was in the throes of modernizing its educational institutions and political cultural ethos, greatly impacted by the emerging corporate capitalist order. The writings about Mexico and the Mexican immigrants, together with the changing U.S. educational system, in no small measure contributed to the formation of the educational experience of the immigrant community, which differed from that experienced by other nationalities in the United States.

The culture of empire modified the educational experience in important ways. Educators in particular had ready access to writings by academic writers regarding the culture and predisposition of the average Mexican immigrant—the crux of the Mexican Problem—and shaped schooling policy in accordance with this information. Unfortunately, the educational materials they availed themselves of provided a set of characteristics of the Mexican that were virtually identical to those of the original American writers on Mexico—for example, Nevin O. Winter, Wallace Thompson, Frederick Starr, and George B. Winton. Such writings were appropriated freely by those charged with educational policy relating to the Mexican community.

The ethnic Mexican historical experience originated in empire and continues to be influenced by the same economic linkages that William Rosecrans set out to establish more than a century ago. The "peaceful conquest" has undergone a number of euphemistic changes of terminology—first to "indissoluble linkages" and "interdependence," and today to "globalization" and "transnationalism." Regardless of the language touch-ups, U.S. foreign policy geared to economic domination has not changed. The images originating from the economic ties binding Mexico to the United States continue to perpetuate the educational experiences found across the Southwest and the nation in relation to the ethnic Mexican community. The historical period entered into in the late nineteenth century marked by the rise of Mexican immigration and the immigrants' economic, social, and political integration, has yet to play itself out. We in the twenty-first century are experiencing that peaceful conquest and living out its social and political consequences.

CONCLUSION

The preceding chapters have presented an entirely different approach to understanding the history of the ethnic Mexican community. The American economic empire, it was argued, is central to an effective historical accounting of the ethnic Mexican peoples. In other words, the United States empire and the history of the ethnic Mexican community are inseparable. In contrast to the cultural approach that traditionally places race and racism at the explanatory center and that usually remains within a national framework, an approach that has strongly influenced the literature, this interpretation focuses on the American economic empire and its imperial dominion over Mexico since the late nineteenth century. In addition, the present study disputes those historical accounts which assert that Chicano history begins with the Mexican-American War of 1848, and that a set of institutionalized public policies and social relations have governed ever since. The present approach argues that the Mexican immigrant community is a twentieth-century phenomenon and that the histories of the conquered Spanish-Mexican settlers must be separated from twentieth-century Mexican immigration in order to fully comprehend the origins and historical evolution of the Mexican immigrant community.

To demonstrate the significance of empire and its importance for explaining the history of the ethnic Mexican community, this work explored the late nineteenth century imperial agenda and activities of Americans involved in shaping the economic expansion of U.S. capital into Mexico. The motive mentioned in the literature for embarking on this "American invasion" of Mexico (as some writers referred to the policy) was the excess of capital and the need to export the surplus as a means of preventing economic stagnation and class tensions at home. Further, just as a policy of capital export and the acquisition of natural resources for cheapening industrial production at home rather than territorial conquest formed the core of the colonial expansionary policies followed by the European colonial powers in the latter nineteenth century, the U.S.

imperial expansion, which began around the 1880s, took the form of an economic rather than a territorial colonization. Much like the British in relation to their colonial possessions, Americans legitimized their expansionist adventures by the self-proclaimed burden of civilizing and "uplifting" less-developed peoples. In other words, the United States launched a foreign policy that largely corresponded to the imperialist endeavors, in an economic and cultural sense, carried out by European powers.

By the turn of the twentieth century, American capital was firmly in command of the key sectors of the Mexican economy, so that the vital sectors of Mexico's national economy came under foreign control. For example, practically the whole of Mexico's mining operations, oil production, rail transport, and key agricultural regions fell under American direction by 1900. Despite the nationalistic and anti-American rhetoric accompanying the 1910 Mexican Revolution, the civil war failed to weaken U.S. influence, and by 1930 the United States held a greater hand in the Mexican economy than it had twenty years previously.

This study is based in its entirety on published writings by Americans, some of whom wrote on Mexico and others on Mexican immigrants. The analysis begins with an examination of a sizable cross section of American writers who addressed themselves to the issues of Mexico. Publications written by diplomats, statesmen, politicians, missionaries, travelers, and retired mining engineers, among others, examined practically every dimension of Mexico, from its biocultural history to its fauna, from its flora to its meteorology and geography. By far, the varied peoples of Mexico and their cultures provided the favorite themes.

What caught the eye of Americans as they traveled in Mexico were the vast cultural differences that separated Americans from Mexicans, and consequently they attempted to define and explain these differences. Americans depicted Mexicans as a hopeless people entangled in a web of cultural and biological pathologies that prevented a self-generated evolution to a modern or higher national culture. Rather than continually repeat the litany of cultural deviations from more highly civilized societies, the phrase "the Mexican Problem" as an explanatory shortcut came into general use.

Writers marveled at the apparent parallels of Mexicans with Egyptians, Indians, and Chinese, who were all then identified as Orientals. Some went so far as to claim that Mexicans were closely related to Orientals, asserting that the Oriental and the Mexican shared many fundamental characteristics, from traditional customs to forms of thinking (both were described as inscrutable). Although one can follow the Mexican as Oriental theme into the 1920s, eventually the more popular term "peon" overtook "Oriental." But the two terms meant the same to American observers. In their respective contexts, "peon" to Americans and "Oriental" to the British meant an adult with a child's mental capacity. And thus the identification of Mexicans as a childlike mass became a common theme in the literature. Consequently, Mexico, a nation of adolescents, required foreign tutelage in order to achieve parity with the industrialized nations. And, of course, Americans selected themselves as tutors for the Mexican transition to national adulthood.

The examination of this literature offers a new perspective on American writing about Mexico and the culture of empire that writers produced. The ideas and images of Mexico eventually became a part of America's popular culture, including film, music, and news media. However, these publications proved more than just an informational tool for those interested in Mexico; the publications came into prominent use for understanding Mexican immigrants after the mass Mexican migrations that began in the first decade of the twentieth century, a social consequence resulting from American capital investments. The extensive and influential body of literature published by American authors impacted deeply on the consciousness of the American public and influenced their perception of Mexican immigrants. The culture of empire developed by a host of American writers did not remain focused on Mexico; it was put into service in the United States for entirely different ends than originally intended by the writers. As Mexican migrants crossed the border, that literature was used to define them.

Migrants integrated into the American economy, performing the labor traditionally reserved for the unskilled and poorest sectors of the American working class, and settled into barrios across the Southwest and Midwest. As migrants proceeded into the core of the industrial economy, public policy makers, from local educators to federal officials, sought an information base to consult in drawing up policies requisite for this new immigrant group. They did not need to search for long. The body of literature on Mexico by American writers was quickly located, and became the informational base that instructed the policy-making community. The speed and ease with which this literature merged into the decision-making boardrooms and influenced the discourse on Mexican immigrants demonstrated the power of imperial cultural writings in constructing domestic policy. This study has focused on the importance of the literature on Mexico in shaping the educational practices applied to the Mexican immigrants. However, it should be kept in mind that the culture of empire did not emerge solely from the imagination of the writers; it was spawned by the economic conquest. The cultural production of authors intent on identifying the keys to understanding Mexico for an American audience, and thereby expanding the economic conquest, eventually served as the keys to understanding the Mexican immigrant. The culture of empire, originally intended to rationalize and demonstrate the efficacy of the American economic empire, later became a means to construct a public policy that served to dominate the Mexican immigrant community and preserve its class status as cheap labor. Nowhere else is that domination so evident as in the public education system.

Educators en masse opted to utilize the writings on Mexico as authoritative sources for information on Mexicans. A wide range of works were incorporated into policy studies, as well as graduate theses written by aspiring school administrators who would later be responsible for the educational programs directed at Mexican immigrants. The literature on Mexico was more than simply a source of information; it was cited and quoted repeatedly, and its representations of Mexico, Mexican culture, and Mexicans in general were incorporated without question into public policy discourses and enactments. Mexican children were segregated partially on the reasoning that Mexicans were culturally polar opposites of Americans and that this difference constituted the Mexican Problem, so that Mexican children could not be integrated with Anglo American children until they were Americanized. Not surprisingly, the argument for the Americanization of Mexico was found throughout the literature on Mexico. Following the prescriptions for salvaging Mexico, American educational officials allowed that a Mexican Problem in the form of a lack of ambition, propensity of handwork, lower moral standards, apathy, and so on could only be resolved through Americanization and a training program adapted to the Mexicans' peculiar abilities. The same cultural stereotypes summed up in the Mexican Problem and used to argue the necessity of the Americanization of Mexico were employed to recommend the Americanization of the Mexican immigrant community.

Mexicans were considered particularly adept at handwork, artistry, music, dance, and singing, but when it came to intellectual ability, Mexicans fell noticeably behind the average American. Dozens of research projects repeated the assertion that Mexicans were "good with their hands but weak with their brains." Given the information gleaned from the alleged experts on Mexico and Mexicans, educators generally upheld segregation and nonacademic training in the form of industrial training as the appropriate school experiences for Mexican children. At school, boys and girls were separated for distinct training programs, with boys in industrial shops and girls in homemaking and domestic training classes. In general, Mexican children were afforded an education commonly reserved for slow learners and educationally mentally retarded students. The training for Mexican children also depended extensively on IQ testing and tracking. But most school practices relied on the common wisdom, collected over the decades, that Mexicans were different and therefore a special educational program adapted to this difference was needed. Often schools dispensed with testing, given the widespread notion that Mexican children were foreordained for the nonacademic levels of the educational mission. Of course, this meant vocational course work, which in many school districts began in the early years of elementary school continued until graduation for children who did not drop out, at which time the graduates would pursue vocational work. Most, however, dropped out long before reaching the twelfth grade.

Community-based and other reformers intending to strike down the extensive practice of segregation were successful in the mid-1940s challenges to the odious practice. Yet the institutionalized reliance on specious, at best, interpretations of Mexican culture and the emphasis on Americanization and vocational training remained. As late the 1950s and 1960s, Americanization, IQ testing, and tracking into vocational coursework remained the staple approach undertaken for ethnic Mexican children in America's public schools. Mexican culture still struck a discordant chord among educators, and images of Mexicans that were first broadcast at the turn of the century were still recycling in the popular mind at midcentury. And while Mexican immigration, migrant integration into the economy as cheap labor, community settlement, and Americanization were issues of major importance in the 1900 to 1930 period, in the first years of the twenty-first century these have remained key topics for political discussion. These factors continue to impact on the unceasing formation and re-formation of the ethnic Mexican community and its political agenda. In addition, the portrayal of Mexicans in ways that mimic the images constructed by American writers in the 1880 to 1930 period are evident today.

The term "peon" assumed new uses within the American lexicon and came to mean someone occupying a position of powerlessness or of employment at the lowest level of the corporate hierarchy. Haven't we all heard the common indictment "He's just a peon"? During the 1940s and 1950s, the term "wetback" meant Mexican, but the meaning metamorphosed into illegal aliens in the 1970s and has been used since then to indicate an invasion of unwelcome peoples. Each term depicted Mexican immigrants as carriers of an oppositional culture, of disease, crime, drugs, and public service parasitism. What is common to both terms is that each represented a migrant population integrated into the core of the American economy as a major sector of the workforce, as maids, nannies, busboys, factory workers, agricultural workers, day laborers and more. Working for minimal wages, they were able to manage poverty, and each was abhorred.

Arousing fears of illegal aliens served as a political ploy to stimulate a rollback of the educational reforms passed during the 1960s and 1970s. Americanization as a response to the increasing numbers of Mexican immigrants reared its head, and a concerted effort was made to remove all bilingual education policies and practices and to return to the English immersion classes of the 1930s. However, just as the economic domination exercised by the United States over Mexico remains stronger than ever, so the Mexican Problem has not gone away but simply been institutionalized.[1] At the threshold of the twenty-first century, the negative images of Mexico and Mexicans, and consequently of the ethnic Mexican community, continue to guide policy makers all along the line. How else does one explain the stampede to pass California's Proposition 187, legislation to bar undocumented immigrant children from public schools, or to create the immigrant control project Operation Gatekeeper (which led to the deaths of thousands of migrants), or to end affirmative action and bilingual education across the nation?

In looking back at the twentieth century, the Mexican economy has become ever more subordinate to the United States and the peaceful conquest has become a reality. The principal industries and employers in Mexico are American corporations, which operate thousands of assembly plants mainly in the northern Mexican states and employ over one million low-wage workers, mainly women. Foreigners dominate the banking system; Citibank Corporation recently purchased Banamex, the largest independent bank of Mexico, and in the process formed the largest financial entity in Latin America. Wal-Mart is the largest retailer in the country. Budweiser owns 50.2 percent of the famous Mexican brewer Grupo Modelo. Meanwhile, Mexico is in debt to foreign lenders to the tune of 160 billion dollars. At the beginning of the twenty-first century, studies show that over 60 percent of the Mexican population lives in poverty (by the standards of Mexico)—the unemployment rate hovers at about 30 percent. And for the fortunate ones, maquila employment means a forty-eight hour workweek that ensures poverty wages and living in shack towns.

The North American Free Trade Agreement, signed in 1993 and touted by the leaders in Washington and elites in Mexico City as a neoliberal boost for Mexico and the United States, promoted one goal above all others: an open door for U.S. capital. Formerly protected state-run businesses such as the air carriers Mexicana and Aeroméxico are now on the auction block (with American, Continental, and Delta expressing keen interest). Other than maquila employment, no NAFTA-propelled economic boost has occurred in Mexico; on the contrary, a disastrous economic depression fell across the nation, causing the middle classes to shrink significantly. And, just as happened at the turn of the twentieth century, U.S. corporations are using low-wage labor, enjoying special governmental protections, and administering and supervising the operations. In the early twentieth century, Mexico became a large exporter of metals and minerals, which were integrated into U.S. industrial production. In the early twenty-first century, Mexico serves as a huge manufacturing site and export platform for goods consumed in the United States. In each case, Americans, not Mexicans, are in charge.

As in the early twentieth century, today's migrants are pushed off their traditional lands by policies shaped by American corporate interests. Mexico's corn farmers are reeling from an influx of cheap U.S. agricultural products that NAFTA enabled to enter Mexico. Today, Mexico allows the annual importation of 2.5 million tons of corn; by the year 2008 there will be no limit to corn importation. Sugarcane producers are similarly affected by the mass import of corn sweeteners from the United States. Small farmers throughout the southern nation are being ruined. They leave their farmlands and their communities and migrate to the cities, causing the widespread abandonment of villages across rural Mexico and the urban overcrowding that John Kenneth Turner attested to in the first decade of the twentieth century. If today's migrants find employment in a maquila plant along the northern border, they will probably eventually migrate to the United States, where they will integrate into the American economy as cheap and easily disposable labor, like millions before them in the past hundred years. In Mexico they are cheap labor for American corporations; in the United States they are cheap labor for American corporations. Meanwhile, they endure the same disdain that has been visited upon Mexican migrants for a century and enter into society that discusses at length the cultural and political dangers posed by the latest version of peon, the "illegal alien."

The recent discussions between the Mexican government and the Bush administration over recreating the old Bracero Program under the sanitized euphemism "Guest Worker Program" indicate the continuing economic domination exerted by the United States over Mexico. Whether or not the plans—regarded by some as a security response to the terrorist attack of September 11, 1901—go forward, the reality is that Mexican labor remains critical to U.S. production. Mexican labor continues integrated into the American economy at the lowest wages possible, and if the Guest Worker Program is enacted the old figure of the wetback will surely surface and overtake the illegal alien image. The Mexican government, under the administration of a former Coca-Cola executive, has made it known that it will provide cheap, disposable labor to do the most arduous types of agricultural work, no matter what the outcome of the Guest Worker Program may be. For a hundred years this has been the experience of Mexican immigrant labor; the only difference between then and now is that the Mexican government under free trader Vicente Fox has declared migrants "heroes." This encomium will afford little change in the economic integration of Mexican migrants, whether legal or not, as they will remain on the lowest, cheapest rungs of labor.

In the course of Chicano history over the twentieth century, there has been much more continuity than change, continuity grounded in the economic domination of the United States over Mexico. The empire has spurred continued, ever increasing migrations, as well as the integration of the migrants at the lowest-paid levels of the U.S. economy and their settlement in barrios. Along the Texas-Mexico border alone, at least 1,800 poverty-ridden colonias are home to hundreds of thousands of Mexican immigrants who, as one commentator noted, "remain out of sight." A resident of the Cameron Park colonia described how non-Mexicans imagine the residents: "When they hear 'Cameron Park' they think, 'trouble.'"[2] We continue to find the general scorn that has been persistently directed at Mexican migrants for the past hundred years, as well as a continuation of the educational experiences first encountered in the early 1900s: segregation, tracking into vocational courses, unequal outcomes, and a reproduction of the class standing of the Mexican community. In the final analysis, the historical epoch experienced by Mexican migrants in the first decades of the twentieth century has not played itself out and persists into the twenty-first. In reviewing the early twentieth century experiences of the Chicano community we survey a process that is evident today; and when we study contemporary ethnic Mexicans we explore experiences lived over the past century. Explaining this historical condition requires centering the American economic empire and its domination of the nation of Mexico.

NOTES

Introduction

1. Gilbert G. González, "The System of Public Education and Its Function in the Chicano Community in Los Angeles, 1920–1930," Ph.D. dissertation, University of California, Los Angeles, 1974; Gilbert G. González, *Chicano Education in the Era of Segregation*.

2. This is not the first study to examine the culture of empire; however, it is the first to study its expression in relation to Mexico in a systematic fashion. A host of authors have, in varying degrees, dealt with the construction of negative stereotypes of Mexican and Latin American culture. See, for example, the following works which explore the culture evoked by Americans in Mexico and Latin America: John Mason Hart, *Empire and Revolution: The Americans in Mexico since the Civil War*, 43–45; Lars Schoultz, *Beneath the United States: A History of U.S. Policy toward Latin America*; and Emily S. Rosenberg, *Financial Missionaries to the World: The Politics and Culture of Dollar Diplomacy, 1900–1930*.

3. Novelists were of lesser significance in the production of a practical culture of empire, that is, a culture of empire that could easily translate into public policy. Among the analytical works on novelists writing on Mexico see, for example, Helen Delpar, *The Enormous Vogue of Things Mexican: Cultural Relations between the United States and Mexico, 1920–1935*; Drewey Wayne Gunn, *American and British Writers in Mexico, 1556–1973*; and Edward Simmen, *Gringos in Mexico*. The reader will notice that the analyses undertaken by these authors leave out any discussion of empire.

4. Amy Kaplan, "'Left Alone with America': The Absence of Empire in the Study of American Culture," in Amy Kaplan and Donald E. Pease, eds., *Cultures of United States Imperialism*.

5. The work of John Mason Hart, historian and specialist on Mexico, is a notable exception to the rule among academics to ignore empire in their analyses, and Hart decidedly is not from the far right. See Hart's *Empire and Revolution*. For a different theoretical approach, see Ramón Eduardo Ruiz, *The People of Sonora and Yankee Capitalists*. Ruiz opts to employ dependency theory to identify U.S.-Mexico relations. Dependency theory, however, is significantly different from the theory of empire. Dependency theory contends that the world has become one large capitalist enterprise with some large capitalists and other, small ones, and that an imbalance of trade is the cause of underdevelopment. However, empire as it is used here refers to imperial domination via financial capital in the form of

loans from international bankers—WTO and World Bank, for example—and investment capital, such as assembly plants along the U.S.-Mexico border, that dominates the internal economic resources of the subject nation. American imperial capital, and not merely trade imbalance, shapes the contours of the Mexican economy.

6. Cited in "Reject Calls for an 'American Empire,'" editorial, *Orange County (Calif.) Register*, October 15, 2001.

7. William Rusher, "U.S. Too Big for Other Countries to Like Us," *Pasadena Star News*, June 5, 2001.

8. See Emily Eakin, "All Roads Lead to D.C.," *New York Times*, March 31, 2002. Eakin writes, "Today America is no mere superpower or hegemony but a full-blown empire in the Roman and British sense. That, at any rate, is the consensus of some of the nation's most notable commentators and scholars." What Eakin fails to note is that this consensus comes from the conservative wing of the political spectrum. What she did document is the respectability with which empire is coming to be treated.

9. Quoted in Robin Wright, "Urgent Calls for Peace in Mideast Ring Hollow As Prospects Dwindle," *Los Angeles Times*, March 31, 2002. The person quoted is Geoffrey Kemp, Mideast policy chief at the National Security Council under President Ronald Reagan.

10. Charles J. Weeks, "The New Frontier, the Great Society, and American Imperialism in Oceania," *Pacific Historical Review* 71, no. 1 (February 2002).

11. A glaring example of the reluctance to develop the field of empire studies, particularly U.S. empire studies, can be found in the flagship journal for historians in the United States, the *Journal of American History*. There is no category for empire in the "Recent Scholarship" section contained in each issue. One may find the latest work on topics related to education, colonial and revolutionary periods, family, civil war and reconstruction, international relations, and more—but nothing on empire. Apparently, the U.S. empire is not a common subject for research, although film studies merits a section.

12. The United States has militarily invaded other nations on at least eighty-four separate occasions over the course of the twentieth century; this number does not count the various declared wars and "police actions" but does include numerous surreptitious actions of the CIA. Source: U.S. Congress, Committee on Foreign Affairs, *Background Information on Use of United States Armed Forces in Foreign Countries*, 91st Congress, 2nd Session (1970).

13. Trumbull White, *Our New Possessions: A Graphic Account, Descriptive and Historical, of the Tropic Islands of the Sea Which Have Fallen under Our Sway, Their Cities, Peoples and Commerce, Natural Resources and the Opportunities They Offer to Americans*, 17. On the title page, White is characterized as "The well known author, historian, war correspondent and traveler—author of 'Our War with Spain for Cuba's Freedom,' etc., etc." White was by no means alone in correctly identifying, then praising, the imperial forays. Writing in *Forum* 26 (September 1898), John R. Proctor submitted that "from the blood of our heroes, shed at Santiago and Manila, there shall arise a New Imperialism, replacing the waning Imperialism of Old Rome; an Imperialism destined to carry world-wide the principles of Anglo-Saxon peace and justice, liberty and law." Cited in Richard E. Welch, Jr., *Imperialists vs. Anti-Imperialists: The Debate over Expansionism in the 1890s*, 26.

14. See, for example, John Dewey's article written after visiting Mexico and published in the *New Republic* in 1926. Dewey never mentioned the word "empire," nor did he castigate in any significant fashion the overwhelming presence of American investments in Mexico. Dewey seemed ill at ease with, as he said, "the contact of a people having an industrialized, Anglo-Saxon psychology with a people of Latin psychology . . . [it] is charged with high explosives." The philosopher urged American investors to take a more sensitive approach when investing in Mexico, an approach that would render "good relations between the two countries." John Dewey, "From a Mexican Notebook," *New Republic* 48 (October 20, 1926): 241. Dewey's contention stood squarely within the framework of the Anti-Imperialist League's platform, which defined imperialism as territorial control. Twenty years after the end of Porfirio Díaz's regime, an administration which had kept an open door for American capital, Dewey refrained from categorizing the Díaz era as imperialist. His reticence stemmed from his notion of empire, one shared by a good many of his cohorts and many academics today. See "Platform of the American Anti-Imperialist League," in Richard Hofstadter, ed., *Great Issues in American History*, vol. 2, pp. 202–204. On the other hand, some anti-imperialists as represented by Stanford University President David Starr Jordan, who shared the vice-presidency of the Anti-Imperialist League (1910–1921) with Dewey, opposed imperialism because, as Jordan claimed, "the proposed colonies are incapable of civilized self-government" and they "live without care, reckless and dirty [and] . . . the lottery, cock-fight and games of chance for excitement [mean] . . . more to them than rapid transit, telegraphic communication, literature, art, education, and all the joys of Saxon civilization ("Colonial Expansion: Address before the Congress of Religions at Omaha in October, 1898").

Not all anti-imperialists misunderstood the historical importance of the policy. Mark Twain comprehended the nature of colonial acquisition, which he expressed in "To the Person Sitting in Darkness." See Jim Zwick, ed., *Mark Twain's Weapons of Satire: Anti-Imperialist Writings on the Philippine-American War.* Twain's contemporary George D. Herron perceived the colonization extraordinarily well and analyzed it for what it was without resorting to racial logic or chauvinistic claims. Herron offered an accurate protest against expansion, one Twain would have agreed with, in an address before an enthusiastic audience at the Chicago Central Music Hall: "We have driven out Spain, but the Secretary of War is proceeding to divide up Cuba among stock speculators and corporate interests. We have driven out medieval tyranny, and American exploitation will take its place." George D. Herron, "American Imperialism," *Social Forum*, vol. 1 (June 1, 1899), cited in *http://www.boondocksnet.com/ai/index.html.*

15. See Hart, *Empire and Revolution*, particularly Chapter 3, "Ubiquitous Financiers"; also Ramón Eduardo Ruiz, *The People of Sonora*; Mark Wasserman, *Capitalists, Caciques, and Revolution: The Native Elite and Foreign Enterprise in Chihuahua, Mexico, 1854–1911*; and Roberto R. Calderón, *Mexican Coal Mining Labor in Texas and Coahuila, 1880–1930.*

16. John Kenneth Turner, *Barbarous Mexico*, 256–257.

17. On the domination of the Mexican economy, see the following: John Coatsworth, *Growth against Development: The Economic Impact of Railroads in Porfirian Mexico*; John Mason Hart, *Revolutionary Mexico: The Coming and Process of the Mexican Revolution*; Hart, *Empire and Revolution*; Ramón Eduardo Ruiz, *The Great Re-*

bellion: Mexico, 1905–1924; Ramón Eduardo Ruiz, *The People of Sonora;* Miguel Tinker Salas, *In the Shadow of the Eagles: Sonora and the Transformation of the Border during the Porfiriato;* Jonathan Brown, *Oil and Revolution in Mexico;* Wasserman, *Capitalists, Caciques, and Revolution;* and Calderón, *Mexican Coal Mining Labor.*

18. David Spurr notes a similar discourse in European colonization projects. His work illustrates how imperialism is basically similar even when contexts differ widely. See David Spurr, *The Rhetoric of Empire: Colonial Discourse in Journalism, Travel Writing, and Imperial Administration,* Chapter 5.

19. See Gilbert G. González and Raúl Fernández, "Empire and the Origins of Twentieth-Century Migration from Mexico to the United States," *Pacific Historical Review* 71, no. 1 (February 2002).

20. On the development of new sets of social relations as a consequence of American capital, see Ramón Eduardo Ruiz, *The People of Sonora,* Chapter 7, "The Making of the Working Class"; Tinker Salas, *In the Shadow of the Eagles,* 88–100; Calderón, *Mexican Coal Mining Labor;* and Hart, *Empire and Revolution,* Chapters 4 and 5.

21. Cecil Robinson, *Mexico and the Hispanic Southwest in American Literature,* 137.

22. See John Mason Hart, *Revolutionary Mexico: The Coming and Process of the Mexican Revolution* and *Empire and Revolution,* and Gilbert G. González and Raúl Fernández, *A Century of Chicano History: Empire, Nations, and Migration.*

1. The Economic Conquest and Its Social Relations

1. Quoted in Percy F. Martin, *Mexico's Treasure-House (Guanajuato): An Illustrated and Descriptive Account of the Mines and Their Operations in 1906,* title page.

2. David M. Pletcher, *Rails, Mines, and Progress: Seven American Promoters in Mexico, 1867–1911,* 38.

3. Ibid., 38, 79–80.

4. F. E. Prendergast, "Railroads in Mexico," *Harper's New Monthly Magazine,* 1881, 276.

5. Chester Lloyd Jones, *Mexico and Its Reconstruction,* 299, 310.

6. George Creel, *The People Next Door: An Interpretive History of Mexico and the Mexicans,* xiii.

7. George B. Winton, *Mexico Past and Present,* 288.

8. J. Park Alexander, *Mexico: Facts about the Republic of Mexico,* 15.

9. Frederick Simpich, "A Mexican Land of Canaan: Marvelous Riches of the Wonderful West Coast of Our Neighbor Republic," *National Geographic,* October 1919, 311. Former U.S. diplomat Chester Lloyd Jones used slightly different phrasing to say the same thing: "Mexico is the most important of the Latin countries as a place for investment of American capital and it may continue to be so" (Chester Lloyd Jones, *Mexico and Its Reconstruction,* 307).

10. Quoted in International Bureau of the American Republics, *Mexico: Geographic Sketch, Natural Resources, Laws, Economic Conditions, Actual Development, Prospects of Future Growth,* 257.

11. Wallace Thompson, *The People of Mexico: Who They Are and How They Live,* 407.

12. Charles Arthur Conant, *The United States in the Orient: The Nature of the Economic Problem*, 75; Conant was not the only economist who pointed to surplus capital. Scott Nearing and Joseph Freeman also emphasized the importance of surplus capital in their book, *Dollar Diplomacy: A Study in American Imperialism*.

13. Conant, *The United States in the Orient*, 63–64.

14. Ibid., vi. For discussions of the alliance of the AFL with the Confederación Regional Obrera Mexicana, see the following: Gilbert G. González, *Mexican Consuls and Labor Organizing: Imperial Politics in the American Southwest*; Gregg Andrews, *Shoulder to Shoulder? The American Federation of Labor, the United States, and the Mexican Revolution*; and Norman Caulfield, *Mexican Workers and the State: From the Porfiriato to NAFTA*.

15. Matías Romero, *Mexico and the United States: A Study of the Subjects Affecting Their Political, Commercial, and Social Relations, Made with a View to Their Promotion*, 395. Romero's contemporary John Kenneth Turner was justly critical of the alliance of Díaz and his cronies with American capital. See Turner, *Barbarous Mexico*, 256–257.

16. Charles W. Toth, "Elihu Root," in Norman A. Graebner, *An Uncertain Tradition: American Secretaries of State in the Twentieth Century*, 46–47. For an in-depth discussion of messianic vision practiced by U.S. political figures, see Emily S. Rosenberg, *Financial Missionaries to the World: The Politics and Culture of Dollar Diplomacy, 1900–1930*.

17. Elihu Root, *Latin America and the United States: Addresses by Elihu Root*, 246–247.

18. Charles Evans Hughes, *Our Relations to the Nations of the Western Hemisphere*, 68.

19. Root, *Latin America and the United States*, 188.

20. Nevin O. Winter, *Mexico and Her People of To-Day*, 53. That "invasion" has been noted by a number of historians, including John Mason Hart, *Empire and Revolution: The Americans in Mexico since the Civil War*; Ramón Eduardo Ruiz, *The People of Sonora and Yankee Capitalists*; and Mark Wasserman, *Capitalists, Caciques, and Revolution: The Native Elite and Foreign Enterprise in Chihuahua, Mexico, 1854–1911*.

21. Juan N. Navarro, "Mexico of Today," *National Geographic* 12 (June 1901): 237.

22. Chester Lloyd Jones, *Mexico and Its Reconstruction*, 307.

23. James Brown Scott, ed. *President Wilson's Foreign Policy*, 219. Woodrow Wilson followed much the same imperial policy as his White House predecessors. On U.S. foreign policy continuity from Roosevelt to Wilson, see Lars Schoultz, *Beneath the United States: A History of U.S. Policy toward Latin America*, Chapter 12.

24. Fred Wilbur Powell, *The Railroads of Mexico*, 119.

25. "Mexican Labor and Foreign Capital," *The Independent* 112, no. 3869 (May 24, 1924): 275. The dominant presence of U.S. capital in railroad construction is analyzed by a number of historians, including John Coatsworth, *Growth against Development: The Economic Impact of Railroads in Porfirian Mexico*; David M. Pletcher, *Rails, Mines and Progress: Seven American Promoters in Mexico, 1867–1911*; and Hart, *Empire and Revolution*.

26. See Gilbert G. González and Raúl Fernández, "Empire and the Origins of

Twentieth-Century Migration from Mexico to the United States," *Pacific Historical Review* 71, no. 1 (February 2002); see also Moisés González Navarro, *El Porfiriato: la vida social.*

27. One of the few analyses of this population in Mexico City is covered by William Schell Jr., *Integral Outsiders: The American Colony in Mexico City, 1876–1911.* My analysis differs in substantial respects from that of Schell, who identifies the relationship between Americans and Mexicans as a "contact zone" and states that the economic relationship between the two countries is an example of "trade diaspora." The presence of U.S. capital interests like those of J. P. Morgan, Gould, or Guggenheim manifested a much more significant relationship than a simple diaspora. The imperial character of U.S.-Mexico relations is clouded by references to a reciprocal "interdependence."

28. Claude T. Rice, "Mines of Penoles Company, Mapimí, Mex.—I," *Engineering and Mining Journal* (hereafter cited as *EMJ*) 86, no. 7 (August 15, 1908): 314.

29. J. B. Empson, "Silver Cyaniding in Mexico," *EMJ* 86, no. 12 (October 3, 1908): 667.

30. E. H. Blichfeldt, *A Mexican Journey*, 231.

31. Several historians have observed evidence for these patterns of social relations. See Wasserman, *Capitalists, Caciques and Revolution*, 6; also Ramón Eduardo Ruiz, *The People of Sonora*, and Miguel Tinker Salas, *In the Shadow of the Eagles.* Tinker Salas writes, "Mining became fertile ground for ethnic and racial strife since Mexicans and Indians constituted the majority of laborers and Anglo-Americans composed the bulk of supervisors and mine owners. Even in cases where Americans worked side by side with Mexicans, a dual wage-system prevailed" (88).

32. Alexander V. Dye, "Railways and Revolutions in Mexico," *Foreign Affairs* 5, no. 2 (January 1927): 321; see also Rodney Anderson, *Outcasts in Their Own Land: Mexican Industrial Workers, 1906–1911.*

33. "Gen. Foster on Mexico," *National Geographic* 12 (1901): 159.

34. See Hart, *Empire and Revolution.* Hart writes: "Aggressive American capitalists began to move forward with commitments to banking, railroads, technology, resource exploitation, and land ownership in Mexico. The bankers gave direction and coordination to this increasing flow of American investments, which deepened the intermixing of American and Mexican businessmen. Leading U.S. bank directors established personal and institutional operations in Mexico" (73). This was more than mere Dollar Diplomacy, a rather tame name that emphasizes political choice and eviscerates the meaning of a policy of expansionism propelled by the very economic order itself, an economically driven imperialist expansion.

35. See Ramón Eduardo Ruiz, *The People of Sonora*, Chapter 7, "The Making of the Working Class," and Tinker Salas, *In the Shadow of the Eagles*, 88–100.

36. Gilbert G. González and Raúl Fernández, "Empire and the Origins of Twentieth-Century Migration from Mexico to the United States"; also Hart, *Empire and Revolution*, 200, and Moisés González Navarro, *El Porfiriato: La Vida Social*, 20.

37. Mrs. Alec Tweedie, *Mexico As I Saw It*, 87.

38. Cy Warman, *The Story of the Railroad*, 89.

39. The work of Jonathan Brown delves into the dependence of the Mexican

oil industry on foreign capital during the Porfiriato. See Jonathan Brown's *Oil and Revolution in Mexico.*

40. Clarence W. Barron, *The Mexican Problem*, 20.

41. Nearing and Freeman, *Dollar Diplomacy*, 87.

42. Wallace Thompson, *Trading with Mexico*, 198.

43. Barron, *The Mexican Problem*, 92.

44. Thompson, *Trading with Mexico*, 202.

45. Jonathan Brown, *Oil and Revolution in Mexico*, 310; Caulfield, *Mexican Workers and the State*, 24.

46. Jonathan Brown, *Oil and Revolution in Mexico*, 80.

47. Second interview with Mr. Edward D. Doheny, File 3283, Interview 503, Doheny Research Foundation. Special Collections, Mary Norton Clapp Library, Occidental College, Los Angeles.

48. Marian Storm, "Wells at the World's End: Life in the Pánuco Oil Region of Mexico," *Atlantic Monthly*, April 1924, 516.

49. Second interview with Mr. Edward D. Doheny. A number of historians have documented the castelike system differentiating Americans from Mexican laborers. See Tinker Salas, *In the Shadow of the Eagles*, 88–92, and Ramón Eduardo Ruiz, *The People of Sonora*, 100–107.

50. Storm, "Wells at the World's End," 514.

51. Ibid.

52. Barron, *The Mexican Problem*, 24.

53. Thompson, *Trading with Mexico*, 207. On Mexican mining the works of Marvin Bernstein, Ramón Eduardo Ruiz, and John Mason Hart are indispensable. See Bernstein, *The Mexican Mining Industry*; Ramón Eduardo Ruiz, *The People of Sonora*; and Hart, *Empire and Revolution.*

54. H. A. C. Jenison, "Mining History of Mexico—II," *EMJ* 115 (March 3, 1923): 401.

55. Franklin Wheaton Smith, "Present Conditions of Mining in Mexico," *EMJ* 86, no 12 (October 3, 1908): 655.

56. James W. Malcolmson, "Mining Development in Mexico during 1902," *EMJ* 75, no. 1 (January 3, 1903): 29.

57. L. H. Jansen, correspondence, *EMJ* 79 (May 25, 1905): 1000. On the dominating presence of U.S. capital, see Tinker Salas, *In the Shadow of the Eagles*. Tinker Salas writes of the copper boomtown Cananea, "American interests hegemonized all major economic activity in Cananea" (176). Similar power relations distinguishing Americans from Mexicans were found throughout Mexico. On the role of U.S. capital on coal mining in Coahuila, Mexico, and the ensuing social relations, see Roberto R. Calderón, *Mexican Coal Mining Labor in Texas and Coahuila, 1880–1930.*

58. Jenison, "Mining History of Mexico—II," 402.

59. Robert T. Hill, "Geographic and Geologic Features of Mexico," *EMJ* 72, no. 18 (November 2, 1901): 561–564. See also James W. Malcolmson, "The Sierra Mojada, Coahuila, Mexico, and Its Ore Deposits," *EMJ* 72, no. 22 (November 30, 1901): 705–710.

60. Malcolmson, "Mining Development in Mexico during 1902," 33.

61. Walter D. Beverly, "Reminiscences of Mining in Durango," *EMJ* 83, no. 14 (October 2, 1909): 636.

62. Robert T. Hill, "The Santa Eulalia District, Mexico," *EMJ* 76, no. 5 (August 1, 1903): 158.

63. International Bureau of the American Republics, *Mexico*, 258.

64. Victor S. Clark, *Mexican Labor in the United States*, 470–471. See also William E. French, *A Peaceful and Working People: Manners, Morals, and Class Formation in Northern Mexico*, 42–43.

65. Morris B. Parker, *Mules, Mines, and Me in Mexico: 1895–1932*, 32–33. Among other insights into mining in Sonora, the discussion of housing in Ramón Eduardo Ruiz's *The People of Sonora* effectively probes the social relations connecting Americans and Mexicans during the Porfirian era. See Chapter 6, "The World of the Miner." See the work of Miguel Tinker Salas, *In the Shadow of the Eagles*, Chapter 8, "The Greatest Mining Camp in Northwest Mexico."

66. Mark R. Lamb, "On Horseback in Western Chihuahua," *EMJ* 86, no. 4 (July 25, 1908): 163–164.

67. Allen H. Rogers, "Character and Habits of Mexican Miners," *EMJ* 85, no. 14 (April 14, 1908): 702.

68. Claude T. Rice, "Smelter of Penoles, Mapimí, Mex.—II," *EMJ* 86, no. 4 (August 22, 1908): 374.

69. Harry A. Franck, *Tramping through Mexico, Guatemala and Honduras*, 63, 99. Ruiz found the same social relations in Sonora; see Ramón Eduardo Ruiz, *The People of Sonora*. Ruiz writes that housing conditions for Mexicans "were abominable" and that "malnutrition stalked Mexican families" (89).

70. Robert T. Hill, "Cananea Revisited," *EMJ* 76, no. 4 (December 31, 1903): 1000.

71. Franck, *Tramping through Mexico, Guatemala and Honduras*, 88.

72. Frederick A. Ober, *Travels in Mexico and Life among the Mexicans*, 616. John Mason Hart includes a very comprehensive study of mining in his most impressive book, *Empire and Revolution*. See Chapter 5, "Silver, Copper, Gold, and Oil." See as well Calderón, *Mexican Coal Mining Labor*, Chapter 2, "Las Minas: Origins and Contours."

73. Parker, *Mules, Mines, and Me in Mexico*, 14.

74. Claude Rice, "The Ore Deposits of Santa Eulalia, Mexico," *EMJ* 85, no. 25 (June 20, 1908): 1229.

75. Ober, *Travels in Mexico*, 615.

76. Marie Robinson Wright, *Mexico: A History of Its Progress and Development in One Hundred Years*, 401–402.

77. James A. Wilson, *Bits of Old Mexico*, 153.

78. Mark R. Lamb, "Stories of Batopilas Mines, Chihuahua," *EMJ* 85, no. 13 (April 4, 1908): 689.

79. Isaac F. Marcosson, "Our Financial Stake in Mexico," *Collier's* 57 (July 1, 1916): 23.

80. Grant Shepherd, *The Silver Magnet: Fifty Years in a Mexican Silver Mine*, 66.

81. B. E. Russell, "Las Chispas Mines, Sonora, Mexico," *EMJ* 86, no. 13 (November 21, 1908): 1007. See also Claude T. Rice, "Ore Sorting at the Cabresante Mine, Santa Barbara, Mexico," *EMJ* 86, no. 10 (September 12, 1908): 465; E. A. H. Tays, "Mining in Mexico, Past and Present," *EMJ* 86, no. 12 (October 3, 1908): 666.

82. Lamb, "Stories of the Batopilas Mines," 691.

83. Lamb, "On Horseback in Western Chihuahua," 160–162.

84. Ralph McA. Ingersoll, *In and under Mexico*, 104. The British and other European usages of the Himalayan Sherpa appear in many ways equivalent to those of the *mozo* in Mexico; see Sherry B. Ortner, *Life and Death on Mt. Everest: Sherpas and Himalayan Mountaineering.*

85. Shepherd, *The Silver Magnet*, 37–38.

86. Ibid., 71–72.

87. Ibid., 37–38.

88. Isaac F. Marcosson, *Metal Magic: The Story of the American Smelting and Refining Company*, 224. For a discussion of mining in Coahuila, see Calderón, *Mexican Coal Mining Labor.*

89. Historian John Mason Hart writes, "Elitism and cultural isolation on the part of American mining industrialists, engineers, and oilmen paralleled the attitudes and practices of American landowners, colonists, and settlers. Their segregationist beliefs and all too frequently haughty manners antagonized Mexicans" (Hart, *Empire and Revolution*, 166). See also Tinker Salas, *In the Shadow of the Eagles*, 88–100. Several authorities have examined the cultural aspects of the evolving U.S. empire. See for example, the work of Lars Schoultz, who examines the racialized utterances and the corresponding imperialist policies fashioned by America's statesmen in the post-Civil War period in his very informative book *Beneath the United States: A History of U.S. Policy toward Latin America*; see also Rosenberg, *Financial Missionaries to the World.* Her discussion in Chapter 2, "Gender Race, National Interest, and Civilization," delves into the culture of empire.

90. Ingersoll, *In and under Mexico*, 26.

91. Ibid., 138.

92. Ibid., 139.

93. Parker, *Mules, Mines, and Me in Mexico*, 16.

94. Ingersoll, *In and under Mexico*, 33, 114.

95. Arthur R. Townsend, "The Ocampo District, Mexico," *EMJ* 77, no. 13 (March 31, 1904): 515.

96. "Labor Conditions in the Mining Industries on the West Coast," Interview no. 570 (June 17, 1918). Doheny Research Foundation Collection, Occidental College, Glendale, California.

97. Ingersoll, *In and under Mexico*, 28. Ingersoll wrote of Monte del Cobre: "Directly above the native shops stood the company store, extending credit the former could not compete with" (28). See also C. Nelson Nelson, "The Sahuaripa District, Sonora, Mexico," *EMJ* 82, no. 13 (October 6, 1906): 628. Nelson wrote: "It is practically necessary for every employer of labor to run a store; of the mining companies this is especially true. If properly run, the store will produce an important revenue without charging excessive prices to the workmen" and later, "It is seldom that a Mexican with a family gets more than $5 cash at the end of the month [and] at current prices the companies make from 30 to 40 percent profit on the actual cost of the goods; this does not include clerk-hire or maintenance costs. The companies thus save handling large sums of cash, which is hard and costly to procure" (631).

98. Ingersoll, *In and under Mexico*, 14.

99. Ibid., 15.

100. Ibid., 52.

101. Ibid., 15.

102. Ibid., 151.

103. Ibid., 161.

104. Parker, *Mules, Mines, and Me in Mexico*, 45, 57–58.

105. William Schell Jr. discusses the American colony in Mexico City in his *Integral Outsiders: The American Colony in Mexico City, 1876–1911*; see also Hart, *Empire and Revolution*, Chapter 7, "Resident American Elite."

106. Charles Macomb Flandrau, *Viva Mexico!* 218.

107. Henry Lane Wilson, *Diplomatic Episodes in Mexico, Belgium, and Chile*, 185; Wilson's perspective is corroborated in Schell's *Integral Outsiders*, 16–17.

108. W. E. Carson, *Mexico: The Wonderland of the South*, rev. ed., 183.

109. Mary Barton, *Impressions of Mexico with Brush and Pen*, 61.

110. John W. Foster, "The New Mexico," *National Geographic* 13, no. 1 (January 1902): 24.

111. Blichfeldt, *A Mexican Journey*, 112.

112. "Mexican Labor and Foreign Capital," *The Independent*, May 24, 1924: 275.

2. American Writers Invade Mexico

1. Francis Hopkinson Smith, *A White Umbrella in Mexico*, 214.

2. Solomon Bulkley Griffin, *Mexico of To-Day*, 48; Charles Macomb Flandrau, *Viva Mexico!* 222.

3. Alfred Oscar Coffin, *Land without Chimneys, or The Byways of Mexico*, ix.

4. Frank Collins Baker, *A Naturalist in Mexico*, preface.

5. William Henry Bishop, *Old Mexico and Her Lost Provinces*, 2.

6. Marie Robinson Wright, *Mexico: A History of its Progress and Development in One Hundred Years*.

7. George G. Street, *Che! Wah! Wah! or, The Modern Montezumas in Mexico*, 79.

8. C. William Beebe, *Two Bird-Lovers in Mexico*, 19.

9. W. E. Carson, *Mexico: The Wonderland of the South*, rev. ed., v.

10. See the following: Francis S. Borton, *Mexico: "Our People Next Door"*; Frederick Starr, *In Indian Mexico: A Narrative of Travel and Labor*; Francis Hopkinson Smith, *A White Umbrella in Mexico*; David A. Wells, *A Study of Mexico*; E. D. Trowbridge, *Mexico To-Day and To-Morrow*; Nevin O. Winter, *Mexico and Her People of To-Day*; E. H. Blichfeldt, *A Mexican Journey*; Flandrau, *Viva Mexico!*; Chester Lloyd Jones, *Mexico and Its Reconstruction*; Wallace Thompson, *The Mexican Mind: A Study of National Psychology* and *The People of Mexico: Who They are and How They Live*; H. A. C. Jenison, "Mining History of Mexico—II," *Engineering and Mining Journal* 115 (March 3, 1923); Robert Glass Cleland, *The Mexican Yearbook*; Earnest Gruening, *Mexico and Its Heritage*; Edward Alsworth Ross, *The Social Revolution in Mexico*; and Doheny Research Foundation Papers.

11. George H. Blakeslee, ed., *Mexico and the Caribbean*.

12. Grant Shepherd, *The Silver Magnet: Fifty Years in a Mexican Silver Mine*, 252.

13. Beebe, *Two Bird-Lovers in Mexico*, vii.

14. Marie Robinson Wright, *Picturesque Mexico*, preface, 423, and 286.

15. Howard Conkling, *Mexico and the Mexicans, or Notes of Travel in the Winter and Spring of 1883*, vii.

16. Starr, *In Indian Mexico*, ix.

17. T. A. Rickard, *Journeys of Observation*, title page.

18. J. Hendrickson McCarty, *Two Thousand Miles through the Heart Of Mexico*, 47.

19. Griffin, *Mexico of To-Day*, 13.

20. Sullivan Holman McCollester, *Mexico, Old and New: A Wonderland*, 8.

21. Harriott Wight Sherrat, *Mexican Vistas Seen from Highways and By-ways of Travel*, 44.

22. Maturin M. Ballou, *Aztec Land*, 47.

23. James A. Wilson, *Bits of Old Mexico*, 2.

24. J. H. Bates, *Notes of a Tour in Mexico and California*, 21.

25. Nevin O. Winter, *Mexico and Her People of To-Day*, 4.

26. Albert Zabriskie Gray, *Mexico As It Is, Being Notes of a Recent Tour in That Country*, 31.

27. Winter, *Mexico and Her People of To-Day*, 5–6. The Reverend Edward E. Hale and his daughter, Susan, observed a similar attraction, which they noted in their book, *A Family Flight through Mexico*. They cheerfully wrote, "The lovely climate, neither too hot nor too cold, the picturesque people, the flowers, so luxuriant even in this autumn of the Mexican year, made up a bundle of pleasures not always found in travelling" (114).

28. George B. Winton, *Mexico To-Day: Social, Political, and Religious Conditions*, 3.

29. James H. Wilkins, *A Glimpse of Old Mexico*, 31.

30. William Henry Bishop, *Old Mexico and Her Lost Provinces*, 94.

31. Baker, *A Naturalist in Mexico*, 34.

32. Marian Storm, "Wells at the World's End: Life in the Pánuco Oil Region of Mexico," *Atlantic Monthly*, April 1924, 516.

33. Winter, *Mexico and Her People of To-Day*, 132.

34. Alden Buell Case, *Thirty Years with the Mexicans: In Peace and Revolution*, 24.

35. W. E. Carson, *Mexico: The Wonderland of the South*, rev. ed., 38.

36. Consul Walter H. Faulkner to the Honorable J. B. Moore, Assistant Secretary of State, October 15, 1898.

37. Wallace Gillpatrick, *The Man Who Likes Mexico*, 7, 321.

38. See the work of Sherry B. Ortner, *Life and Death on Mt. Everest: Sherpas and Himalayan Mountaineering*. The descriptions of the British use of guides for scaling the Himalayas were very reminiscent of Americans and their exploitation of servants in Mexico.

39. Beebe, *Two Bird-Lovers in Mexico*, 124, 160, 266, 352, 372.

40. Wilkins, *A Glimpse of Old Mexico*, 79.

41. Rickard, *Journeys of Observation*, 106.

42. Percy F. Martin, *Mexico's Treasure-House (Guanajuato)*, 66.

43. Starr, *In Indian Mexico*, 379.

44. William Henry Bishop, *Old Mexico and Her Lost Provinces*, 158.

45. Griffin, *Mexico of To-Day*, 185.

46. Gillpatrick, *The Man Who Likes Mexico*, 12–13,

47. Coffin, *Land without Chimneys, or The Byways of Mexico*, 72, 303.

48. Sherrat, *Mexican Vistas Seen from Highways and By-ways of Travel*, 113.

49. Reau Campbell, *Complete Guide and Descriptive Book of Mexico*; also, Mc-Collester, *Mexico, Old and New*.

50. Gillpatrick, *The Man Who Likes Mexico*, 125.

51. Shepherd, *The Silver Magnet*, 263.

52. Ballou, *Aztec Land*, 18.

53. Frederick R. Guernsey, "The Year in Mexico," *Atlantic Monthly* 97 (February 1906): 220.

54. James A. Wilson, *Bits of Old Mexico*, 126.

55. Edward M. Conley, "The Americanization of Mexico," *American Monthly Review of Reviews* 32 (1907): 724.

56. James Creelman, *Díaz, Master of Mexico*, 1–2.

57. Ibid., v.

58. Borton, *Mexico: "Our People Next Door,"* 52.

59. Harry L. Foster, *A Gringo in Mañana-Land*, 174.

60. C. S. Babbitt, *A Remedy for the Decadence of the Latin Race*, 47. Paul J. Vanderwood's very insightful and informative study, *Disorder and Progress: Bandits, Police and Mexican Development*, corroborates much of the evidence cited here. Vanderwood writes, "So the Rurales all along served the needs of international capitalism, the cornerstone of the Porfirian dictatorship" (119).

61. Harry L. Foster, *A Gringo in Mañana-Land*, 174.

62. Campbell, *Complete Guide and Descriptive Book of Mexico*, 52.

63. Frederick A. Ober, *Travels in Mexico and Life among the Mexicans*, 285.

64. Wilkins, *A Glimpse of Old Mexico*, 12–13.

65. Fanny Gooch (Inglehart), *Face to Face with the Mexicans*, 243.

66. Winter, *Mexico and Her People of To-Day*, 333.

67. See Trowbridge, *Mexico To-Day and To-Morrow*, 105.

68. Isaac F. Marcosson, "Our Financial Stake in Mexico," *Collier's* 57 (July 1, 1916): 22.

69. Blichfeldt, *A Mexican Journey*, 245.

70. Frederick Simpich, "Mexico's Agrarian Experiment," *The Independent* 116, no. 3948 (January 30, 1926): 142.

71. James Carson, "Upon the Indian Depends Mexico's Future," in Blakeslee, *Mexico and the Caribbean*, 43.

72. Fred Wilbur Powell, "The Railroads of Mexico," in Robert Glass Cleland, *The Mexican Yearbook, 1922–1924*, 169.

73. Franklin Wheaton Smith, "Present Conditions of Mining in Mexico," *EMJ* 86, no. 12 (October 3, 1908): 655.

74. Herbert Corey, "Adventuring Down the West Coast of Mexico," *National Geographic* 42, no. 5 (November 1922): 496.

75. Kamar Al-Shimas, *The Mexican Southland*, viii.

76. Frederick Simpich, "A Mexican Land of Canaan: Marvelous Riches of the Wonderful West Coast of Our Neighbor Republic," *National Geographic*, October 1919, 307.

77. Ballou, *Aztec Land*, 25.

78. Martin, *Mexico's Treasure-House (Guanajuato)*, 10, 13–14.

79. International Bureau of the American Republics. *Mexico: Geographic Sketch, Natural Resources, Laws, Economic Conditions, Actual Development, Prospects of Future Growth*, 257.

80. Juan N. Navarro, "Mexico of Today," *National Geographic* 12 (June 1901): 237.

81. *National Geographic* 30 (July 1916).

82. Marie Robinson Wright, *Picturesque Mexico*, 444.

83. Wilkins, *A Glimpse of Old Mexico*, 99.

84. Wallace Thompson, *Trading with Mexico*, xi. See also the following books by Thompson: *The People of Mexico: Who They Are and How They Live* and *The Mexican Mind: A Study of National Psychology*.

85. Charles Johnston, "The Two Mexicos," *Atlantic Monthly*, November 1920, 709.

86. Juan N. Navarro, "Mexico of Today," *National Geographic* 12 (April 1901).

87. There is evidence that some studies of Mexico were taken for the expressed purpose of reporting on investment potentials. Anthropologist Carl Lumholtz wrote *New Trails in Mexico: An Account of One Year's Exploration in North-western Sonora, Mexico, and South-western Arizona, 1909–1910* partially in response to an invitation by, as Lumholtz put it, "some influential friends to look into certain economical possibilities of the arid and little known country along the upper part of the Gulf of California, east of the Colorado River . . . lying, so to speak, at the door of the great empire of Yankee enterprise." (vii).

88. John W. Foster, "The New Mexico," *National Geographic* 13, no. 1 (January 1902): 24.

89. Flandrau, *Viva Mexico!* 207.

90. Corey, "Adventuring Down the West Coast of Mexico," *National Geographic* 42, no. 5 (November 1922): 485.

91. Harry Carr, *Old Mother Mexico*, 52.

92. Storm, "Wells at the World's End," 516.

93. Simpich, "A Mexican Land of Canaan," 318.

94. W. E. Carson, *Mexico: The Wonderland of the South*, rev. ed., 433.

3. The Imperial Burden

1. Frederick A. Ober, *Travels in Mexico and Life among the Mexicans*, 270.

2. Wallace Thompson, *The People of Mexico: Who They Are and How They Live*, 3.

3. William H. Prescott, "The Luster of Ancient Mexico," *National Geographic* 30, no. 1 (July 1916): 3; Maturin M. Ballou, *Aztec Land*; Susan Hale, *Mexico*; Solomon Bulkley Griffin, *Mexico of To-Day*.

4. William Joseph Showalter, "Mexico and the Mexicans," *National Geographic* 25, no. 5 (May 1914): 471.

5. Nevin O. Winter, *Mexico and Her People of To-Day*, 9.

6. Wallace Thompson, *The Mexican Mind*, 28.

7. C. S. Babbitt, *A Remedy for the Decadence of the Latin Race.*

8. Chester Lloyd Jones, *Mexico and Its Reconstruction*, 18.

9. George B. Winton, *Mexico To-Day: Social, Political, and Religious Conditions*, 2.

10. Ibid., 24; The eminent historian Hubert Howe Bancroft reached a similar conclusion: "The assumption that the half-breed of Mexico inherits the worst traits of their progenitors is hardly correct. If these characteristics appear conspicuous, with a stronger stamp of the inferior race, it is due rather to his equivocal position which places obstacles, especially of a social nature, against his efforts for higher models." However, in the previous paragraph Bancroft states that the mestizo lacks "depth and earnestness" and exhibits "conceit, bombast, and irresolution" (*History of Mexico, 1861–1887*, vol. 14 of *The Works of Hubert Howe Bancroft*, 607).

11. Frederick Starr, "The Mexican People," in George H. Blakeslee, ed., *Mexico and the Caribbean*, 23.

12. Charles W. Hamilton, *Early Day Oil Tales of Mexico*, 11.

13. Jack London, "Our Adventures in Tampico," *Collier's* 53, no. 15 (June 27, 1914): 7.

14. Walter E. Weyl, *Labor Conditions in Mexico*, 4.

15. Sullivan Holman McCollester, *Mexico, Old and New: A Wonderland*, 32.

16. Reau Campbell, *Mexico: Tours through the Egypt of the New World*.

17. Winton, *Mexico To-Day*, 30.

18. Winter, *Mexico and Her People of To-Day*.

19. Matías Romero, *Mexico and the United States: A Study of the Subjects Affecting Their Political, Commercial, and Social Relations, Made with a View to Their Promotion*, 10.

20. Mary Elizabeth Blake, "Picturesque Mexico," in Mary Elizabeth Blake and Margaret F. Sullivan, *Mexico*, 39.

21. Herbert Corey, "The Isthmus of Tehuantepec," *National Geographic* 45, no. 5 (May 1924): 550.

22. Marie Robinson Wright, *Picturesque Mexico*, 438.

23. C. Reginald Enock, *Mexico: Its Ancient and Modern Civilisation*, 35.

24. Percy F. Martin, *Mexico of the Twentieth Century*, 211.

25. E. H. Blichfeldt, *A Mexican Journey*, 45.

26. Ballou, *Aztec Land*, 6.

27. William Henry Bishop, *Old Mexico and Her Lost Provinces*, 84.

28. Charles Johnston, "The Two Mexicos," *Atlantic Monthly*, November 1920, 708.

29. George B. Winton, *Mexico Past and Present*, 32.

30. Charles W. Drees, *Thirteen Years in Mexico*, ed. Ada M. C. Drees, 51.

31. Winton, *Mexico To-Day*, 2.

32. Ernest Gruening, "The Mexican Renaissance," *The Century Magazine* 85 (February 1924): 526.

33. James Creelman, *Díaz, Master of Mexico*, 17.

34. Rudyard Kipling, "The Epics of India," *Civil and Military Gazette*, August 24, 1886, in Thomas Pinney, ed., *Kipling's India: Uncollected Sketches, 1884–88*, 178.

35. Pinney, ed., *Kipling's India*, 19.

36. David A. Wells, *A Study of Mexico*, 27; Wells writes: "The laboring-classes in Mexico—the so called "peons" who comprise the great bulk of the population—are chiefly Indians, or descendents of Indians, and are a different race than their employers."

37. W. E. Carson, *Mexico: The Wonderland of the South*, rev. ed., 187.

38. Martin, *Mexico of the Twentieth Century*, x.

39. "Mexico: An Impartial Survey," typed ms. prepared by G. W. Scott (1918), Doheny Research Foundation Collection, Special Collections, Mary Norton Clapp Library, Occidental College, Glendale, California. Bancroft, *History of Mexico, 1861–1867*, 611–612.

40. Wallace Gillpatrick, *The Man Who Likes Mexico*, 337.

41. Frank H. Probert, "The Treasure Chest of Mercurial Mexico," *National Geographic* 30, no. 1 (July 1916): 43.

42. Allen H. Rogers, "Character and Habits of Mexican Miners," *EMJ* 85, no. 14 (April 14, 1908): 700.

43. Blichfeldt, *A Mexican Journey*, 64.

44. Francis Hopkinson Smith, *A White Umbrella in Mexico*, 67–68.

45. Evan Fraser-Campbell, "The Management of Mexican Labor," *EMJ* 90 (June 3, 1911): 1104.

46. J. Nelson Nevius, Letter to the Editor, *EMJ*, 78, no. 6 (August 11, 1904), 213.

47. Eva Frank, "The Mexican 'Just Won't Work,'" *The Nation* 125, no. 3241 (July 17, 1927): 156, cited in Helen Walker, "The Conflict of Cultures in First Generation Mexicans in Santa Ana, California," master's thesis, University of Southern California, 1928: 18.

48. W. E. Carson, *Mexico: The Wonderland of the South*, rev. ed., 188.

49. Griffin, *Mexico of To-Day*, 160.

50. McCollester, *Mexico, Old and New: A Wonderland*, 237.

51. Weyl, *Labor Conditions in Mexico*, 48.

52. W. E. Carson, *Mexico: The Wonderland of the South*, 1st ed., 188. Mrs. Alec Tweedie, a British professional traveler, thought the exact same idea. She wrote, "There is a hopeless apathy about him. He never thinks about saving money; he sees no comfort in independence, cares for nothing higher than the position and circumstances in which he was born. . . . Mexicans are able to live on little" (*Mexico As I Saw It*, 64).

53. Herbert Corey, "Adventuring Down the West Coast of Mexico," *National Geographic* 42, no. 5 (November 1922): 460.

54. J. Park Alexander, *Mexico: Facts about the Republic of Mexico*, 15.

55. Winter, *Mexico and Her People of To-Day*, 200.

56. Charles F. Lummis, *The Awakening of a Nation: Mexico of To-Day*, 76.

57. Wells, *A Study of Mexico*, 30–31.

58. J. H. Bates, *Notes of a Tour in Mexico and California*, 23.

59. William Henry Bishop, *Old Mexico and Her Lost Provinces*, 100.

60. Winter, *Mexico and Her People of To-Day*, 192.

61. London, "Our Adventures in Tampico," 7.

62. Harry L. Foster, *A Gringo in Mañana-Land*, 8.

63. John J. Johnson, *Latin America in Caricature*. See Chapter 4, titled "The Re-

publics as Children"; editorial cartoons regularly carried images of Latin Americans as children in need of a stern parent. John Mason Hart also discusses the Mexican-as-child theme in *Empire and Revolution: The Americans in Mexico since the Civil War*, 43–45.

64. Edward Alsworth Ross, *The Social Revolution in Mexico*, 14.

65. J. Hendrickson McCarty, *Two Thousand Miles through the Heart of Mexico*, 126.

66. Ralph McA. Ingersoll, *In and under Mexico*, 45.

67. C. S. Thomas, "Traveling in Mexico," *EMJ* 91, no. 24 (June 17, 1911): 1201.

68. Franklin Wheaton Smith, "Present Conditions of Mining in Mexico," *EMJ* 86, no. 12 (October 3, 1908): 656.

69. Thompson, *The Mexican Mind*, 134.

70. Ibid., 171.

71. Bancroft, *History of Mexico, 1861–1887*.

72. Griffin, *Mexico of To-Day*, 128.

73. William Henry Bishop, *Old Mexico and Her Lost Provinces*, 90.

74. Ballou, *Aztec Land*, 147.

75. Cy Warman, *The Story of the Railroad*, 218.

76. Frederick Simpich, "Along Our Side of the Mexican Border," *National Geographic* 38, no. 1 (July 1920): 63.

77. Alexander, *Mexico: Facts about the Republic of Mexico*, 15.

78. Stanton Davis Kirkham, *Mexican Trails: A Record of Travel in Mexico, 1904–1907, and a Glimpse of the Life of the Mexican Indian*, 153.

79. W. E. Carson, *Mexico: The Wonderland of the South*, rev. ed., 38.

80. Alfred Oscar Coffin, *Land without Chimneys, or The Byways of Mexico*, 25. Coffin wrote: "There are many Americans in Monterey, and they are trying very hard to implant their customs upon the country, one of which is the color line in public places" (25).

81. Griffin, *Mexico of To-Day*, 152.

82. Alden Buell Case, *Thirty Years with the Mexicans: In Peace and Revolution*, 228.

83. Ross, *The Social Revolution in Mexico*, 16.

84. McCarty, *Two Thousand Miles through the Heart of Mexico*, 116.

85. Creelman, *Díaz, Master of Mexico*, 396.

86. Blakeslee, *Mexico and the Caribbean*, viii.

87. Thompson, *The People of Mexico*, 35.

88. Chester Lloyd Jones, *Mexico and Its Reconstruction*, viii.

89. Clarence W. Barron, *The Mexican Problem*, xi.

90. Chester Lloyd Jones, *Mexico and Its Reconstruction*, 5.

91. Barron, *The Mexican Problem*, 12–13.

92. Chester Lloyd Jones, *Mexico and Its Reconstruction*, 27.

93. Ibid., 115.

94. Ross, *The Social Revolution in Mexico*, 7.

95. Harriott Wight Sherrat, *Mexican Vistas Seen from Highways and By-ways of Travel*, 20.

96. Edward M. Conley, "The Americanization of Mexico," *American Monthly Review of Reviews* 32 (1907): 724.

97. Winter, *Mexico and Her People of To-Day*, 20.

98. Ingersoll, *In and under Mexico*, 117–118.

99. Winter, *Mexico and Her People of To-Day*, 395.

100. Ballou, *Aztec Land*, 348.

101. Griffin, *Mexico of To-Day*, 197.

102. Frederick Simpich, "A Mexican Land of Canaan: Marvelous Riches of the Wonderful West Coast of Our Neighbor Republic," *National Geographic*, October 1919, 309.

103. Howard Conkling, *Mexico and the Mexicans*, 256–257.

104. Ober, *Travels in Mexico*, 616.

105. Kirkham, *Mexican Trails*, 50.

106. Thompson, *The Mexican Mind*, 10.

107. Wallace Thompson, *Trading with Mexico*, 268.

108. Barron, *The Mexican Problem*, 14.

109. Gruening, "The Mexican Renaissance," 525.

110. Thompson, *The Mexican Mind*, 175.

111. Case, *Thirty Years with the Mexicans*, 199–200; See also McCarty, *Two Thousand Miles through the Heart of Mexico*, 102–103.

112. For a thorough review of the conduct of American missionaries around the world, see Emily S. Rosenberg, *Spreading the American Dream: American Economic and Cultural Expansion, 1890–1945*, Chapter 2. American missionaries in Mexico were no different from those proselytizing in other nations under foreign domination.

113. Winton, *Mexico To-Day*, 156.

114. Ibid., 154–155.

115. Mrs. John W. Butler, "The Women of Mexico," *Missionary Review of the World* 39 (January–June, 1916): 186.

116. John Wesley Butler, *History of the Methodist Episcopal Church in Mexico*, 145.

117. Drees, *Thirteen Years in Mexico*, ed. Ada M. C. Drees, 222.

118. McCarty, *Two Thousand Miles through the Heart of Mexico*, 288.

119. Thompson, *Trading with Mexico*, 137.

120. Thompson, *The People of Mexico*, 207. Thompson argued that the "Negro Problem" in the United States and the "Mexican Problem" were comparable and required similar solutions. In both situations, neither constituent was capable of independently overcoming political or economic problems that beset them without outside tutelage, hence the transnational "white man's burden."

121. John Wesley Butler, *History of the Methodist Episcopal Church in Mexico*, 59.

122. Francis S. Borton, *Mexico: "Our People Next Door"*, 36.

123. Blichfeldt, *A Mexican Journey*, 126.

124. Samuel Guy Inman, *Intervention in Mexico*, 138, 140–41.

125. Gruening, "The Mexican Renaissance," 535. On this literary groundswell of a more positive image of Mexico and its culture, promoted by Gruening and others—albeit not in contradiction to the peaceful conquest—see Hart, *Empire and Revolution*, 367–370.

126. On this matter the work of Robert Freeman Smith is most informative. Robert Freeman Smith, *The United States and Revolutionary Nationalism in Mexico*,

1916–1932. According to Smith, the United States "expanded its presence" in the 1920s beyond the levels of the Díaz era (149). Also see William Schell Jr., *Integral Outsiders: The American Colony in Mexico City, 1876–1911,* 163–175.

127. Charles Bernard Nordhoff, "The Human Side of Mexico," *Atlantic Monthly* 124 (1919): 503. The "good will" initiative predated a similar policy, instituted in the 1960s, which created the Peace Corps to correct the Ugly American syndrome (and national liberation movements as well); the Corps was to fashion a new culture within Latin America as well, a culture that would be responsive to the exigencies resulting from foreign-inspired modernization. Thus the Peace Corps was intended to give the Third World a pacific and wholesome image of Americans while simultaneously seeking to reform the culture of the Third World.

128. Editorial, *The Survey* 59, no. 3 (November 1, 1927): 156.

129. Inman, *Intervention in Mexico,* 212. See also Samuel Guy Inman, "The Young Mexicans," *The Survey* 42 (August 30, 1919), in which Inman argued against armed intervention and for better relations with Mexico: "We can strike hands in friendship and cooperate if we only have the heart and good sense to do so" (767). See also John Palmer Gavit, "Through Neighbors' Doorways," *The Survey* 59, no. 5 (December 1, 1927): 322; of the "New American" in Mexico and their liberalized thinking on Mexicans, Gavit wrote, "It takes so little in human relations to turn a current of thought in the opposite direction! These, believe me, are *people,* like ourselves" (322).

130. John Palmer Gavit, "Mexico and an Awakened Administration," *The Independent* 119 (December 31, 1927): 645.

131. Helen Delpar, *The Enormous Vogue of Things Mexican,* 73. On the Friends of the Mexicans conferences I suggest the work of Matt García, *A World of Its Own: Race, Labor, and Citrus in the Making of Greater Los Angeles, 1900–1970.*

132. Inman, *Intervention in Mexico,* 213.

133. George Agnew Chamberlain, *Is Mexico Worth Saving?* 243.

134. Robert Freeman Smith, *The United States and Revolutionary Nationalism in Mexico,* 201–202. Smith finds that U.S. corporate investors controlled substantial portions of Mexico's economy by 1930, capturing 95 percent of refined sugar, 98 percent of all mining establishments, 86 percent of cotton production, 94 percent of oil production, and 100 percent of bananas and other fruits. For a review of the continuity of U.S. economic domination into the twenty-first century, see the concluding chapter, titled "Imperial America," in Hart's *Empire and Revolution.*

4. The Peaceful Conquest and Mexican Migration within Mexico and to the United States

1. Samuel Bryan, "Mexican Immigrants in the United States," *The Survey* 28, no. 23 (September 7, 1912): 726–730.

2. Robert N. McLean, *That Mexican! As He Really Is, North and South of the Rio Grande,* 120.

3. Richard Warner Van Alstyne, *The Rising American Empire.*

4. For a more complete discussion of this theoretical approach to a century of Mexican migration, see Gilbert G. González and Raúl Fernández, "Empire and

the Origins of Twentieth-Century Migration from Mexico to the United States," *Pacific Historical Review* 71, no. 1 (February 2002).

5. Cy Warman, *The Story of the Railroad*, 246.

6. John H. Coatsworth, *Growth against Development: The Economic Impact of Railroads in Porfirian Mexico*, 123–124; also John Mason Hart, *Revolutionary Mexico: The Coming and Process of the Mexican Revolution*, 41, 170.

7. Moisés González Navarro, *El Porfiriato: La Vida Social*, 20. On land seizures see John Mason Hart, *Revolutionary Mexico: The Coming and Process of the Mexican Revolution*, 41, 170; William E. French, *A Peaceful and Working People: Manners, Morals, and Class Formation in Northern Mexico*, 37–47; Ramón Eduardo Ruiz, *The People of Sonora and Yankee Capitalists*, 16–17; and Mark Wasserman, *Capitalists, Caciques, and Revolution: The Native Elite and Foreign Enterprise in Chihuahua, Mexico*, 109.

8. Michael Johns, *City of Mexico in the Age of Díaz*, 64.

9. Victor S. Clark, *Mexican Labor in the United States*, U.S. Department of Commerce and Labor, Bureau of Labor Bulletin no. 78, pp. 470–471, 515.

10. Franklin Wheaton Smith, "Present Conditions of Mining in Mexico," *EMJ* 86, no. 12 (October 3, 1908): 656.

11. Dwight E. Woodbridge, "La Cananea Mining Camp," *EMJ* 82, no. 14 (October 6, 1906): 623.

12. H. J. Baron, "Río Plata Mine and Mill, Western Chihuahua," *EMJ* 87, no. 3 (January 16, 1909): 151.

13. Clark, *Mexican Labor in the United States*, 470–471. On the recruitment and migration of coal mining labor from Mexico to Texas, see the very informative work by Roberto R. Calderón, *Mexican Coal Mining Labor in Texas and Coahuila, 1880–1930*. Calderón writes: "The coal industries of Coahuila and Texas shared a common transnational history. American capital and Mexican labor were important components. . . . Texas coal operators had a ready source of labor in northern Mexico" (78).

14. Of Texas coal mining Calderón writes: "Miners from Coahuila were present in the Texas coalfields throughout the industries' existence because companies in Texas typically recruited them at the border in places like Laredo and Eagle Pass." See Calderón, *Mexican Coal Mining Labor*, 213.

15. Ibid. 470.

16. Ibid. 471.

17. Ibid. 476.

18. Senate, Reports of the Immigration Commission, *Abstracts of Reports of the Immigration Commission*, 682–683; see also Bryan, "Mexican Immigrants in the United States," 727.

19. Victor S. Clark, *Mexican Labor in the United States*, 470.

20. Senate, Reports of the Immigration Commission, *Abstracts of Reports of the Immigration Commission*, 684.

21. Interview by author with Antonio J. González, November 2, 1980, Alhambra, California. At the age of fifteen, González, along with his uncle Ubiliado González, signed on to work with a railroad. When they discovered that they were working for nothing, given that their room and board equaled their one dollar per day in wages, they jumped camp in New Mexico without finishing their contracts

and gradually worked their way to California's San Joaquin Valley. Their story must have been the same as countless migrants'.

22. Antonio Ríos-Bustamante, "As Guilty as Hell: Mexican Copper Miners and Their Communities in Arizona, 1920–1950," in John Mason Hart, ed., *Border Crossings: Mexican and Mexican American Workers* (Wilmington, Del.: Scholarly Resources, 1998), 164. See Roberto R. Calderón, *Mexican Coal Mining Labor.* Calderón notes the high proportion of the Mexican population in certain coal mining regions of south Texas by 1910 in Chapter Four. Calderón states: ". . . the mining population of the border mining communities was a predominantly immigrant and ethnically Mexican population." (112).

23. Jeffrey Marcos Garcilazo, "Traqueros: Mexican Railroad Workers in the United States, 1870–1930," typescript, 1998, 1.

24. Vernon Monroe McCombs, *From over the Border: A Study of the Mexicans in the United States,* 21.

25. On acreage in Colorado see Carey McWilliams, *North from Mexico: The Spanish Speaking People of the United States,* 180–181; and Robert N. McLean, *The Northern Mexican,* 8.

26. Jay S. Stowell, *The Near Side of the Mexican Question,* 36.

27. McWilliams, *North from Mexico,* 186.

28. Jay Stowell wrote: "The Mexican who comes across the international line to work in the United States does not, however, come alone. He brings his wife and family with him" (*The Near Side of the Mexican Question,* 42). Virtually every student of Mexican immigration came to the same conclusion, and many fretted over having a new racial group "taint" American culture and society.

29. Paul S. Taylor, "Mexicans North of the Rio Grande," *The Survey* 65, no. 3 (May 1, 1931): 197.

30. See McLean, *The Northern Mexican.* McLean wrote: "Usually the farmer who employs the Mexican furnishes houses also. In newer beet districts the types of housing furnished is naturally less adequate than in communities where beet work has gone on for a considerable number of years. In some of these new communities shacks, sheds, barns and even stables were hastily remodeled and utilized to house the Mexican worker and his family. The Great Western Sugar Company in its effort to stabilize its Mexican labor has gone to considerable effort and expense to provide adequate housing" (18).

31. Mario T. García, *Desert Immigrants: The Mexicans of El Paso, 1880–1920,* 62.

32. "Labor Conditions in the Southwest," editorial, *EMJ* 77, no. 13 (March 31, 1904): 510; see also Ríos-Bustamante, "As Guilty as Hell: Mexican Copper Miners and Their Communities in Arizona, 1920–1950."

33. Garcilazo, "Traqueros," 229.

34. McWilliams, *North from Mexico,* 175.

35. Bertram H. Mautner and W. Lewis Abbot, *Child Labor in Agriculture and Farm Life in the Arkansas Valley of Colorado,* 29.

36. For a thorough discussion to Mexican labor in the citrus industry, see Gilbert G. González, *Labor and Community: Mexican Citrus Worker Villages in a Southern California County, 1900–1950.*

37. Copy found in the Doheny Foundation Research Collection, File K, Special Collections, Main Library, Occidental College, Glendale, California.

38. "The Well Housed Employee," *The California Citrograph* 3, no. 9 (September 1918): 253.

39. Placentia (Calif.) Orange Growers Association, *Manager's Annual Report* (1925).

40. George Hodgkin, "Making the Labor Camp Pay," *The California Citrograph* (August 1921), quoted in Jessie Hayden, "The La Habra Experiment in Mexican Social Education," master's thesis, Claremont Colleges, 1934: 44.

41. An excellent example of the use of model camps as a means to augment control over labor is revealed in an editorial on Arizona mines published in *EMJ* in 1904. The editorial states, "Morenci and Bisbee impress one as model camps. . . . the employees of the Detroit Copper Company enjoy . . . a well equipped gymnasium . . . billiard tables and bowling alleys. At Bisbee the Copper Queen has been no less liberal to its employees. This camp is one of a very few in the West that has never witnessed a strike, or any serious disagreement between the company and the miners" ("Labor Conditions in the Southwest," editorial, *EMJ* 11, no. 13 [March 31, 1904]: 510).

42. Interview with J. R. Silva, employment agent for Mexican agricultural laborers, El Paso, Texas, File 103–107a, Contractors and Agencies, Paul S. Taylor Collection, Bancroft Library, University of California, Berkeley.

43. Mautner and Abbot, *Child Labor in Agriculture and Farm Life*, 29; Roberto R. Calderón also found the emphasis on hiring men with families in the coal mining districts of the Texas border. Calderón writes, "It is evident, then, that the mine operators chose instead, by design or default, to discourage unattached male workers and encourage a labor force increasingly bound by kinship and regional . . . ties" (*Mexican Coal Mining Labor*, 128).

44. Sara Brown, Robie O. Sargent, and Clara B. Armentrout, *Children Working in the Sugar Beet Fields of Certain Districts of the South Platte Valley, Colorado*, 28.

45. Amber A. Warburton, Helen Wood, and Marian M. Crane, *The Work and Welfare of Children of Agricultural Laborers in Hidalgo County, Texas*, 30.

46. On cannery workers see Vicki Ruiz, *Cannery Women, Cannery Lives: Unionization and the Food Processing Industry, 1930–1940.*

47. California Mexican Fact-Finding Committee, *Mexicans in California: Report of Governor C. C. Young's Mexican Fact-Finding Committee*, 87–88. Emory Bogardus reported that in the early 1930s, "the number of [Mexican women] who are going into homes as workers by the day or hour is slowly increasing" (*The Mexican in the United States*, 43). See also Rosalinda Mendez Gonzalez, "Chicanas and Mexican Immigrant Families 1920–1940: Women's Subordination and Family Exploitation," in Lois Scharf and Joan Jensen, eds., *Decades of Discontent: The Women's Movement, 1920–1940*, 66–67.

48. Mario T. García, *Desert Immigrants*, 60.

49. McWilliams, *North from Mexico*, 187.

50. Mining engineer Claude T. Rice noted: "Most of the ore is mined on contract, the men paying for their own dynamite and fuse. The price paid for drilling and breaking varies between 0.60 and 1 peso per ton. Drilling when done with a machine is paid 15 centavos per meter. Several Murphy hammer drills are used. The men on large piston machines work on day's pay or on contract" ("The Working Mines of Guanajuato," *EMJ* 86 [October 24, 1908]: 806). Another wrote

that in the northern Chihuahua district of Ocampo, "most development work is done on contract, from $25 to $50 (Mex) per m. being paid for cross-cutting and driving" (Arthur R. Townsend, "The Ocampo District, Mexico," *EMJ* 78, no. 13 [March 31, 1904]: 516).

51. McWilliams, *North from Mexico*, 172–173.

52. Bogardus, *The Mexican in the United States*, 39–40.

53. Mark Reisler, *By the Sweat of Their Brow: Mexican Immigrant Labor in the United States, 1900–1940*, 100.

54. Ernesto Galarza, an early student and civil rights advocate of the ethnic Mexican community, described the migratory process a half a century ago with particular attention to the actions and effects of American capital on the people of Mexico. He maintained that the migrant "is forced to seek better conditions north of the border by the slow but relentless pressure of United States' agricultural, financial, and oil corporate interests on the entire economic and social evolution of the Mexican nation" ("Program for Action," *Common Ground* 10, no. 4 [1949]).

55. Paul S. Taylor, "Mexicans North of the Rio Grande," 135.

5. The Transnational Mexican Problem

1. James Hoffman Batten, "Mexicans are People," *The Survey* 61, no. 7 (January 1, 1929): 477.

2. "An Eye on the Little Brown Brother," editorial, *The Independent* 119, no. 4037 (October 8, 1927): 347; "Barriers to the Little Brown Brother," editorial, *The Independent* 120 (February 1928), 242; see also Frederick Simpich, "The Little Brown Brother Treks North," *The Independent* 116 (1924): 237–239; and Frederick Simpich, "Along Our Side of the Mexican Border," *National Geographic* 38, no. 1 (July 1920).

3. C. Reginald Enock, *Mexico: Its Ancient and Modern Civilisation*.

4. Frederick Starr, *In Indian Mexico: A Narrative of Travel and Labor*.

5. E. D. Trowbridge, *Mexico To-Day and To-Morrow*.

6. Nevin O. Winter, *Mexico and Her People of To-Day*.

7. George B. Winton, *Mexico To-Day: Social, Political and Religious Conditions*.

8. Bogardus listed two of Wallace Thompson's imperial-minded books: *The People of Mexico: Who They are and How They Live* and *The Mexican Mind: A Study of National Psychology*.

9. Robert N. McLean, *That Mexican! As He Really Is, North and South of the Rio Grande*.

10. Reau Campbell, *Mexico and the Mexicans: The Material Matters and Mysterious Myths of That Country and Its People*.

11. Susan Hale, *Mexico*.

12. Alden Buell Case, *Thirty Years with the Mexicans: In Peace and Revolution*.

13. Percy F. Martin, *Mexico of the Twentieth Century*.

14. Edward Alsworth Ross, *The Social Revolution in Mexico*.

15. Simpich, "The Little Brown Brother Treks North."

16. Clarence W. Barron, *The Mexican Problem*.

17. Hubert Howe Bancroft, *History of Mexico, 1861–1887*, vol. 14 of *The Works of Hubert Howe Bancroft*.

18. George H. Blakeslee, ed., *Mexico and the Caribbean.*

19. Robert Glass Cleland, *The Mexican Year Book, 1922–1924.*

20. Edward M. Conley, "The Americanization of Mexico," *American Monthly Review of Reviews* 32 (1907): 724–725.

21. Lewis Spence, *Mexico of the Mexicans.*

22. Emory Bogardus, *The Mexican in the United States,* 122.

23. Clara Gertrude Smith, "The Development of the Mexican People in the Community of Watts, California," master's thesis, University of Southern California, 1933.

24. Harry Carr, *Old Mother Mexico.*

25. Ernest Gruening, *Mexico and Its Heritage.*

26. Mary Lanigan, "Second Generation Mexicans in Belvedere," master's thesis, University of Southern California, 1932.

27. George B. Winton, *Mexico Past and Present.*

28. Albert Turner Kaderli, "The Educational Problem in the Americanization of the Spanish-Speaking Pupils of Sugar Land, Texas," master's thesis, University of Texas, Austin, 1940: 14.

29. Emory Bogardus, *Essentials of Americanization,* 179–180.

30. McLean, *That Mexican!* 34–35.

31. California Mexican Fact-Finding Committee, *Mexicans in California: Report of Governor C. C. Young's Mexican Fact-Finding Committee,* 41. The committee quoted from Princeton economist Robert E. Foerster, who must have dizzied everyone within hearing distance. He testified: "From the survey which has been given of the population of Mexico, it must be plain that the pure Spanish element is small. . . . and that the basic race of the country is Indian. . . . Common estimates of the pure Indian stock place it *at five or six millions;* of the *white stock at one and one-half to less than three million* . . . of the mestizo stock about *seven or eight millions.* If the smaller of the estimate for the Indian stock is preferred, the larger must be taken for the mestizo. *Of the mestizo stock a part is half-Indian and half-white,* another part is more than half-white and less than half-Indian, and still another part is more than half Indian and less than half white. Since the pure Indian stock greatly outnumbers the pure white it is safe to infer that that part of the mestizo which is more than half Indian greatly exceeds that part which is more that half white" (Hearings before the House Committee on Immigration and Naturalization, 68th Cong., 2d sess., March 3, 1925, 307).

32. Enock, *Mexico.*

33. John Emanuel Kienle, "Housing Conditions among the Mexican Population of Los Angeles," master's thesis, University of Southern California, 1912: 3.

34. Wallace Thompson, *The Mexican Mind: A Study of National Psychology,* quoted in Jessie Hayden, "The La Habra Experiment in Mexican Social Education," master's thesis, University of Southern California, 1934: 2.

35. Grace Elizabeth Reeves, "Adult Mexican Education in the United States," master's thesis, Claremont Colleges, 1929: 51.

36. Jay S. Stowell, *The Near Side of the Mexican Question,* 17.

37. Vernon Monroe McCombs, *From over the Border: A Study of the Mexicans in the United States,* 57.

38. McLean, *That Mexican!* 176–177.

39. Ibid. 182.

40. Charles A. Thomson, "What of the Bracero? The Forgotten Alternative in Our Immigration Policy," *The Survey* 54, no. 5 (June 1, 1925): 292.

41. Carey McWilliams, *North from Mexico: The Spanish Speaking People of the United States*, 206. The full meaning of the term "the Mexican Problem" has been misunderstood for sometime now. I am referring to the tendency to restrict the analysis of the term to domestic origins and use. For example, in David Montejano's very valuable work *Anglos and Mexicans in the Making of Texas, 1836–1986*, the Mexican Problem is defined within a strictly national scope, as if it developed on U.S. soil and only in relation to Mexican immigrants. Others have followed Montejano's example. See Roberto R. Calderón, *Mexican Coal Mining Labor*, 6–7.

42. Bogardus, *Essentials of Americanization*, 179.

43. Simpich, "The Little Brown Brother Treks North," 239.

44. Merton E. Hill, *The Development of an Americanization Program*, 5.

45. Charles Clifford Carpenter, "A Study of Segregation versus Non-segregation of Mexican Children," master's thesis, University of Southern California, 1935: 27.

46. Elizabeth Fuller, *The Mexican Housing Problem* (originally published in 1921), in *Perspectives on Mexican-American Life*, The Mexican American Series, ed. Carlos Cortes et al., 1.

47. William Edward Garnett, "Immediate and Pressing Race Problems of Texas," in Southwestern Political and Social Science Association, *Proceedings* (sixth annual meeting, 1925), 32.

48. Herschel T. Manuel, *The Education of Mexican and Spanish-Speaking Children in Texas*, v, 1–2.

49. Edward Everett Davis, "A Report on Illiteracy in Texas," University of Texas Bulletin no. 2328, cited in Marvin Ferdinand Doerr, "Problem of the Elimination of Mexican Pupils from School," master's thesis, University of Texas, Austin: 1.

50. Thomson, "What of the Bracero?" 291.

51. See Betty Gould, "Methods of Teaching Mexicans," master's thesis, University of Southern California, 1932. Gould wrote, "The ever increasing number of Mexican pupils in the schools of California today has presented a problem of major importance to the educational system" (1).

52. Stowell, *The Near Side of the Mexican Question*, 118–119.

53. McCombs, *From over the Border*, 38.

54. Simon Ludwig Treff, "The Education of Mexican Children in Orange County," master's thesis, University of Southern California, 1934: 10.

55. Chester H. Crowell, "Why Make Mexico an Exception?" *The Survey* 64, no. 3 (May 1, 1931): 180.

56. Simpich, "The Little Brown Brother Treks North," 238.

57. McCombs, *From over the Border*, 62.

58. Herschel T. Manuel, The *Education of Mexican and Spanish-Speaking Children in Texas*, 8.

59. Stowell, *The Near Side of the Mexican Question*, 32.

60. Simpich, "The Little Brown Brother Treks North," 238.

61. Frank Callcott, "The Mexican Peon in Texas," *The Survey* 44 (June 26, 1920): 437.

62. Helen Walker, "Mexican Immigrants and Citizenship," *Sociology and Social Research* 13, no. 1 (1929): 466.

63. Merton E. Hill, *The Development of an Americanization Program*, 35.

64. Richard Lee Strout, "A Fence for the Rio Grande," *The Independent* 120, no. 4070 (June 2, 1928): 518.

65. Simpich, "Along Our Side of the Mexican Border," 63.

66. Ibid., 71.

67. Bogardus, *The Mexican in the United States*, 24.

68. Gould, "Methods of Teaching Mexicans," 3.

69. Victor S. Clark, *Mexican Labor in the United States*, 500.

70. Katherine Hollier Meguire, "Educating the Mexican Child in the Elementary School," master's thesis, University of Southern California, 1938: 6.

71. Laura Lucille Lyon, "Investigation of the Program for the Adjustment of Mexican Girls to the High Schools of the San Fernando Valley," master's thesis, University of Southern California, 1933: 8.

72. Samuel Bryan, "Mexican Immigrants in the United States," *The Survey* 28, no. 23 (September 7, 1912): 729–730.

73. Manuel, *The Education of Mexican and Spanish-Speaking Children in Texas*, 23–24.

74. Walker, "Mexican Immigrants and Citizenship," 466.

75. Bogardus, *The Mexican in the United States*, 65.

76. Hazel Peck Bishop, "A Case Study of the Improvement of Mexican Homes through Instruction in Homemaking," master's thesis, University of Southern California, 1937: 5–6.

77. Gould, "Methods of Teaching Mexicans," 96.

78. Lawrence Otto Barfell, "A Study of the Health Program among Mexican Children with Special Reference to the Prevalence of Tuberculosis and Its Causes," master's thesis, University of Southern California, 1937: 71.

79. Treff, "The Education of Mexican Children in Orange County," 16.

80. Bogardus, *The Mexican in the United States*, 47.

81. Gould, "Methods of Teaching Mexicans," 2.

82. Ibid., 73.

83. Bogardus, *Essentials of Americanization*, 181.

84. California Commission of Immigration and Housing, *First Annual Report*, 239. The *Report* describes the Mexican immigrant as one who suffers from a "lack of initiative [and a] roving temper."

85. Eva Frank, "The Mexican 'Just Won't Work,'" *The Nation* 125, no. 3241 (August 17, 1927): 156, cited in Helen Walker, "The Conflict of Cultures in First Generation Mexicans in Santa Ana, California," master's thesis, University of Southern California, 1928: 18.

86. Helen D. Marston, "Mexican Traits," *The Survey* 44 (August 2, 1920): 563.

87. Helen Walker, "Mexican Immigrants as Laborers," *Sociology and Social Research* 13 (September, 1928): 62

88. Walker, "Mexican Immigrants and Citizenship," 466.

89. Vera Sturges, "The Progress and Adjustment in Mexican and United States Life," in National Conference on Social Welfare, *Proceedings* (1920), 486.

90. Bogardus, *The Mexican in the United States*, 65, 66–67.

91. The training manual for elementary school teachers prepared by Mary

Bess Henry, an Americanization teacher, is illustrative of the general tendency to divide the alleged qualities into good side and bad. She wrote:

> In spite of these very common faults of improvidence, apparent shiftlessness, lack of ambition, and moral carelessness, they have many likeable qualities. Their good nature and naïve pleasure in things that interest them, their loyalty to each other and to their friends, their utter disregard for worry, their generosity and courtesy make them happy among themselves. (*Santa Ana's Problem in Americanization*, 14)

92. Clark, *Mexican Labor in the United States*, 496.

93. Bogardus, *The Mexican in the United States*, 52.

94. Clara Gertrude Smith, "The Development of the Mexican People in the Community of Watts, California," 9.

95. Ibid., 26.

96. Anna Christine Lofstedt, "A Study of the Mexican Population in Pasadena, California," master's thesis, University of Southern California, 1922: 6.

97. Sturges, "The Progress and Adjustment in Mexican and United States Life," 483.

98. Of the mythical Juan García, considered the typical Mexican, Robert McLean wrote, "But the greatest ill from which Mexico suffers is one which seems to go down to the very well-springs of her life. Everywhere there is lack of conscience; no love for right, because it is right; no hatred for wrong, because it is wrong." And later, "The Aztecs taught chastity; the Spaniards came with unbridled passions . . . [and] instead of being an example of sobriety, of gentleness and chastity, . . . [were] usually the opposite of all these virtues" (*That Mexican!* 43).

99. Clark, *Mexican Labor in the United States*, 482.

6. Empire, Domestic Policy, and the Education of Mexican Immigrants

1. Gilbert G. González, *Chicano Education in the Era of Segregation*.

2. The master's theses and doctoral dissertations which examined various themes concerning the Mexican Problem or cited authors of works on Mexico here discussed numbered no less than twenty-six. Along with those noted in the body of the narrative, the following graduate studies also made one or more of such claims or citations: Emma E. Valle, "The Adjustment of Migrant Pupils in a Junior High School," master's thesis, University of Texas, 1953; Grace Elizabeth Reeves, "Adult Mexican Education in the United States," master's thesis, Claremont Colleges, 1929; Charles Dinnijes Withers, "Problems with Mexican Boys," master's thesis, University of Southern California, 1942; Marvin Ferdinand Doerr, "Problem of the Elimination of Mexican Pupils from School," master's thesis, University of Texas, 1938; Herman A. Buckner, "A Study of Pupil Elimination and Failure among Mexicans," master's thesis, University of Southern California, 1935; Gladys Riskin Wueste, "A Survey of Factors Relating to the Education of the Children of Migratory Parents of Eagle Pass, Texas," master's thesis, University of Texas, Austin, 1950; William Nathan Wilson, "An Analysis of the Academic and Home Problems of the Pupils in a Mexican Junior High School," mas-

ter's thesis, University of Southern California, 1938; Helen Summers, "An Evaluation of Certain Procedures in the Teaching of the Non-English Speaking Mexican Child," master's thesis, University of California, Los Angeles, 1939; Eunice Elvira Parr, "A Comparative Study of Mexican and American Children in the Schools of San Antonio, Texas," Ph.D. dissertation, University of Chicago, 1926; Mary C. Sauter, "Arbol Verde: Cultural Conflict and Accommodation in a California Mexican Community," master's thesis, Claremont Colleges, 1933; William Wilson McEuen, "A Survey of the Mexicans in Los Angeles," master's thesis, University of Southern California, 1914.

3. Helen Walker, "The Conflict of Cultures in First Generation Mexicans in Santa Ana, California," master's thesis, University of Southern California, 1928.

4. Anna Christine Lofstedt, "A Study of the Mexican Population in Pasadena, California," master's thesis, University of Southern California, 1922.

5. Mary Lanigan, "Second Generation Mexicans in Belvedere," master's thesis, University of Southern California, 1932.

6. George Curtiss Gillette, "A Diagnostic Study of the Factors Affecting the Low Scores of Spanish Speaking Children on Standardized Tests," master's thesis, University of Southern California, 1941.

7. Laura Lucille Lyon, "Investigation of the Program for the Adjustment of Mexican Girls to the High Schools of the San Fernando Valley," master's thesis, University of Southern California, 1933.

8. Victor H. Kelley, "Teaching the Spanish Speaking Child in Arizona," in Arizona State Department of Education, *Course of Study for Elementary Schools of Arizona*, Bulletin no. 13, p. 3.

9. Albert Turner Kaderli, "The Educational Problem in the Americanization of the Spanish-Speaking Pupils of Sugar Land, Texas," master's thesis, University of Texas, Austin, 1940: 14. Kaderli cited a number of works on Mexico, including Ernest Gruening's *Mexico and Its Heritage*, as well as Emory Bogardus' *Essentials of Americanization*. Kaderli was certainly not alone in suggesting that the background be investigated. The Arizona State Department of Education recommended to the teaching corps the following:

The development of a sympathetic attitude toward the Mexican or Spanish-speaking child involves knowing his or her background. . . . Teachers of non-English speaking children must understand and appreciate the races and nationalities of which the children are a product, because they differ in background, in habits, in point of view, and in ambition. (Kelley, "Teaching the Spanish Speaking Child in Arizona," 3)

10. Jessie Hayden, "The La Habra Experiment in Mexican Social Education," master's thesis, University of Southern California, 1934: 27.

11. Wallace Thompson, *The Mexican Mind: A Study of National Psychology*, 41.

12. Hazel Peck Bishop, "A Case Study of the Improvement of Mexican Homes through Instruction in Homemaking," master's thesis, University of Southern California, 1937: 5–6.

13. Simon Ludwig Treff, "The Education of Mexican Children in Orange County," master's thesis, University of Southern California, 1934: 1.

14. See for example, James Kilbourne Harris, "A Sociological Study of a Mexican School in San Antonio, Texas," master's thesis, University of Texas, 1927; and Mary Bess Henry, *Santa Ana's Problem in Americanization.* Henry wrote: "In spite of these very common faults of improvidence, apparent shiftlessness, lack of ambition, and moral carelessness, they have many likeable qualities. Their good nature and naïve pleasure in things that interest them, their loyalty to each other and to their friends, their utter disregard for worry, their generosity and courtesy make them happy among themselves" (14).

15. John Leonard Vandenbergh, "The Mexican Problems in the Schools," *Los Angeles School Journal* 11 (May 14, 1928): 154.

16. Edward Alsworth Ross, *Social Control: A Survey of the Foundations of Order;* see also Ross's *Sin and Society: An Analysis of Latter-Day Iniquity.*

17. On the concept of intelligence, see Gilbert G. González, "The Historical Development of the Concept of Intelligence," *Review of Radical Political Economics* 11, no. 2 (summer 1979).

18. William James, *Principles of Psychology.*

19. Lewis Terman, *Intelligence Tests and School Reorganization;* also Lewis Terman, "Intelligence and Its Measurement," *Journal of Educational Psychology* 12, no. 3 (March 1921).

20. Clara Gertrude Smith, "The Development of the Mexican People in the Community of Watts, California," master's thesis, University of Southern California, 1933: 9; Jessie Hayden, "The La Habra Experiment in Social Education," 112.

21. Herschel Manuel, *The Education of Mexican and Spanish-Speaking Children in Texas,* 20.

22. Hazel Peck Bishop, "A Case Study of the Improvement of Mexican Homes through Instruction in Homemaking," 6.

23. In his master's thesis, Charles Clifford Carpenter wrote, "Many school districts in Southern California have attempted to solve the problem presented by large numbers of Mexican children in their schools by organizing special rooms and segregating Mexican children from the American children" ("A Study of Segregation versus Non-segregation of Mexican Children," master's thesis, University of Southern California, 1935: 27).

24. Ward William Leis, "The Status of Education for Mexican Children in Four Border States," master's thesis, University of Southern California, 1931: 72.

25. Carpenter, "A Study of Segregation versus Non-segregation of Mexican Children," 152. Carpenter, later the school superintendent at the Westminster School District in Orange County, was not alone in stressing the alleged differences. Lawrence Otto Barfell, his colleague at the University of Southern California, wrote: "There is a logical reasoning for this non-mixing policy. The Mexican child was older and his health standards were low. Many Mexican children were unclean, physically as well as mentally. . . . Mental aspects are varied" ("A Study of the Health Program among Mexican Children with Special Reference to the Prevalence of Tuberculosis and Its Causes," master's thesis, University of Southern California, 1937: 62).

26. Edward Everett Davis, "A Report on Illiteracy in Texas," University of Texas Bulletin no. 2328, 30, cited in Marvin Ferdinand Doerr, "Problem of the Elimination of Mexican Pupils from School," master's thesis, University of Texas,

Austin, 1938: 1. A second writer noted that in Texas "whenever it is possible . . . separate schools, especially for the grammar grades, are provided for whites and for the Mexicans, as this has been found more satisfactory for all concerned" (Frank Callcott, "The Mexican Peon in Texas," *The Survey* 44 (June 26, 1920): 438.

27. Merton E. Hill, *The Development of an Americanization Program*, 106.

28. Treff, "The Education of Mexican Children in Orange County," 133.

29. Manuel, *The Education of Mexican and Spanish-Speaking Children in Texas*, 68.

30. Grace Stanley, "Special Schools for Mexicans," *The Survey* 44 (September 15, 1920): 714.

31. See Gilbert G. González, *Labor and Community: Mexican Citrus Worker Villages in a Southern California County*, Chapter 4, "Schooling Village Children."

32. Davis, "A Report on Illiteracy in Texas," 29.

33. Annie Reynolds, "The Education of Spanish-Speaking Children in Five Southwestern States," U.S. Office of Education Bulletin no. 11, p. 48.

34. Susan B. Dorsey, "Mrs. Pierce and Mrs. Dorsey Discuss Matters before the Principals' Club," *Los Angeles School Journal* 6, no. 25 (March 5, 1923): 59.

35. Emory Bogardus, *Essentials of Americanization*, 179.

36. Merton E. Hill, *The Development of an Americanization Program*, 5.

37. Quoted in Manuel, *The Education of Mexican and Spanish-Speaking Children in Texas*, 126–127.

38. Katherine Hollier Meguire, "Educating the Mexican Child in the Elementary School," master's thesis, University of Southern California, 1938: 121.

39. J. T. Taylor, "The Americanization of Harlingen's Mexican School Population," *Texas Outlook* 18 (September 1934): 38.

40. Emory Bogardus, *The Mexican in the United States*.

41. Helen Walker, "Mexican Immigrants and Citizenship," *Sociology and Social Research* 13 (1929), no. 1 (September–October): 466–467.

42. Jay S. Stowell, *The Near Side of the Mexican Question*, 82.

43. Ibid., 80.

44. Linna E. Bressette, *Mexicans in the United States: A Brief Report of a Survey*, 29.

45. Stowell, *The Near Side of the Mexican Question*, 84. Stowell's colleague in missionary work, Vernon Monroe McCombs, exclaimed that

> just as millions of the great American desert have been transformed into paradise by water, cultivation, and patience, so can these potentially brilliant, passionate Mexican young people be transformed into the flower of human culture. Thus he who says, "It cannot be done," is already being interrupted by people saying, "It is being done." Some day it will be said of the products of our mission schools for Mexicans, "Ye are God's tilled land." Sympathetic trained American teachers in these schools are leaving the impress of their lives upon their plastic students by giving practical training amid surroundings where all possible racial and hereditary handicaps have been removed. (McCombs, *From over the Border: A Study of the Mexicans in the United States*, 122)

46. Gilbert G. González, *Chicano Education in the Era of Segregation*, 47–61.

47. *La Habra (Calif.) Star*, May 22, 1925.

48. Betty Gould, "Methods of Teaching Mexicans," master's thesis, 1932: 118.

Gould wrote: "Bring children in contact with American homes to teach principles of sanitation. . . . They should contact American homes and see the advantages of clean sheets, fresh air, and sanitary surroundings" (118).

49. Merton E. Hill, *The Development of an Americanization Program*, 97.

50. George Alan Works, "The Non-English Speaking Child and the Public School," in *General Report*, Texas Educational Survey Report, vol. 8, p. 211.

51. John Branigan, "Education of Over-Age Mexican Children," *Sierra Educational News* 12 (December 1929): 37.

52. William E. Garnett, "Immediate and Pressing Race Problems of Texas," in Southwestern Political and Social Science Association, *Proceedings* (sixth annual meeting, 1925), 43.

53. C. R. Tupper, "The Use of Intelligence Tests in the Schools of a Small City," in Lewis Terman, ed., *Intelligence Tests and School Reorganization*, 95.

54. Merton E. Hill, *The Development of an Americanization Program*, 96.

55. Reynolds, "The Education of Spanish-Speaking Children in Five Southwestern States."

56. Harold J. Jones, "All-Mexican School: A Need for Learning Is Satisfied in an All-Mexican School," *Sierra Educational News* 36 (November 1940): 17.

57. Leis, "The Status of Education for Mexican Children in Four Border States," 72. Leis cited Thompson's *The Mexican Mind* and *The People of Mexico*. Another reviewer's systematic examination of the literature on the education of Mexican children found unsurprising results. The author reported that "early segregation, special guidance programs, and specialized curricula were recommended for dealing with the problem of educating the Mexican child" (William Nathan Wilson, "An Analysis of the Academic and Home Problems of the Pupils in a Mexican Junior High School," 15).

58. Vera A. Chase, "Instruction of Bilingual Children," in Arizona State Department of Education, *Course of Study for Elementary Schools of Arizona*, Bulletin no. 13, p. 13.

59. H. Frank Gifford, "The Mexican Child in Our American School," *Arizona Teacher-Parent* 27 (March 1939): 198.

60. *Los Angeles School Journal* 9 (February 15, 1926): 41.

61. Los Angeles City Schools. *Third Yearbook of the Department of Psychology and Educational Research*, Los Angeles School District School Publication no. 185, p. 87.

62. Meguire, "Educating the Mexican Child in the Elementary School," 117. See also Pearl Idelia Ellis, *Americanization through Homemaking*, who wrote (among other things): "Since only about five percent of Mexican girls who graduate from the eighth grade enter high school, their ability as seamstresses must be developed in the elementary schools" (13).

63. Meguire, "Educating the Mexican Child in the Elementary School," 80.

64. "The Public Schools in San Antonio," *San Antonio Public Schools Bulletin* 2, no. 1, p. 70.

65. Gould, "Methods of Teaching Mexicans," 69, 92.

66. Dorothy M. Kress, "The Spanish-Speaking School Child in Texas," *Texas Outlook* 18, no. 24 (December 1934): 24.

67. Tupper, "The Use of Intelligence Tests in the Schools of a Small City," 102.

68. *Los Angeles School Journal* 6 (June 4, 1923): 23.

69. Manuel, *The Education of Mexican and Spanish-Speaking Children in Texas*, 36.

70. See González, *Chicano Education in the Era of Segregation*, Chapter 7.

71. Margaret Mead, ed., *Cultural Patterns and Cultural Change*, quoted in Paula Roden, "A Study of Relationships among Various Intelligence Test and Reading Test Results Obtained with Latin American Second Grade Children," master's thesis, University of Texas, 1955: 4.

72. Florence Rockwood Kluckhohn, "Cultural Factors in Social Work Practice and Education," *Social Service Review* 25, no. 1 (March 1951): 44.

73. Perry Morris Broom, "An Interpretive Analysis of the Economic and Educational Status of Latin Americans in Texas," Ph.D. dissertation, University of Texas, 1942: 167.

74. Ignacio Reyes, "A Survey of the Problems Involved in the Americanization of the Mexican American," master's thesis, University of Southern California, 1957: 24.

75. Dorothy K. Chang, "A Guide for the Understanding and Teaching of Mexican American Adolescents," master's thesis, University of Southern California, 1957: 14, 17.

76. James Clifford Safley, *Mexican Vistas*, 2, 13, 19, 22,

77. Quoted in Carey McWilliams, *North from Mexico: The Spanish-Speaking People of the United States*, 234.

Conclusion

1. On June 15, 1993, a major metropolitan newspaper, the *Orange County Register*, ran an article entitled "Mexico Is Shedding Its *Manana* [*sic*] Image," a conceptualization that Americans could easily grasp at the end of the twentieth century. The article originally appeared in the *Dallas Morning News;* its author, Richard Estrada, was the associate editorial page editor of the *Dallas Morning News*.

2. Lee Hockstader, "Immigrants from Mexico Take Steps toward Hope," *Washington Post*, August 25, 2002. The *Washington Post* journalist noted: "Health conditions are poor, residents suffer from sky-high rates of diabetes, cancer, asthma, hypertension and cardiovascular diseases. Most colonia residents have no medical insurance, which means no private hospital will treat them except in an emergency. The nearest hospital to Cameron Park and the other 100 colonias in Cameron County is in Galveston, Tex., about a 480 mile drive north."

BIBLIOGRAPHY

Abbreviation: *EMJ* = *Engineering and Mining Journal.*

Alexander, J. Park. *Mexico: Facts about the Republic of Mexico Gathered in a Recent Brief Visit and Informally Set Down in Letters to His Family.* Akron, Ohio: Beacon Publishing Co., 1890.

Al-Shimas, Kamar. *The Mexican Southland.* Fowler, Ind.: Benton Review Shop, 1922.

Anderson, Rodney. *Outcasts in Their Own Land: Mexican Industrial Workers, 1906–1911.* De Kalb: Northern Illinois University, 1976.

Andrews, Gregg. *Shoulder to Shoulder? The American Federation of Labor, the United States, and the Mexican Revolution.* Berkeley: University of California Press, 1991.

Babbitt, C. S. *A Remedy for the Decadence of the Latin Race.* Pamphlet. El Paso: El Paso Publishing Company, 1999.

Baker, Frank Collins. *A Naturalist in Mexico: Being a Visit to Cuba, Northern Yucatan, and Mexico.* Chicago: David Oliphant, 1895.

Ballou, Maturin M. *Aztec Land.* Boston: Houghton Mifflin and Co., 1890.

Bancroft, Hubert Howe. *History of Mexico, 1861–1887.* Vol. 14 of *The Works of Hubert Howe Bancroft.* San Francisco: The History Company, 1888.

Barfell, Lawrence Otto. "A Study of the Health Program among Mexican Children with Special Reference to the Prevalence of Tuberculosis and Its Causes." Master's thesis, University of Southern California, 1937.

Baron, H. J. "Río Plata Mine and Mill, Western Chihuahua." *EMJ* 87, no. 3 (January 16, 1909): 147–51.

"Barriers to the Little Brown Brother." Editorial. *The Independent* 120 (February 1928), 242.

Barron, Clarence W. *The Mexican Problem.* Boston: Houghton Mifflin Co., 1917.

Barton, Mary. *Impressions of Mexico with Brush and Pen.* London: Methuen, [1911].

Bates, J. H. *Notes of a Tour in Mexico and California.* New York: Burr Printing House, 1887.

Batten, James Hoffman. "Mexicans are People." *The Survey* 61, no. 7 (January 1, 1929): 447–48.

Beebe, C. William. *Two Bird-Lovers in Mexico.* Boston: Houghton Mifflin Co., 1905.

Bernstein, Marvin. *The Mexican Mining Industry, 1890–1950.* Albany: State University of New York, 1964.

Beverly, Walter D. "Reminiscences of Mining in Durango," *EMJ* 83, no. 14 (October 2, 1909): 635–639.

Bishop, Hazel Peck. "A Case Study of the Improvement of Mexican Homes through Instruction in Homemaking." Master's thesis, University of Southern California, 1937.

Bishop, William Henry. *Old Mexico and Her Lost Provinces: A Journey in Mexico, Southern California, and Arizona by Way of Cuba*. New York: Harper and Brothers, 1883.

Blake, Mary Elizabeth. "Picturesque Mexico." In Mary Elizabeth Blake and Margaret F. Sullivan, *Mexico*. New York: Lee and Shepherd, 1888.

Blakeslee, George H., ed. *Mexico and the Caribbean*. Clark University Addresses. New York: G. E. Stechert and Co., 1920.

Blichfeldt, E. H. *A Mexican Journey*. New York: Thomas Y. Crowell Co., 1912.

Bogardus, Emory. *Essentials of Americanization*. Los Angeles: University of Southern California, 1919.

———. *The Mexican Immigrant: An Annotated Bibliography*. Los Angeles: Council on International Relations, 1929.

———. *The Mexican in the United States*. University of Southern California School of Research Studies, no. 5, Los Angeles: University of Southern California Press, 1934.

Borton, Francis S. *Mexico: "Our People Next Door."* New York: Missionary Society of the Methodist Episcopal Church, 1904.

Branigan, John. "Education of Over-Age Mexican Children." *Sierra Educational News* 12 (December 1929): 25–29.

Bressette, Linna E. *Mexicans in the United States: A Brief Report of a Survey*. Washington, D.C.: National Catholic Welfare Conference, 1929.

Broom, Perry Morris. "An Interpretive Analysis of the Economic and Educational Status of Latin Americans in Texas." Ph.D. dissertation, University of Texas, Austin, 1942.

Brown, Jonathan. *Oil and Revolution in Mexico*. Berkeley: University of California Press, 1993.

Brown, Sara, Robie O. Sargent, and Clara Armentrout. *Children Working in the Sugar Beet Fields of Certain Districts of the South Platte Valley, Colorado*. New York: National Child Labor Committee, 1925.

Bryan, Samuel. "Mexican Immigrants in the United States." *The Survey* 28, no. 23 (September 7, 1912): 726–730.

Buckner, Herman A. "A Study of Pupil Elimination and Failure among Mexicans." Master's thesis, University of Southern California, 1935.

Butler, John Wesley. *History of the Methodist Episcopal Church in Mexico*. New York: Methodist Book Concern, 1918.

Butler, Mrs. John W. "The Women of Mexico." *Missionary Review of the World* 39 (January–June 1916): 181–186.

Calderón, Roberto R. *Mexican Coal Mining Labor in Texas and Coahuila, 1880–1930*. College Station: Texas A&M Press, 2000.

California. Commission of Immigration and Housing. *First Annual Report*. San Francisco: State Building, 1915.

California. Mexican Fact-Finding Committee. *Mexicans in California: Report of Governor C. C. Young's Mexican Fact-Finding Committee.* San Francisco: State Building, 1930.

Callcott, Frank. "The Mexican Peon in Texas." *The Survey* 44 (June 26, 1920): 437–438.

Campbell, Reau. *Complete Guide and Descriptive Book of Mexico.* Mexico City: Sonora News Co., 1899.

———. *Mexico and the Mexicans: The Material Matters and Mysterious Myths of That Country and Its People.* Mexico City: Sonora News Agency, 1892.

———. *Mexico: Tours through the Egypt of the New World.* New York: G. G. Crawford, 1890.

Carpenter, Charles Clifford. "A Study of Segregation versus Non-segregation of Mexican Children." Master's thesis, University of Southern California, 1935.

Carr, Harry. *Old Mother Mexico.* Boston: Houghton Mifflin Co., 1931.

Carson, James. "Upon the Indian Depends Mexico's Future." In George H. Blakeslee, ed., *Mexico and the Caribbean: Clark University Addresses.* New York: G. E. Stechert and Co., 1920.

Carson, W. E. *Mexico: The Wonderland of the South.* 1st ed., New York: MacMillan Co., 1909; rev. ed., New York: MacMillan Co., 1914.

Case, Alden Buell. *Thirty Years with the Mexicans: In Peace and Revolution.* New York: Fleming H. Revell Co., 1917.

Caulfield, Norman. *Mexican Workers and the State: From the Porfiriato to NAFTA.* Fort Worth: Texas Christian University Press, 1998.

Chamberlain, George Agnew. *Is Mexico Worth Saving?* Indianapolis: Bobbs-Merrill Co., 1920.

Chang, Dorothy K. "A Guide for the Understanding and Teaching of Mexican American Adolescents." Master's thesis, University of Southern California, 1957.

Chase, Vera A. "Instruction of Bilingual Children." In Arizona State Department of Education, *Course of Study for Elementary Schools of Arizona,* Bulletin no. 13 (1939).

Clark, Victor S. *Mexican Labor in the United States.* U.S. Department of Commerce and Labor, Bureau of Labor Bulletin no. 78. Washington, D.C.: U.S. Government Printing Office, 1908.

Cleland, Robert Glass. *The Mexican Year Book, 1922–1924.* Los Angeles: Times-Mirror Press, 1924.

Coatsworth, John H. *Growth against Development: The Economic Impact of Railroads in Porfirian Mexico.* De Kalb: Northern Illinois University, 1981.

Coffin, Alfred Oscar. *Land without Chimneys, or The Byways of Mexico.* Cincinnati: Editor Publishing Co., 1898.

Conant, Charles Arthur. *The United States in the Orient: The Nature of the Economic Problem.* 1900; reprint, Port Washington, N.Y.: Kennikat Press, 1971.

Conkling, Howard. *Mexico and the Mexicans, or Notes of Travel in the Winter and Spring of 1883.* New York: Taintor Brothers, Merrill and Co., 1883.

Conley, Edward M. "The Americanization of Mexico." *American Monthly Review of Reviews* 32 (1907): 724–725.

Corey, Herbert. "Adventuring Down the Coast of Mexico." *National Geographic* 42, no. 5 (November 1922): 451–503.

———. "The Isthmus of Tehuantepec." *National Geographic* 45, no. 5 (May 1924): 549–578.

Creel, George. *The People Next Door: An Interpretive History of Mexico and the Mexicans.* New York: John Day Co., 1926.

Creelman, James. *Díaz, Master of Mexico.* New York: D. Appleton and Co., 1911.

Crowell, Chester H. "Why Make Mexico an Exception?" *The Survey* 66, no. 3 (May 1, 1931): 180.

Delpar, Helen. *The Enormous Vogue of Things Mexican: Cultural Relations between the United States and Mexico, 1920–1935.* Tuscaloosa: University of Alabama Press, 1992.

Doerr, Marvin Ferdinand. "Problem of the Elimination of Mexican Pupils from School." Master's thesis, University of Texas, 1938.

Doheny, Edward D. Second interview with Mr. Edward D. Doheny. File 3283, Interview 503. Doheny Research Foundation Collection. Special Collections, Mary Norton Clapp Library, Occidental College, Glendale, California.

Dorsey, Susan B. "Mrs. Pierce and Mrs. Dorsey Discuss Matters before the Principals' Club." *Los Angeles School Journal* 6, no. 25 (March 5, 1923): 59.

Drees, Charles W. *Thirteen Years in Mexico.* Edited by Ada M. C. Drees. New York: Abingdon Press, 1915.

Dye, Alexander V. "Railways and Revolutions in Mexico." *Foreign Affairs* 5, no. 2 (January 1927): 321–323.

Eakin, Emily. "All Roads Lead to D.C." *New York Times,* March 31, 2002.

Editorial. *The Survey* 59, no. 3 (November 1, 1927): 155–156.

Ellis, Pearl Idelia. *Americanization through Homemaking.* Los Angeles: Wetzel Publishing Company, 1929.

Empson, J. B. "Silver Cyaniding in Mexico." *EMJ* 86, no. 12 (October 3, 1908): 667–668.

Enock, C. Reginald. *Mexico: Its Ancient and Modern Civilisation, History and Political Conditions, Topography and Natural Resources, Industries and General Development.* New York: Scribner, 1909.

Estrada, Richard. "Mexico Is Shedding Its *Manana* Image." *Orange County Register,* June 15, 1993.

"An Eye on the Little Brown Brother." Editorial. *The Independent* 119, no. 4037 (October 8, 1927): 347.

Faulkner, Consul Walter H. to the Honorable J. B. Moore, assistant secretary of state, October 15, 1898. National Archives Records of the Department of State, microfilms.

Flandrau, Charles Macomb. *Viva Mexico!* New York: D. Appleton and Co., 1908.

Foster, Harry L. *A Gringo in Mañana-Land.* New York: Dodd, Mead and Co., 1924.

Foster, John W. "The New Mexico." *National Geographic* 13, no. 1 (January 1902).

Franck, Harry A. *Tramping through Mexico, Guatemala and Honduras.* New York: Century Co., 1916.

Fraser-Campbell, Evan. "The Management of Mexican Labor." *EMJ* 90 (June 3, 1911): 1104–1105.

French, William E. *A Peaceful and Working People: Manners, Morals, and Class Formation in Northern Mexico*. Albuquerque: University of New Mexico Press, 1996.

Fuller, Elizabeth. *The Mexican Housing Problem*. In *Perspectives on Mexican American Life*. The Mexican American Series, ed. Carlos Cortes et al. 1921 (monograph); New York: Arno Press, 1974.

Galarza, Ernesto. "Program for Action." *Common Ground* 10, no. 4 (1949): 27–38.

García, Mario T. *Desert Immigrants: The Mexicans of El Paso, 1880–1920*. New Haven: Yale University Press, 1981.

García, Matt. *A World of Its Own: Race, Labor, and Citrus in the Making of Greater Los Angeles, 1900–1970*. Chapel Hill: University of North Carolina Press, 2001.

Garcilazo, Jeffrey Marcos. "Traqueros: Mexican Railroad Workers in the United States, 1870–1930." Typescript, 1998.

Garnett, William Edward. "Immediate and Pressing Race Problems of Texas." In Southwestern Political and Social Science Association, *Proceedings* (sixth annual meeting, 1925).

Gavit, John Palmer. "Mexico and an Awakened Administration." *The Independent* 119 (December 31, 1927): 645.

———. "Through Neighbors' Doorways." *The Survey* 59, no. 5 (December 1, 1927): 322.

"Gen. Foster on Mexico." *National Geographic* 12 (1901): 159–160.

Gifford, H. Frank. "The Mexican Child in Our American School." *Arizona Teacher-Parent* 27 (March 1939).

Gillette, George Curtiss. "A Diagnostic Study of the Factors Affecting the Low Scores of Spanish Speaking Children on Standardized Tests." Master's thesis, University of Southern California, 1941.

Gillpatrick, Wallace. *The Man Who Likes Mexico*. New York: Century Co., 1911.

González, Antonio José. Interview with author, November 2, 1980.

González, Gilbert G. *Chicano Education in the Era of Segregation*. Philadelphia: Balch Institute Press, 1990.

———. "The Historical Development of the Concept of Intelligence." *Review of Radical Political Economics* 11, no. 2 (summer 1979).

———. *Labor and Community: Mexican Citrus Worker Villages in a Southern California County, 1900–1950*. Urbana: University of Illinois Press, 1994.

———. *Mexican Consuls and Labor Organizing: Imperial Politics in the American Southwest*. Austin: University of Texas Press, 1999.

———. *Progressive Education: A Marxist Interpretation*. Minneapolis: Marxist Educational Press, 1982.

———. "The System of Public Education and Its Function in the Chicano Community in Los Angeles, 1920–1930." Ph.D. dissertation, University of California, Los Angeles, 1974.

González, Gilbert G., and Raúl Fernández. "Empire and the Origins of Twentieth-Century Migration from Mexico to the United States." *Pacific Historical Review* 71, no. 1 (February 2002): 19–51.

———. *A Century of Chicano History: Empire, Nations, and Migration*. New York: Routledge, 2003.

González Navarro, Moisés. *El Porfiriato: la vida social.* Vol. 4 of *Historia moderna de México,* ed. Daniel Cosío Villegas. Mexico City: Editorial Hermes, 1957.

Gooch (Inglehart), Fanny. *Face to Face with the Mexicans.* 1887; rev. ed., edited and with an introduction by C. Harvey Gardiner, Carbondale, Ill.: Southern Illinois University, 1966.

Gould, Betty. "Methods of Teaching Mexicans." Master's thesis, University of Southern California, 1932.

Gray, Albert Zabriskie. *Mexico as It Is, Being Notes of a Recent Tour in That Country.* New York: E. P. Dutton, 1878.

Griffin, Solomon Bulkley. *Mexico of To-Day.* New York: Harper and Brothers, 1886.

Gruening, Ernest. "The Mexican Renaissance." *Century Magazine* 85 (February 1924): 520–535.

———. *Mexico and Its Heritage.* New York: Century Co., 1928.

Guernsey, Frederick R. "The Year in Mexico." *Atlantic Monthly* 97 (February 1906): 219–231.

Gunn, Drewey Wayne. *American and British Writers in Mexico, 1556–1973.* Austin: University of Texas Press, 1974.

Hale, E. E., and Susan Hale. *A Family Flight through Mexico.* Boston: Lothrop, Lee and Shepherd, 1886.

Hale, Susan. *Mexico.* New York: Putnam, 1889.

Hamilton, Charles W. *Early Day Oil Tales of Mexico.* Houston: Gulf Publishing Co., 1966.

Harris, James Kilbourne. "A Sociological Study of a Mexican School in San Antonio, Texas." Master's thesis, University of Texas, Austin, 1927.

Hart, John Mason. *Empire and Revolution: The Americans in Mexico since the Civil War.* Berkeley: University of California Press, 2002.

———. *Revolutionary Mexico: The Coming and Process of the Mexican Revolution.* Berkeley: University of California Press, 1987.

———, ed. *Border Crossings: Mexican and Mexican American Workers.* Wilmington, Del.: Scholarly Resources, 1998.

Hayden, Jessie. "The La Habra Experiment in Mexican Social Education." Master's thesis, University of Southern California, 1934.

Henry, Mary Bess. *Santa Ana's Problem in Americanization.* Santa Ana, Calif.: Santa Ana Board of Education, 1920.

Hill, Merton E. *The Development of an Americanization Program.* Ontario, Calif.: Chaffey Union High School Board of Trustees, 1928.

Hill, Robert T. "Cananea Revisited." *EMJ* 76, no. 4 (December 31, 1903): 1000.

———. "Geographic and Geologic Features of Mexico." *EMJ* 72, no. 18 (November 2, 1901): 561–564.

———. "The Santa Eulalia District, Mexico." *EMJ* 76, no. 5 (August 1, 1903): 158–160.

Hockstader, Lee. "Immigrants from Mexico Take Steps toward Hope." *Washington Post,* August 25, 2002.

Hofstadter, Richard, ed. *Great Issues in American History: A Documentary Record,* vol. 2. New York: Vintage Books, 1958.

Hughes, Charles Evans. *Our Relations to the Nations of the Western Hemisphere.* Princeton: Princeton University Press, 1928.

Ingersoll, Ralph McA. *In and under Mexico.* New York: Century Co., 1924.

Inman, Samuel Guy. *Intervention in Mexico.* New York: George H. Doran Co., 1919.

———. "The Young Mexicans." *The Survey* 42 (August 30, 1919): 767–771.

International Bureau of the American Republics. *Mexico: Geographic Sketch, Natural Resources, Laws, Economic Conditions, Actual Development, Prospects of Future Growth.* Washington, D.C.: U.S. Government Printing Office, 1904.

James, William. *Principles of Psychology.* New York: Dover, 1950.

Jansen, L. H. Correspondence. *EMJ* 79 (May 25, 1905): 1000.

Jenison, H. A. C. "Mining History of Mexico—II." *EMJ* 115 (March 3, 1923): 364–403.

Johns, Michael. *City of Mexico in the Age of Díaz.* Austin: University of Texas Press, 1997.

Johnson, John J. *Latin America in Caricature.* Austin: University of Texas Press, 1980.

Johnston, Charles. "The Heart of the Trouble in Mexico." *Atlantic Monthly* 124 (October 1919): 554–561.

———. "The Two Mexicos." *Atlantic Monthly,* (November 1920): 703–709.

Jones, Chester Lloyd. *Mexico and Its Reconstruction.* New York: D. Appleton, 1921.

Jones, Harold J. "All-Mexican School: A Need for Learning Is Satisfied in an All-Mexican School." *Sierra Educational News* 36 (November 1940): 17.

Jordan, David Starr. "Colonial Expansion: Address before the Congress of Religions at Omaha in October, 1898." http://www.boondocksnet.com/ai/alltexts/Jordon01.html

Kaderli, Albert Turner. "The Educational Problem in the Americanization of the Spanish-Speaking Pupils of Sugar Land, Texas." Master's thesis, University of Texas, 1940.

Kaplan, Amy. "'Left Alone with America': The Absence of Empire in the Study of American Culture." In Amy Kaplan and Donald Pease, eds., *Cultures of United States Imperialism.* Durham, N.C.: Duke University Press, 1993.

Kelley, Victor H. "Teaching the Spanish Speaking Child in Arizona." In Arizona State Department of Education, *Course of Study for Elementary Schools of Arizona,* Bulletin no. 13 (1939).

Kienle, John Emanuel. "Housing Conditions among the Mexican Population of Los Angeles." Master's thesis, University of Southern California, 1912.

Kipling, Rudyard. "The Epics of India." *Civil and Military Gazette,* August 24, 1886. In Thomas Pinney, ed., *Kipling's India: Uncollected Sketches, 1884–88.* London: Macmillan Press, 1986.

Kirkham, Stanton Davis. *Mexican Trails: A Record of Travel in Mexico, 1904–1907, and a Glimpse of the Life of the Mexican Indian.* New York: G. P. Putnam's Sons, 1909.

Kluckhohn, Florence Rockwood. "Cultural Factors in Social Work Practice and Education." *Social Service Review* 25, no. 1 (March 1951): 38–46.

Kress, Dorothy M. "The Spanish-Speaking School Child in Texas." *Texas Outlook* 18, no. 24 (December 1934): 24.

"Labor Conditions in the Mining Industries on the West Coast." Interview no. 570 (June 17, 1918). Doheny Research Foundation Collection. Occidental College, Glendale, California.

"Labor Conditions in the Southwest." Editorial. *EMJ* 77, no. 13 (March 31, 1904): 510.

Lamb, Mark R. "On Horseback in Western Chihuahua." *EMJ* 86, no. 4 (July 25, 1908): 159–164.

———. "Stories of Batopilas Mines, Chihuahua." *EMJ* 85, no. 13 (April 4, 1908): 689–691.

Lanigan, Mary. "Second Generation Mexicans in Belvedere." Master's thesis, University of Southern California, 1932.

Leis, Ward William. "The Status of Education for Mexican Children in Four Border States." Master's thesis, University of Southern California, 1931.

Lofstedt, Anna Christine. "A Study of the Mexican Population in Pasadena, California." Master's thesis, University of Southern California, 1922.

London, Jack. "Our Adventures in Tampico." *Collier's* 53, no. 15 (June 27, 1914): 5–7, 24.

Los Angeles City Schools. *Third Yearbook of the Department of Psychology and Educational Research.* Los Angeles School District School Publication no. 185 (1929).

Los Angeles School Journal 6 (June 4, 1923); and 9 (February 15, 1926).

Lumholtz, Carl. *New Trails in Mexico: An Account of One Year's Exploration in North-western Sonora, Mexico, and South-western Arizona, 1909–1910.* New York: Charles Scribner's, 1912.

Lummis, Charles F. *The Awakening of a Nation: Mexico of To-Day.* New York: Harper and Brothers, 1898.

Lyon, Laura Lucille. "Investigation of the Program for the Adjustment of Mexican Girls to the High Schools of the San Fernando Valley." Master's thesis, University of Southern California, 1933.

Malcolmson, James W. "Mining Development in Mexico during 1902." *EMJ* 75, no. 1 (January 3, 1904).

———. "The Sierra Mojada, Coahuila, Mexico, and Its Ore Deposits." *EMJ* 72, no. 22 (November 30, 1901): 705–710.

Manuel, Herschel. *The Education of Mexican and Spanish-Speaking Children in Texas.* Austin: Fund for the Research in the Social Sciences, University of Texas, 1930.

Marcosson, Isaac F. *Metal Magic: The Story of the American Smelting and Refining Company.* New York: Farrar, Strauss and Co., 1949.

———. "Our Financial Stake in Mexico." *Collier's* 57 (July 1, 1916): 22–24.

Marston, Helen D. "Mexican Traits." *The Survey* 44 (August 2, 1920): 563.

Martin, Percy F. *Mexico of the Twentieth Century.* London: Edward Arnold, 1907.

———. *Mexico's Treasure-House (Guanajuato): An Illustrated and Descriptive Account of the Mines and Their Operations in 1906.* New York: Cheltenham Press, 1906.

Mautner, Bertram H., and W. Lewis Abbot. *Child Labor in Agriculture and Farm Life in the Arkansas Valley of Colorado.* Colorado College General Series, no. 164, Studies Series no. 2. Colorado Springs: Colorado College, 1929.

McCarty, J. Hendrickson. *Two Thousand Miles through the Heart of Mexico.* New York: Phillips and Hunt, 1886.

McCollester, Sullivan Holman. *Mexico, Old and New: A Wonderland.* Boston: Universalist Publishing House, 1899.

McCombs, Vernon Monroe. *From over the Border: A Study of the Mexicans in the United States.* New York: Council of Women for Home Missions and Missionary Education Movement, 1925.

McEuen, William Wilson. "A Survey of the Mexicans in Los Angeles." Master's thesis, University of Southern California, 1914.

McLean, Robert N. *The Northern Mexican.* New York: Home Missions Council, 1930.

————. *That Mexican! As He Really Is, North and South of the Rio Grande.* New York: Fleming H. Revell Co., 1928.

McWilliams, Carey. *North from Mexico: The Spanish Speaking People of the United States.* Philadelphia: J. B. Lippincott, 1949.

Meguire, Katherine Hollier. "Educating the Mexican Child in the Elementary School." Master's thesis, University of Southern California, 1938.

Mendez Gonzalez, Rosalinda. "Chicanas and Mexican Immigrant Families 1920–1940: Women's Subordination and Family Exploitation." In Lois Scharf and Joan Jensen, eds., *Decades of Discontent: The Women's Movement, 1920–1940* (Westport, Conn.: Greenwood Press, 1983).

"Mexican Labor and Foreign Capital." *The Independent* 112, no. 3869 (May 24, 1924): 275–276.

Montejano, David. *Anglos and Mexicans in the Making of Texas, 1836–1986.* Austin: University of Texas Press, 1987.

Navarro, Juan N. "Mexico of Today." *National Geographic* 12 (April 1901): 153–179.

————. "Mexico of Today." *National Geographic* 12 (June 1901): 235–238.

Nearing, Scott, and Joseph Freeman. *Dollar Diplomacy: A Study in American Imperialism.* New York: B. W. Huebsch and Viking Press, 1925.

Nelson, C. Nelson. "The Sahuaripa District, Sonora, Mexico." *EMJ* 82, no. 13 (October 6, 1906).

Nevius, J. Nelson. Letter to the editor. *EMJ* 78, no. 6 (August 11, 1904): 213.

Nordhoff, Charles Bernard. "The Human Side of Mexico." *Atlantic Monthly* 124 (1919): 502–509.

Ober, Frederick A. *Travels in Mexico and Life among the Mexicans.* San Francisco: J. Dewing and Co., 1884.

Ortner, Sherry B. *Life and Death on Mt. Everest: Sherpas and Himalayan Mountaineering.* Princeton, N.J.: Princeton University Press, 1999.

Parker, Morris B. *Mules, Mines, and Me in Mexico: 1895–1932.* Tucson: University of Arizona Press, 1979.

Parr, Eunice Elvira. "A Comparative Study of Mexican and American Children in the Schools of San Antonio, Texas." Ph.D. dissertation, University of Chicago, 1926.

Pinney, Thomas, ed. *Kipling's India: Uncollected Sketches, 1884–1888.* London: Macmillan Press, 1986.

Placentia (Calif.) Orange Grower's Association, *Manager's Annual Report* (1925).

Pletcher, David M. *Rails, Mines, and Progress: Seven American Promoters in Mexico, 1867–1911.* Ithaca: Cornell University Press, 1958.

Powell, Fred Wilbur. *The Railroads of Mexico.* Boston: Stratford Co., 1921.

————. "The Railroads of Mexico." In Robert Glass Cleland, *The Mexican Yearbook, 1922–1924.* Los Angeles: Times-Mirror Press, 1924.

Prendergast, F. E. "Railroads in Mexico." *Harper's New Monthly Magazine,* 1881, 276–281.

Prescott, William H. "The Luster of Ancient Mexico." *National Geographic* 30, no. 1 (July 1916): 1–32.

Probert, Frank H. "The Treasure Chest of Mercurial Mexico." *National Geographic* 30, no. 1 (July 1916): 34–68.

"The Public Schools in San Antonio." *San Antonio Public Schools Bulletin* 2, no. 1 (1924).

Reeves, Grace Elizabeth. "Adult Mexican Education in the United States." Master's thesis, Claremont Colleges, 1929.

Reisler, Mark. *By the Sweat of Their Brow: Mexican Immigrant Labor in the United States, 1900–1940.* Westport, Conn.: Greenwood Press, 1976.

"Reject Calls for an 'American Empire.'" Editorial. *Orange County (Calif.) Register,* October 15, 2001.

Reyes, Ignacio. "A Survey of the Problems Involved in the Americanization of the Mexican American." Master's thesis, University of Southern California, 1957.

Reynolds, Annie. "The Education of Spanish-Speaking Children in Five Southwestern States." U.S. Office of Education Bulletin no. 11. Washington, D.C.: U.S. Government Printing Office, 1933.

Rice, Claude T. "Mines of Penoles Company, Mapimí, Mex.—I." *EMJ* 86, no. 7 (August 15, 1908): 309–314.

————. "The Ore Deposits of Santa Eulalia, Mexico." *EMJ* 85, no. 25 (June 20, 1908): 1229–1233.

————. "Ore Sorting at the Cabresante Mine, Santa Barbara, Mexico." *EMJ* 86, no. 10 (September 12, 1908): 464–468.

————. "Smelter of Penoles, Mapimí, Mex.—II." *EMJ* 86, no. 4 (August 22, 1908): 373–374.

————. "The Working Mines of Guanajuato." *EMJ* 86, no. 16 (October 24, 1908): 806–808.

Rickard, T. A. *Journeys of Observation.* San Francisco: Dewey Publishing Co., 1907.

Ríos-Bustamante, Antonio. "As Guilty as Hell: Mexican Copper Miners and Their Communities in Arizona, 1920–1950." In John Mason Hart, ed., *Border Crossings: Mexican and Mexican American Workers.* Wilmington, Del.: Scholarly Resources, 1998.

Robinson, Cecil. *Mexico and the Hispanic Southwest in American Literature.* Tucson: University of Arizona Press, 1977.

Roden, Paula. "A Study of Relationships among Various Intelligence Test and Reading Test Results Obtained with Latin American Second Grade Children." Master's thesis, University of Texas, Austin, 1955.

Rogers, Allen H. "Character and Habits of Mexican Miners." *EMJ* 85, no. 14 (April 14, 1908): 700–702.

Romero, Matías. *Mexico and the United States: A Study of the Subjects Affecting Their Political, Commercial, and Social Relations, Made with a View to Their Promotion.* New York: G. P. Putnam's Sons, 1898.

Root, Elihu. *Latin America and the United States: Addresses by Elihu Root.* Cambridge, Mass.: Harvard University Press, 1917.

Rosenberg, Emily S. *Financial Missionaries to the World: The Politics and Culture of Dollar Diplomacy, 1900–1930.* Cambridge, Mass.: Harvard University Press, 1999.

———. *Spreading the American Dream: American Economic and Cultural Expansion, 1890–1945.* New York: Hill and Wang, 1982.

Ross, Edward Alsworth. *Sin and Society: An Analysis of Latter-Day Iniquity.* Boston: Houghton, Mifflin, 1907.

———. *Social Control: A Survey of the Foundations of Order.* New York: Macmillan, 1912.

———. *The Social Revolution in Mexico.* New York: Century Co., 1923.

Ruiz, Ramón Eduardo. *The People of Sonora and Yankee Capitalists.* Tucson: University of Arizona Press, 1988.

Ruiz, Vicki. *Cannery Women, Cannery Lives: Unionization and the Food Processing Industry, 1930–1940.* Albuquerque: University of New Mexico Press, 1987.

Rusher, William. "U.S. Too Big for Other Countries to Like Us." *Pasadena Star News,* June 5, 2001.

Russell, B. E. "Las Chispas Mines, Sonora, Mexico." *EMJ* 86, no. 13 (November 21, 1908): 1006–07.

Safley, James Clifford. *Mexican Vistas.* San Diego, Calif.: Union-Tribune Publishing Co., 1952.

Sauter, Mary C. "Arbol Verde: Cultural Conflict and Accommodation in a California Mexican Community." Master's thesis, Claremont Colleges, 1933.

Schell, William, Jr. *Integral Outsiders: The American Colony in Mexico City, 1876–1911.* Wilmington, Del.: Scholarly Resources, 2001.

Schoultz, Lars. *Beneath the United States: A History of U.S. Policy toward Latin America.* Cambridge, Mass.: Harvard University Press, 1998.

Scott, G. W. "Mexico: An Impartial Survey." Typescript (1918). Doheny Research Foundation Collection. Special Collections, Mary Norton Clapp Library, Occidental College, Glendale, California.

Scott, James Brown, ed. *President Wilson's Foreign Policy.* New York: Oxford University Press, 1918.

Shepherd, Grant. *The Silver Magnet: Fifty Years in a Mexican Silver Mine.* New York: E. P. Dutton and Co., 1938.

Sherrat, Harriott Wight. *Mexican Vistas Seen from Highways and By-ways of Travel.* Chicago: Rand, McNally and Co., 1899.

Showalter, William Joseph. "Mexico and the Mexicans." *National Geographic* 25, no. 5 (May 1914): 471–493.

Silva, J. R. Interview with J. R. Silva, employment agent for Mexican agricultural laborers, El Paso, Texas. File 103–107a, Contractors and Agents. Paul S. Taylor Collection, Bancroft Library, University of California, Berkeley.

Simmen, Edward. *Gringos in Mexico.* Fort Worth: Texas Christian University Press, 1988.

Simpich, Frederick. "Along Our Side of the Mexican Border." *National Geographic* 38, no. 1 (July 1920): 61–80.

————. "The Little Brown Brother Treks North." *The Independent* 116 (1924): 237–239.

————. "A Mexican Land of Canaan: Marvelous Riches of the Wonderful West Coast of Our Neighbor Republic." *National Geographic* 37, no. 10 (October 1919): 307–330.

————. "Mexico's Agrarian Experiment." *The Independent* 116, no. 3948 (January 30, 1926): 124–126, 142.

Smith, Clara Gertrude. "The Development of the Mexican People in the Community of Watts, California." Master's thesis, University of Southern California, 1933.

Smith, Francis Hopkinson. *A White Umbrella in Mexico.* Boston and New York: Houghton Mifflin, 1895.

Smith, Franklin Wheaton. "Present Conditions of Mining in Mexico." *EMJ* 86, no. 14 (October 3, 1908).

Smith, Robert Freeman. *The United States and Revolutionary Nationalism in Mexico, 1916–1932.* Chicago: University of Chicago Press, 1972.

Spence, Lewis. *Mexico of the Mexicans.* New York: Charles Scribner's Sons, 1918.

Spurr, David. *The Rhetoric of Empire: Colonial Discourse in Journalism, Travel Writing, and Imperial Administration.* Durham: Duke University Press, 1993.

Stanley, Grace. "Special Schools for Mexicans." *The Survey* 44 (September 15, 1920): 714–715.

Starr, Frederick. *In Indian Mexico: A Narrative of Travel and Labor.* Chicago: Forbes and Co., 1908.

————. "The Mexican People." In George H. Blakeslee, ed., *Mexico and the Caribbean: Clark University Addresses.* New York: G. E. Stechert and Co., 1920.

Storm, Marian. "Wells at the World's End: Life in the Pánuco Oil Region of Mexico." *Atlantic Monthly*, April 1924, 513–526.

Stowell, Jay S. *The Near Side of the Mexican Question.* New York: George H. Doran Co., 1921.

Street, George G. *Che! Wah! Wah! or, The Modern Montezumas in Mexico.* Rochester, N.Y.: E. R. Andrews, Printer and Bookbinder, 1883.

Strout, Richard Lee. "A Fence for the Rio Grande," *The Independent* 120, no. 4070 (June 2, 1928): 518–520.

Sturges, Vera. "The Progress and Adjustment in Mexican and United States Life." National Conference on Social Welfare. *Proceedings* (1920): 481–486.

Summers, Helen. "An Evaluation of Certain Procedures in the Teaching of the Non-English Speaking Mexican Child." Master's thesis, University of California, Los Angeles, 1939.

Taylor, J. T. "The Americanization of Harlingen's Mexican School Population." *Texas Outlook* 18 (September 1934): 37–38.

Taylor, Paul S. "Mexicans North of the Rio Grande." *The Survey* 65, no. 3 (May 1, 1931): 135–140, 197.

Tays, E. A. H. "Mining in Mexico, Past and Present." *EMJ* 86, no. 12 (October 3, 1908): 665–667.

————. "Present Labor Conditions in Mexico." *EMJ* 84, no. 14 (October 5, 1907): 621–624.

Terman, Lewis. "Intelligence and Its Measurement." *Journal of Educational Psychology* 12, no. 3 (March 1921).

———. *Intelligence Tests and School Reorganization.* Yonkers-on-the-Hudson, N.Y.: World Book Co., 1922.

Thomas, C. S. "Traveling in Mexico." *EMJ* 91, no. 24 (June 17, 1911): 1201–1203.

Thompson, Wallace. *The Mexican Mind: A Study of National Psychology.* New York: Little, Brown and Co., 1922.

———. *The People of Mexico: Who They Are and How They Live.* New York: Harper and Brothers, 1921.

———. *Trading with Mexico.* New York: Dodd, Mead and Co., 1921.

Thomson, Charles A. "What of the Bracero? The Forgotten Alternative in Our Immigration Policy." *The Survey* 54, no. 5 (June 1, 1925): 291–292.

Tinker Salas, Miguel. *In the Shadow of the Eagles: Sonora and the Transformation of the Border during the Porfiriato.* Berkeley: University of California Press, 1997.

Toth, Charles W. "Elihu Root." In Norman Graebner, *An Uncertain Tradition: American Secretaries of State in the Twentieth Century.* New York: McGraw Hill, 1961.

Townsend, Arthur R. "The Ocampo District, Mexico." *EMJ* 78, no. 13 (March 31, 1904): 515–516.

Treff, Simon Ludwig. "The Education of Mexican Children in Orange County, California." Master's thesis, University of Southern California, 1934.

Trowbridge, E. D. *Mexico To-Day and To-Morrow.* New York: MacMillan Co., 1919.

Tupper, C. R. "The Use of Intelligence Tests in the Schools of a Small City." In Lewis Terman, ed., *Intelligence Tests and School Reorganization.* Yonkers-on-the-Hudson: World Book Co., 1922.

Turner, John Kenneth. *Barbarous Mexico.* Chicago: Charles H. Kerr and Co., 1911.

Tweedie, Mrs. Alec. *Mexico As I Saw It.* London: Hurst and Blackett, 1901.

U.S. Congress. House. Committee on Foreign Affairs. *Background Information on the Use of United States Armed Forces Foreign Countries.* 91st Congress, 2nd Session. Washington, D.C.: U.S. Government Printing Office, 1970.

U.S. Congress. House. Committee on Immigration and Naturalization. Hearings. 68th Cong., 2d sess., March 3, 1925.

U.S. Congress. Senate. Reports of the Immigration Commission. *Abstracts of Reports of the Immigration Commission.* Washington, D.C.: U.S. Government Printing Office, 1911.

Valle, Emma E. "The Adjustment of Migrant Pupils in a Junior High School." Master's thesis, University of Texas. 1953.

Van Alstyne, Richard Warner. *The Rising American Empire.* New York: Oxford University Press, 1960.

Vandenbergh, John Leonard. "The Mexican Problem in the Schools." *Los Angeles School Journal* 11 (May 14, 1928): 153–154.

Vanderwood, Paul J. *Disorder and Progress: Bandits, Police, and Mexican Development.* Wilmington, Del.: Scholarly Resources, 1992.

Walker, Helen. "The Conflict of Cultures in First Generation Mexicans in Santa Ana, California." Master's thesis, University of Southern California, 1928.

———. "Mexican Immigrants and Citizenship." *Sociology and Social Research* 13, no. 1 (September–October 1929): 464–471.

———. "Mexican Immigrants as Laborers." *Sociology and Social Research* 13 (September 1928): 45–62.

Warburton, Amber A., Helen Wood, and Marian M. Crane, M.D. "The Work and Welfare of Children of Agricultural Laborers in Hidalgo County, Texas." U.S. Department of Labor, Children's Bureau Publication no. 298. Washington, D.C.: U.S. Government Printing Office, 1943.

Warman, Cy. *The Story of the Railroad.* New York: D. Appleton and Co., 1899.

Wasserman, Mark. *Capitalists, Caciques, and Revolution: The Native Elite and Foreign Enterprise in Chihuahua, Mexico, 1854–1911.* Chapel Hill: University of North Carolina Press, 1984.

Weeks, Charles J. "The New Frontier, the Great Society, and American Imperialism in Oceania." *Pacific Historical Review* 71, no. 1 (February 2002): 91–125.

Welch, Richard E. *Imperialists vs. Anti-Imperialists: The Debate over Expansionism in the 1890s.* Itasca, Ill.: F. E. Peacock, 1972.

"The Well Housed Employee." *The California Citrograph* 3, no. 9 (September 1918): 253.

Wells, David A. *A Study of Mexico.* New York: D. Appleton and Co., 1887.

Weyl, Walter E. *Labor Conditions in Mexico.* Department of Labor Bulletin no. 38. Washington, D.C.: U.S. Government Printing Office, 1902.

White, Trumbull. *Our New Possessions: A Graphic Account, Descriptive and Historical, of the Tropic Islands of the Sea Which Have Fallen under Our Sway, Their Cities, Peoples and Commerce, Natural Resources and the Opportunities They Offer to Americans.* Chicago: Thompson and Hood, 1898.

Wilkins, James H. *A Glimpse of Old Mexico.* San Rafael, Calif.: James A. Wilkins, 1901.

Wilson, Henry Lane. *Diplomatic Episodes in Mexico, Belgium, and Chile.* New York: Doubleday and Co., 1927.

Wilson, James A. *Bits of Old Mexico.* San Francisco: James A. Wilson, 1910.

Wilson, William Nathan. "An Analysis of the Academic and Home Problems of the Pupils in a Mexican Junior High School." Master's thesis, University of Southern California, 1938.

Winter, Nevin O. *Mexico and Her People of To-Day.* Boston: L. C. Page and Co., 1907.

Winton, George B. *Mexico Past and Present.* Nashville, Tenn.: Cokesbury Press, 1928.

———. *Mexico To-Day: Social, Political, and Religious Conditions.* New York: Missionary Education Movement, 1913.

Withers, Charles Dinnijes. "Problems with Mexican Boys." Master's thesis, University of Southern California, 1942.

Woodbridge, Dwight E. "La Cananea Mining Camp." *EMJ* 87, no. 14 (October 6, 1906): 624–627.

Works, George Alan. "The Non-English Speaking Child and the Public Schools." In George Alan Works, *General Report.* Texas Educational Survey Report, vol. 8. Austin: Texas Educational Survey Commission, 1925.

Wright, Marie Robinson. *Mexico: A History of Its Progress and Development in One Hundred Years.* Philadelphia: George Barrie and Sons, 1910.

———. *Picturesque Mexico.* Philadelphia: J. B. Lippincott Co., 1897.

Wright, Robin. "Urgent Calls for Peace in Mideast Ring Hollow As Prospects Dwindle." *Los Angeles Times,* March 31, 2002.

Wueste, Gladys Riskin. "A Survey of Factors Relating to the Education of the Children of Migratory Parents of Eagle Pass, Texas." Master's thesis, University of Texas, 1950.

Zwick, Jim, ed. *Mark Twain's Weapons of Satire: Anti-Imperialist Writings on the Philippine-American War.* Syracuse: Syracuse University Press, 1992.

INDEX